A Folk Song History
of America

Samuel L. Forcucci, a published composer, teaches music theory and education at the State University of New York at Cortland. He is professor and chairman of the Department of Music.

A
Folk Song
History
of America

America Through Its Songs

Samuel L. Forcucci

PRENTICE-HALL, INC., Englewood Cliffs, New Jersey 07632

Library of Congress Cataloging in Publication Data

FORCUCCI, SAMUEL L.
    A folk song history of America.

    Includes index.
        1. Folk music—United States—History and criticism.
    2. Folk-songs, English—United States—History and criti-
    cism.   3. Music, Popular (Songs, etc.)—United States—
    History and criticism.   I. Title.
    ML3551.F7   1984   784.4′973′09   83–24610
    ISBN   0–13–323130–5
    ISBN   0–13–323122–4 (A Reward book : pbk.)

Editorial/production supervision and interior design by Fred Bernardi
Cover design by Hal Siegel
Manufacturing buyer: Pat Mahoney

Printed in the United States of America

10   9   8   7   6   5   4   3   2   1

ISBN   0-13-323130-5

ISBN   0-13-323122-4 {pbk.}

Prentice-Hall International, Inc., *London*
Prentice-Hall of Australia Pty. Limited, *Sydney*
Editora Prentice-Hall do Brasil, Ltda., *Rio de Janeiro*
Prentice-Hall Canada Inc., *Toronto*
Prentice-Hall of India Private Limited, *New Delhi*
Prentice-Hall of Japan, Inc., *Tokyo*
Prentice-Hall of Southeast Asia Pte. Ltd., *Singapore*
Whitehall Books Limited, *Wellington, New Zealand*

Dedicated to
My wife Anna and our sons Jay, Joseph, and David

Contents

Preface

My keen interest in American folk music began when I was an elementary school teacher of vocal music. While in the process of teaching music to my students from nursery school through the eighth grade, I learned on the average of thirty to forty new songs each week. Through experience, I soon discovered that the easiest songs to learn and the most enjoyable to sing were those generally classified as folk songs. Ironically enough, these were the same songs that my students learned easily, always remembered, and enjoyed the most. Those so-called contrived songs about community helpers, the seasons of the year, Halloween goblins, and Thanksgiving turkeys were received with interest yet only superficially enjoyed. The real essence of my professional endeavors was imbedded in the philosophy that I would teach songs to my students that they would remember and enjoy the rest of their lives. Those songs that best met that worthy goal were folk songs and, more important, American folk songs.

If this in and of itself was not revealing enough, I soon learned through my research on folk materials that I had gathered some fascinating bits and pieces of information related to the origins and evolution of American folk songs. In the process of presenting new songs, every music teacher finds it advantageous to give students some facts about the songs because it generates interest and enhances learning. As I began to collect more and more information on American folk music, I found I had compiled a folk history of the American people. In reality, I had become a self-styled folklorist, a collector and "dispenser" of a huge storehouse of stories and songs about the American people.

Later, when I became a college professor, I found that my love for and interest in American folk music had not diminished. Although my formal musical training was steeped in the great music of Bach, Mozart, and Stravinsky, I nevertheless believed there was yet another creditable body of good music known as folk music that rightfully should be presented to students in an academic framework. As a result, I organized a college course entitled, "American Folk Music and Jazz," which dealt expressly with the more informal musical expressions of the American people. It became a very popular course, one in which students gained a greater understanding and appreciation for that music which, in essence, was an integral part of their lives as Americans. This book is an outgrowth of the many years I have spent in collecting American folk songs, reading about them, listening to them, thinking about them, and sharing them with hundreds of students in a classroom atmosphere.

Many books dealing with the broad sweep on the subject present their materials either in a general chronological order or by dealing with the expressions of individual groups of Americans. After addressing some basic information that is absolutely essential if one is to both understand and fully appreciate folk music, I have attempted to incorporate the best of both approaches, thus giving the reader a logical progression of materials on the evolution of American folk music.

In preparing this book, it was my hope that I could develop in my readers a greater understanding and love for the music; perhaps even more, it was my ardent desire to solicit a greater admiration and respect for that segment of our heritage that we have come to know simply as American folk music.

I am deeply indebted to the thousands of Americans who shared their dreams, aspirations, humor, trials and tribulations in songs—such people as John and Alan Lomax, Carl Sandburg, John Jacob Niles, Pete Seeger, Burl Ives, Woody Guthrie, and numerous others, who early in this century took it upon themselves to begin to preserve and popularize our American folk songs. I am grateful to the Library of Congress, to the several college and community libraries where I spent many enjoyable hours, and especially to the Cortland Free Library and its Director, Warren S. Eddy. I would also like to thank the State University College, Cortland, New York, for giving me the time to pull together my materials, and finally, the hundreds of students who allowed me the opportunity to literally "think out loud" as I tried to crystallize my thoughts on my "avocational" interest.

S.L.F.

1
The Characteristics of Song

Song is a particular medium of musical expression. It is music intended for performance with the human voice as compared with performance on a mechanical gadget known as an instrument. Simply put, song belongs to that category known as vocal music as contrasted with instrumental music. Many songs are played on musical instruments and indeed played easily and effectively; parenthetically, many instrumental pieces are often sung and sung reasonably well. The difference lies essentially in the intent of the creation regarding which musical medium best lends itself to the production of the sounds.

The human voice is a fascinating musical medium. Although man has devised hundreds of instruments capable of producing a myriad of sounds, accurate rapid-firing responses, and harmony, covering the whole range of sounds that the human ear can register, the voice still remains the most beautiful and intimate of music-producing bodies available to man. Perhaps the greatest compliment one can pay to an instrumentalist is to tell him that he practically "sang through his instrument."

Of even greater importance, the human voice is the only musical medium capable of producing both music and words at the same time. In reality, every human being is a musical instrument, capable of communicating a wide range of musical/verbal thought. Some of our finest songs are examples of music for which the voice conceivably was the medium used in their initial utterance; nonetheless, there exists an abundance of outstanding vocal music that has been created for the voice by highly talented composers. The former, more simplistic in nature, are best suited to the amateur singer. The latter are more often much more complex in content and are intended, therefore, for the trained singer. For any song to be considered worthwhile, it must be what

1

is termed *singable,* an elusive quality that allows the singer to produce and respond to its sounds easily and effectively.

The Musical Properties of Song

Many songs are simply called *melodies.* This, of course, is an inaccurate analogy. A melody is a select arrangement and succession of sounds that the mind perceives as a whole. Such familiar songs as "America the Beautiful" or "Sweet Betsy from Pike," for example, illustrate this point. Both songs contain a select arrangement of tones from our musical sound system and proceed in a succession of tones from beginning to end as compared with a simultaneous sounding that constitutes harmony. (These melodies can, of course, be harmonized.) Finally, the mind collects together all the tones included in each song, thus making them entities unto themselves.

There are instrumental melodies as well as vocal melodies. These are better described as themes. The melodies we recall from a symphony, for example, represent the more melodic aspects of the music, that is, those portions that the mind more easily assimilates and perceives as an entity. The other bursts of tones that we find more difficult to assimilate are generally identified as nonmelodic or transitory in nature. Songs, therefore, best illustrate what melody is all about, although the term is not exclusively reserved for this type of musical media.

Songs usually encompass a limited or small range of musical sounds. Those songs intended for the average singer generally do not go beyond the outer limits of a seven- or eight-note scale; however, those songs intended for the trained singer challenge the outer limits of the human voice. Our national anthem, "The Star Spangled Banner," well illustrates this point. One of the song's major criticisms is its lack of singability, or to state it more accurately, its excessive vocal demands. The range of sounds included in the song exceeds that normally found in the usual repertoire of singable songs. Listen to a rendition of the song as performed by the crowd at an athletic event. One cannot help but notice the singers' struggle with its wide range of sounds. Thus, easy-to-sing songs confine themselves to a narrow range of sounds to accommodate the untrained singer. Songs intended for trained singers, on the other hand, may involve a more ambitious extension of musical tones.

The setting of the vocal mechanism (the expansion and contraction of the vocal cords in the voice box), although seemingly a natural reflex, in essence, demands careful listening if one is to sing accurately. For this reason, songs intended for the ordinary singer make few demands on the relationship or process of going from one tone to the other. In musical parlance, such songs are said to contain simple intervals or easy skips/steps in going from one tone to the next. Again, songs intended for the trained singer are far more complex and make greater demands on the singer's ability to reproduce more intricate intervals between tones.* Music for the voice, there-fore, must take into consideration the elasticity of the vocal cords and limit itself to simple to reproduce intervals as compared with instrumental music in which the tones are easily reproduced through mechanical devices.

Music for singing must also give attention to a free-flowing contour or melodic line. The human voice comprises a maze of muscles. A good song, therefore, would have well-patterned highs and lows structured within it in order to make the physical reproduction of its sounds an almost effortless task. Comparatively speaking, this is not a major factor with music for the piano or tympani; but it does become a factor with such instruments as the trumpet or clarinet, where lip muscles are involved in the sound-producing process. The melodic contour, then, must be such that the vocal cords—a set of muscles subject to strain and fatigue—can respond to easily and sensibly.

Finally, songs usually contain considerable repetition in the use of all elements of music. On close scrutiny, one soon learns that the best songs ordinarily contain melodic/rhythmic units that are repeated throughout. Rep-etition has been aptly defined as the "glue" of music. It is essential for a song to contain a limited number of poignant musical clusters or units that are used repeatedly in order that the singer may easily retain and respond to the musical portions of the song.

HOT CROSS BUNS   Traditional

A: exact repetition, melodically, rhythmically, and verbally

B: sequential, melodically; exact repetition, rhythmically; words quite similar

The Verbal Properties of Song

It is often difficult for musicians to give proper attention to a song's words because their primary focus is most often directed toward the accuracy and

---

*In instrumental music, such as piano music, the mechanical element within the instru-ment makes the sound, so there is little need for adjustment of the highness or lowness (musical pitch). The pianist, for example, need only press down the correct key and use an appropriate touch to strike the desired pitch.

beauty of the musical sounds. Conversely, there are top pop and folk singers who are more enamored with the verbal message of a song rather than with its musical message. Actually, both the musical and verbal messages are of equal importance and are, in fact, a unified whole. What is being communicated involves both musical sounds and verbal sounds all joined together.

The words of a song, or the *lyrics,* must be classified as poetry rather than prose, that is, they must evoke rhythmic beats and accents. These rhythmic beats and their resulting accents must, in turn, be accurately joined with the rhythms and accents contained in the musical portions of the song. The two must not only be compatible, but more important, they must also be bonded together as a unit.

Similarly, the expressiveness of the words must be reflected in the expressiveness of the music and vice versa. The particular distribution of highs and lows that one would necessarily give attention to in the expressive recitation of the words must also be evidenced in the complementary use of highs and lows in the musical line. However, this does not present as much of a problem as it would appear. Creators of songs handle this component instinctively rather than mechanically.

Music has often been called the "language of emotions." One can easily transmit and experience the entire spectrum of emotions from bitter sorrow through euphoric happiness through the effective use of musical sounds. Music tends to heighten the emotional content of words. Take, for example, the opening line of the hymn, "Rock of Ages": "Rock of Ages, Cleft for me, Let me hide myself in thee." When recited by even the most gifted actor, these words have far less emotional impact than when they are sung. To be sure, the reverse is also true. A hymn is actually a prayer emotionally heightened by the addition of musical tones. The lyrics of any song are given emotional emphasis with the addition of music. An excellent example of the emotional impact of music is the background music used in movies or television programs. The music effectively heightens the impact of the visual–verbal–scenic–dramatic elements of the media. One can examine even the simplest of songs to discover the importance of the musical line in reinforcing the emotional message contained in the words. The use of other musical elements, such as harmony, volume, and so on, also adds to the emotional impact of the story line.

Just as there is considerable repetition in the musical content of songs, there is repetition in the verbal content as well. Interestingly enough, this verbal and musical repetition are most often found together. Indeed, the whole purpose of repetition is to present a verbal/musical message in the most emotional and effective manner possible.

A final and perhaps more subtle aspect of words in song addresses itself to the use of original lyrics as compared with modified lyrics or translations. Many people ask why operas are not consistently sung in English when performed in the United States, as opposed to the original French, Italian, or German language. As many of us already know just from dealing with language in everyday usage, even the best translation becomes a mere facsimile of the original and loses something in the process. Given the added problem of combining words with their attendant accents and rhythmic beats along with the accents and rhythmic beats of the accompanying music, the loss becomes all the more pronounced. In addition, word syllables have unique sounds that influence the musical sounds assigned to them by the creator of the song. Words used in translation more often have their own, and oftentimes different, sounds, which tend to give the song a kind of awkwardness or artificiality about it when it is sung in translation. For example, in the aria "Largo al factotum" from *The Barber of Seville,* the words "Per un barbiere, di qualita" would translate as "That of a barber, used to high life." One would have to agree that the aria sounds more authentic and certainly more musical when sung in the original language.

Regarding the modification or refinement of original lyrics, we need only turn to the great black spiritual, "Nobody Knows the Trouble 'Ob Seen." Refined, it would become, "No one Here Knows the Difficulties I've Experienced." To be sure, this is not an improvement on the original. It is about as out of place as the satirical cheer often heard at football games, "Harass them, harass them, make them relinquish the ball."

The Elements of Music

It is generally accepted that European culture was transported in wholesale fashion into the New World and totally dominated the emerging American culture. Music, of course, was a part of that cultural exodus. Even today, American music of every description can be traced to the base roots and early practices of the music of Western civilization. This is important to keep in mind as we discuss the individual elements of music. American music, or more especially, American song is distinctive, yet it belongs to a much broader family of musics closely connected with Western cultural traditions. Thus, as we scrutinize the elements of American music we are, in effect, looking at the musical elements contained in music of the Western hemisphere.

Melody

American music uses twelve tones within the octave, with each tone a semitone or half-step apart. Our music is created or written to accommodate these tones and our instruments are built to produce them. Anything outside this system is considered to be out of tune (that is, sharp or flat).

For the most part, eight of these twelve tones are selected and arranged in systems called *scales*. The great majority of our songs are based on the Major scale; the remainder are based on the Minor scale. A smattering of other scales occasionally appear in some of our songs (such as the pentatonic scale, the whole-tone scale, and so on).* The other tones, not considered a part of the basic scale, often appear in songs and are known as *chromatic tones*. These tones, as their name (*kroma* or *chroma*) suggests, are employed to give a splash of "color" to a particular place in the music.

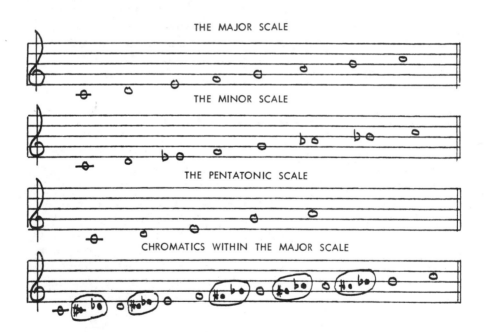

THE MAJOR SCALE

THE MINOR SCALE

THE PENTATONIC SCALE

CHROMATICS WITHIN THE MAJOR SCALE

It is interesting to note that one of the tones in each of the systems serves as the tone from which the scale is derived and also as the tone toward which each member tone is attracted.

---

*A number of our urban folk songs have been based on systems known as modes.

6

The following square dance tag beautifully illustrates the tendency toward a tonal center. Play or sing it delaying the sounding of the last tone for an extra moment.

SQUARE DANCE TAG

Any tone in the sound system can serve as the tone of origin or tonal center, thus allowing us several opportunities to reproduce the same sounding scale although other sets of tones are being used. This has the ultimate effect of placing a song in different parts of the singing voice because the tonal center or key center has changed to a higher or lower position in the sound system. The key or tonal center is chosen to best suit the particular singing voice or instrument performing the music. The following songs illustrate all the references made to melody as discussed above.

AMERICA THE BEAUTIFUL

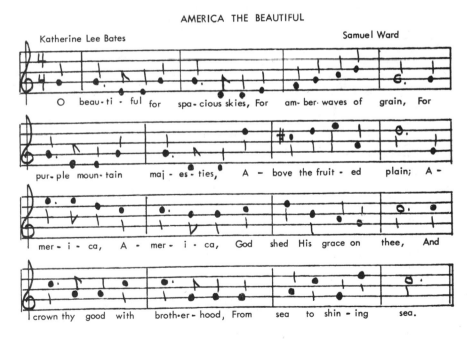

This song is based on the C Major scale with the tone C serving as the tonal center.

SKIP TO MY LOU

Traditional

This song is based on the E-flat Major scale with the tone E-flat as the tonal center.

Rhythm

There are three aspects of musical rhythm that must be understood if one is to both perform and respond intelligently. All human beings "feel" rhythm; however, very few respond musically as can be verified by anyone witnessing a dance floor filled with people who are going through all the requisite physical gyrations, but very few of whom are dancing to the beat of the music. Rhythm is one of the main elements of music and many musicologists claim that primitive man devised rhythm before melody.

The first aspect of rhythm is *heartbeat, pulsation,* or sometimes, just plain *beat,* that is, the persistent pulsation that underlies the majority of music we hear. Sometimes it is strongly pronounced; other times, it is subtly in evidence. These pulsations are each equidistant from one another. Their rate of recurrence is established by the leader of a musical group, or in the case of an individual performer, in his own mind prior to beginning the music. The bass drummer in a marching band is the exclusive guardian of this element, as is the rhythm guitarist in a rock or dance band or the conductor of a symphony orchestra. It is this heartbeat that keeps the music moving from beginning to end, or that keeps a small or large group of performers performing as a single unit.

The second aspect of rhythm, known as *meter,* involves the arrangement of these pulsations into groups. These groups come in simple units of twos or threes or in larger groups of fours, fives, sixes, and so on. What distinguishes meter from beat is the added dimension of accent. We hear certain beats receiving a greater stress or accent. This always occurs on the first beat of every group and on other beats when the grouping is larger than simple groups of twos or threes. Persons paying particular attention to meter in music will be heard or seen counting *One*–two, or *One*–two–three, or *One*–two–three–four, and so on. Generally, music that moves in twos or multiples of two evokes a feeling for dancing or marching (down–up, down–up), music composed of threes or multiples of three usually evokes a feeling for circular movement (*One*–two three, *One* two three, and so on).

The third and most sophisticated aspect of rhythm deals with the interplay of the various durational lengths of sounds. This interplay ranges from sounds of even duration, which are the least exciting, to sounds that are uneven in duration, such as long–short or the reverse. The kind of musical notes used will indicate their duration; for example, two quarter notes ♩♩ (even duration), or a quarter note followed by an eighth note ♩♪ (long–short), or the reverse ♪♩ (short–long).

There are even more subtle rhythmic techniques used in music, such as the use of dotted notes to give the music a nervous or jumpy effect, as in military or patriotic music.* Another popular rhythmic technique is *syncopation,* in which normal accents delineated in meter are placed elsewhere in the group where they would be least expected to appear. This technique of surprise evokes a sudden jolt in the music, making the rhythm all the more exciting. Both jazz and Latin-American music make abundant use of syncopation. Basic jazz syncopation takes a normal group of four beats with the accent on one and three and places them on the opposite beats of two and four (1–2–3–4 to 1–2–3–4).

The selection of a particular type of rhythm and the employment of some of the other rhythmic techniques described here do much to communicate the exact musical message desired. Creators and performers of music give special attention to these rhythmic resources.

Harmony

Harmony is the most sophisticated of the three main musical elements and is utilized only by more advanced cultures. It involves the simultaneous sound-

---

*This effect can be easily demonstrated by performing the "Battle Hymn of the Republic," first with even rhythms and then with dotted notes, as originally conceived.

ing of tones and as such is the most profound of the musical elements. Therefore, primitive cultures, and even advanced cultures where persons performing are laymen in the trained musical sense, limit their attention to rhythm and melody.

Each particular scale has its own set of harmonies achieved through adding tones to each member of the scale. For example, a melody based on a major scale from C would logically be harmonized with chords constituted from adding tones above each of the member tones of the scale. A unit of harmony is known as a *chord*. Each significant tone in a melody demands a particular harmony, usually one that contains that melodic tone. To understand this concept, think of a person who is playing a melody at the piano, searching for the right harmony to go with it. He knows immediately when the right chord has been struck.

Some harmonies evoke a feeling of restfulness and complete compatibility and are described as consonant harmonies. Others evoke a feeling of restlessness and relative incompatibility and are described as dissonant harmonies. This interplay between consonant and dissonant harmonies keeps the music flowing from beginning to end as we sense tension–release and again tension–release. The science of harmony has been advanced to the point where we have the simplest of combined sounds to some very involved harmonies ranging from the most simple and romantic to the most clashing and mind-boggling.

Mention must be made of a system of harmonic identification devised by musical laymen and commonly used by folk singers and jazz–rock artists. This method of chord identification and retrieval is very different from that used by academic music theorists. In this method, chords are identified by letter names rather than by Roman numeral names. It is a fast, functional way of finding the chords on an instrument. Performers using this method read the chord symbols in the music (C, or dm, or G_7) rather than all of the notes contained in the music. Because it is so efficient, this method has been of great help for getting such performers as guitarists, pianists, and so on, to harmonize music readily.

ON TOP OF OLD SMOKY

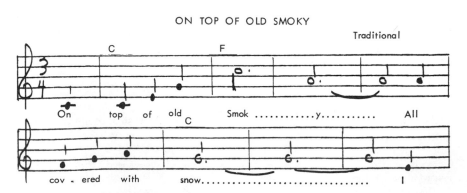

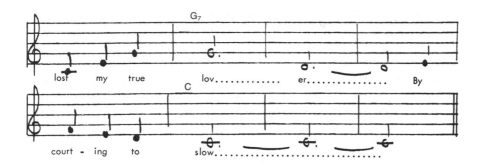

The Expressive Elements

Beyond the three main elements of melody, rhythm, and harmony lies an almost endless list of particular musical "additives" which directly affect the expressive aspects of music. We will concern ourselves here with some of the most important ones.

Musical *dynamics* refers to the amount of sound or volume produced. A piece of music performed on a generally low level of volume would evoke one kind of response as compared with the piece performed at a high level of volume. Beyond this, we can use more subtle shadings with gradual or sudden changes in the levels of volume. In musical terms this is indicated as *piano* (soft) or *forte* (loud), along with gradations of these two general levels. It is interesting to note that the instrument we generally call the piano is really the pianoforte; it was the first keyboard instrument to produce both soft and loud sounds by the mere touch of the keys. There are some general understandings among musicians regarding what is soft and what is loud, but beyond this the topic becomes most subjective. Suffice it to say that musical performers are cognizant of this expressive element and work with it to achieve the ultimate in dramatic effect.

The rate of speed or *tempo* at which a piece of music moves can also effect the expressiveness of the music. A selection that moves at a generally slow pace evokes a feeling different from that experienced when the same piece is taken at a rapid pace. (Consider, for example, the "Battle Hymn of the Republic" played first at a slow pace, then at a fast pace.) There is a whole range of tempi at which music can move from extremely slow (*grave*) to extremely fast (*vivace*). Like musical dynamics, there exist more subtle markings that allow a gradual increase or decrease in tempo along with the inclusion of sudden and abrupt changes. The performer pays special attention to finding just the right tempo and when it is found he will say that he is "in the groove" or really "rolling."

Musical *style* is yet another expressive element. Musical tones can be played or sung in a romantic, sorrowful, or happy and spirited way, to name a few. In the manipulation of musical tones, the performer keeps in mind the

11

particular style appropriate to his interpretation. Obviously, the manner in which he uses both volume and tempo will enable him to achieve the right musical style.

There are any number of additional techniques that have a direct bearing on the expressiveness of music. As a final example, the particular instrument or combination of instruments used in performance would be worthy of mention. The same selection performed by a string quartet, a jazz band, or a single singer with or without guitar certainly changes the manner in which the music is being expressed. Each instrument has its own individual sound or musical *timbre*. A bassoon sounds like a bassoon, a piano sounds like a piano, and a female singer distinctively sounds like a female singer. The manner in which the musical sound is physically produced determines its unique timbre or musical quality. Thus, persons who perform or compose music must take the instrumentation of the music carefully into consideration because they are sensitive to its effect on the musical timbre or quality.

Musical Structure

Music must be organized or structured, otherwise it would not have logic or even hold together. A piece of music is composed of small clusters or units of tones that would be loosely analogous to words in the English language. These musical ideas, as they are called, combine into musical phrases that are analogous to a sentence in the English language. Dealing specifically on a musical level, we are referring to *musical form, structure,* or *organization.**

Most of our short, simple pieces of music are based on three or four musical structures. The simplest and perhaps oldest of these is the Two-Part Song Form. The music is actually made up of two bodies of musical material. The first part (labeled A) is often thought of as the "question" or antecedent; the second part (labeled B) as the "answer" or consequent ("America," "Ten Little Indians").

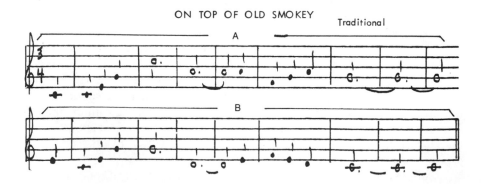

ON TOP OF OLD SMOKEY

Traditional

*The analogy between the component parts of musical form and language is used only as a means of illustrating comparative component units. It bears no direct relationship to music beyond this point.

The Three-Part Song Form is even more popularly used than the Two-Part Song Form insofar as it contains a return of the first body of musical material (A B A), thus giving more continuity or balance to the piece ("Marine's Hymn," "America the Beautiful").

OLD FOLKS AT HOME

Stephen Foster

The blues, although basically a Two-Part Song Form, is unique enough to merit special consideration. The blues, incidentally, is not a particular song or number of songs; it is a strict form, poetically as well as musically.

ORPHAN BLUES

S. L. F.

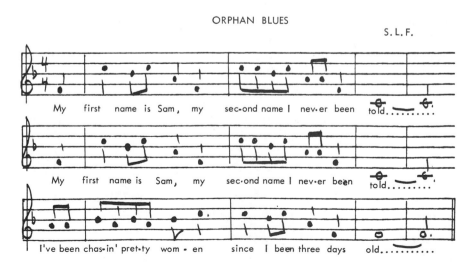

These simple song forms are compounded into larger types of forms to accommodate longer pieces of music. Many of our folk songs or hymn-type songs are structured in a verse–chorus form. In essence, this is a kind of two-part structure. The *chorus* or *refrain* is perhaps the most melodic portion of the song and the part that ordinarily has the same set of lyrics (part B). The *verse* is usually more diverse and accommodates the several sets of words or lyrics needed in the unfolding of the story connected with the music (part A).

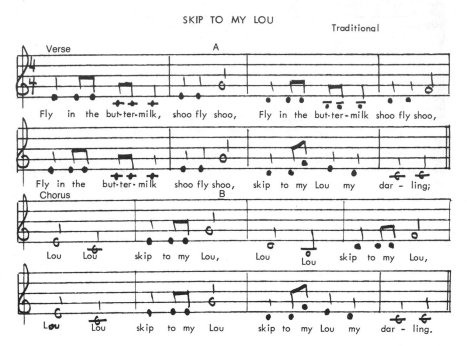

There are a number of hybrid examples such as that in "Sourwood Mountain," (page 15) in which the verse–chorus idea is more compressed and used in smaller units as compared to the two large, distinct units. This type of structure is more frequently used in the music of the American blacks in which immediate responses are required.

Songs should never be listened to on a purely intellectual–technical level. However, if one understands the basic elements of music as presented in this chapter, and is sensitive to their presence in the music they are experiencing, the end result cannot help but be one of total enjoyment.

SOURWOOD MOUNTAIN

Traditional

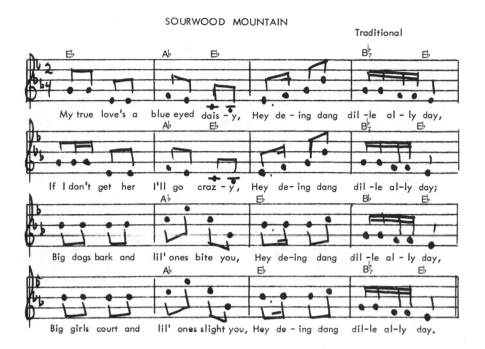

My true love's a blue eyed dais - y, Hey de - ing dang dil -le al -ly day,

If I don't get her I'll go craz - y, Hey de - ing dang dil -le al-ly day;

Big dogs bark and lil' ones bite you, Hey de-ing dang dil -le al - ly day,

Big girls court and lil' ones slight you, Hey de - ing dang dil-le al-ly day.

2

The Characteristics of Folk Song

Although folk music has been with us since the dawn of history, we have only recently begun to realize the great wealth of musical material it embraces. There has been much discussion over the years regarding the origins of folk song. It is generally agreed that they are the songs of the people and that they are the creation of one or more persons working singly or in groups. They are the songs created by common people who use this medium of human expression to describe their way of life.

Folk songs tell about human experiences and for this reason we have many varieties of folk songs. There are work songs, love songs, cradle songs, drinking songs, war songs, play songs, songs of mourning, and on and on. They vary in mood reflecting the patterns of life in a particular area and within a particular society. A mother singing to her baby may have expressed her love for her child with her own special words and tune. A workman may have poured out his feelings, sad or glad, making his work less burdensome and temporarily finding an emotional outlet through song. Others may have been inspired from the events of a very special moment and suddenly burst into song. In most cases, the creator was soon forgotten; nevertheless, the song was remembered by someone and passed on from person to person, group to group, and generation to generation. As often was the case, the song would undergo changes in transmission, either in words and/or music. Some additions or modifications often were included. Because folk songs were communicated through oral transmission rather than through the printed page, the temptation to make changes was all the more inviting.

These changes may have been inadvertent—a misheard lyric or a poorly remembered tune. Often changes were made in a deliberate attempt to add "improvements"; just as with common "gossip," the song was slightly

16

altered in order to make the communication worth repeating. Whether inadvertent or willful, what has come down to us are a number of folk songs that were achieved after hundreds of singers over the generations had had their crack at them. Although even today there are songs that are being passed on from singer to singer just as they were in the past, the process has almost come to a complete halt as most of our songs, both traditional and modern, are now written in musical notation, printed in book form, and delivered via concerts, TV, and recordings.

Folk songs from every nation, region, and group are enjoyed by people from other nations, regions, and walks of life because they deal with universal human experiences, with which everyone can in some way identify. These songs belong to no one in particular, yet to everyone in general. They are community property in the very real sense. It must be added, however, that their universal appeal is also due, in part, to their singability. They are as enjoyable to sing as they are to hear.

The shape or musical structure of folk songs is influenced by two important factors. First, the lyrics of the song, although poetic in genre, are more conversational than conventional poetry. Second, the speech patterns of a people tend to influence the musical properties of the song. Everything about the song is colloquial or provincial and tends to mirror the basic, unblemished cultural patterns of their originators. There is no attempt to use affected or sophisticated texts or music. These so-called musical biographies are plain tales told by plain people in their own plain language.

The great majority of folk songs consist of a simple melody to which several verses are added. This is joined to a chorus or refrain which is also a simple melody, but it uses the same words with each stanza. This would suggest that the verses or storytelling part of the song were probably made up and sung by particular individuals with the whole group joining in on the chorus each time this part came around in the song. In this process, particular individuals were given the opportunity to think up new verses or contribute one they already knew, after which the entire group would add its stamp of approval by singing the chorus. This process is much like that of a prayer meeting where one or more persons has the opportunity to add some religious wisdom as the mood moves them, and then everyone in the congregation may confirm these items with a collective affirmation. The singing of the chorus section also gave the individual soloists an opportunity to prepare the next verse or to fill in while deciding who should be the next contributor. This kind of spontaneous or unrehearsed approach accounts, in part, for the absence of any sensible story line or logical progression of ideas in some of our songs. "Skip to My Lou," "Clementine," and "Sweet Betsy from Pike" are examples of this type of folk song.

There are other songs that allow the individual singer an opportunity to give his contribution in small bits and pieces throughout which the group will come in almost immediately and in short bursts, similar to a preacher's calling out bits of wisdom to which the congregation will quickly respond with an "Amen" or "Hallelujah." Such songs as "Sourwood Mountain," "Liza Jane," and the great spiritual "Little David" are perfect examples of this type of song.

The ballad is the most distinguished of all the types of folk songs. This type of song is intended as a solo song rather than a group song, although they are often sung well by groups. The ballad is a longer song, and like its counterpart in literature, has short stanzas, although many more of them. Normally, they provide for the telling of a narrative, that is, the unfolding of a story, happening, or event. The ballad is usually cast in the third person, rarely in the first person. In these songs the story line is carefully organized. The singer assumes the role of the minstrel-of-old, thus becoming a true storyteller. Songs like "Barbara Allen," "Pretty Polly," or Woody Guthrie's "Pretty Boy Floyd" are examples of the folk-song ballad. These songs become the *pièce de resistance* for the best of our folk singers and perhaps bring the greatest satisfaction to the most discriminating of their listeners.

It is difficult to devise a short, succinct definition for folk song. First off, they are songs that have depended on oral transmission for their existence; however, modern practice makes this description obsolete. Most songs today are delivered via mass media and are immediately preserved. This is why folk songs today are categorized either as folk (traditional) songs or as urban (modern) folk songs. The following list presents a number of generalizations against which one can measure a song to distinguish it as a folk song rather than as some other type of song.

1. Folk songs represent the musical expressions of the common people.
2. These songs are not composed in that they are not the works of skilled, tutored musicians. It is more accurate to say that they have been created rather than composed.
3. These songs are ordinarily the product of an unknown person or group of persons. The credits often read: Anonymous; American Folk Song; Traditional; or Southern Mountain Song.*
4. The words or lyrics of folk songs are usually colloquial in nature to reflect the speech patterns and expressions of a particular people or region.
5. These songs are highly singable, primarily because they were first presented with the singing voice rather than having been written down in musical notation beforehand.
6. Folk songs are simply structured, both musically and verbally. It is their naiveté that gives them their charm.
7. These songs can be effectively performed without instrumental accompaniment. When they are accompanied, a less formal instrument (such as the guitar, banjo, accordion, dulcimer, or Autoharp) is considered appropriate.

---

*It should be noted that there are some songs of known authorship that are also classified as folk songs, for example, the songs of Stephen Foster. These songs are folklike in character and are patterned to fit the mold of what typical American folk songs should sound like.

8. Folk songs are indigenous to a particular region or people because they reflect the musical/verbal preferences of that people or region in their materials.

Folk songs tell a large variety of stories, share "gems" of wisdom, channel innermost feelings, and bring personal satisfaction to both the singer and the listener. They can lull us to sleep, call us to battle, fill us with hope, strike out at our shortcomings, herald our victories, caution the calloused, mourn our dead, and bring joy to lovers or peace to the troubled. Folk music, then, is music for all seasons and all peoples.

The Folk Singer

There is an art to folk singing. The practice of folk singing goes back to the beginnings of modern civilization. History records accounts of the bards of old, the ancient minstrels, the troubadors and trouvères of France, the minnesingers of Germany, and other classes of singers, on down to our present-day folk singers. It is an ancient art, to be sure, and one that demands special talents and skills.

Essentially, the folk singer is a storyteller. He must always be true to the intent of the song, because his *primary* responsibility is to the song he sings, not to the audience for whom he is singing. In and of itself, this attitude distinguishes folk singing from all other types of vocal performance. The folk singer's role is to share with his audience rather than to perform for them. It is the cardinal rule of folk performance, and as such, should never be violated.

An authentic folk singer sings his songs by "heart," a word which in this context signifies more than the obvious meaning that the singer should not be reading from a book during his performing. More importantly, it means that the music must come from the singer's heart because it represents a personal outpouring of his musical message. The successful folk singer, then, will make his listeners feel his very presence as he shares a part of himself with them. This level of intimacy with the audience should be easy for the singer to achieve because it is within the very nature of folk music itself to require the individual personalization of the materials being presented.

Folk singers are expected—indeed, encouraged—to personalize their utterance. The term *version* is revered in folk circles, because it is the opportunity to do it "my way" that makes each new presentation of a folk song a vibrant, unique experience. This is not the case in performance of composed music where the recreation process must be true to the intent of the composer. This license to personalize expression extends well beyond the interpretation stage. The singer may change some of the tones, alter rhythms, devise new harmonies, modify or paraphrase lyrics, even create his own accompaniment, from the selection of instrument(s) all the way to the method of playing technique. The public is accustomed to selecting a Beethoven symphony, for example, played by a certain orchestra under the baton of a certain conductor. In such a case, the parameters of personal interpretation are somewhat limited in the real sense of taking liberties; however, with folk singing, all stops are out and the singer is "free" in the most liberal meaning of the word. The folk singer, then, is encouraged to personalize his expression and, more important, he is *expected* to do so.

Two versions of the same folk song are presented below. They might be described as essentially the same song. On closer scrutiny, however, one discovers that the titles are different, as well as the melodies, and especially, the lyrics. This example clearly illustrates that in the "hand-me-down" process, as in the personalizing process, folk songs do change.

I NEVER SHALL MARRY

Sea Chantey

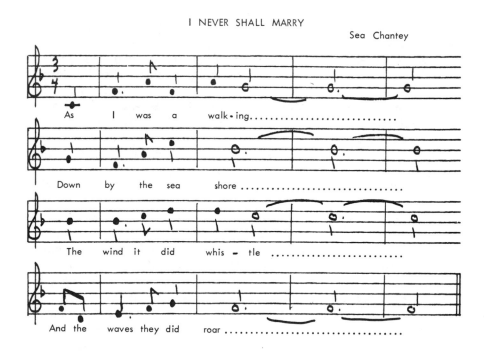

2. I spied a young maiden,
   So wond'rously fair;
   But her poor heart was broken,
   As she stood weeping there.

3. The shells in the ocean,
   Will be my death bed;
   The fish in deep water,
   Will swim over my head.

4. I Never Shall Marry,
   I'll be no man's wife;
   I intend to live single,
   The rest of my life.

5. As I went a-walking,
   Down by the seashore;
   The wind it did whistle,
   And the water did roar.

Sea Chantey

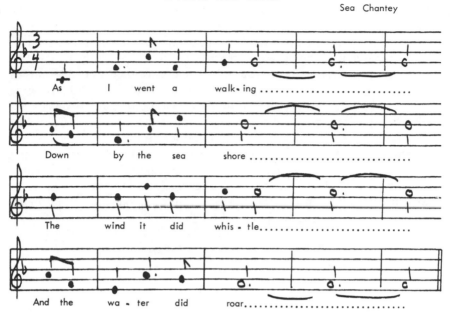

As I went a walk-ing ....

Down by the sea shore ....

The wind it did whis-tle...........................

And the wa-ter did roar...........................

2. I heard a young woman
   Make a pitiful cry
   Said "I Never Will Marry,"
   All the days of my life.

3. (*Repeat first verse*)

The folk singer should not be overly scientific or refined in his presentation. To do so would be to lose the essence of the art. The folk singer should have a natural and effortless singing voice. However, the voice should be rich in terms of musical quality. The ability to articulate the music and the lyrics so that the message is communicated effectively is equally important. Furthermore, the essential musicianship needed to handle all the musical elements involved in the performance is a desirable asset. What is not needed is the kind of refined singing that more appropriately belongs on the concert or operatic stage rather than on the back porch or in a student lounge.

Finally, a folk singer is more at harmony with his art when he is performing in an informal atmosphere. Folk music is essentially intimate music and it is best communicated in a small area to a small group of people. Today, of necessity, folk singers travel the world concertizing their music in huge auditoriums, stadiums, or domes. Obviously, something is lost in this type of setting; however, through modern technical assistance, every attempt is made to narrow the aesthetic distance between singer and listener to make the music more immediately communicative.

Mention must be made of the current practice of arranging folk songs in elaborate settings. Although this is not an authentic treatment of the music, one can easily understand the temptation for experimentation that these fine songs present to the highly skilled arranger. Equally, we can understand the interest of large performing organizations, choral or instrumental, to present folk songs that can fully utilize the full spectrum of their available musical resources. To be sure, these grand arrangements of folk songs are great audience pleasers. The practice is similar to that of a theater company that presents a Shakespearean play in period costume in a reconstructed Elizabethan theater rather than in a modern theater, in modern dress.

At any rate, whether folk songs are presented in a small, intimate setting or in a large, sophisticated one, they can still be enjoyed by both performers and listeners alike. It is left to the individual to choose from either the more simplistic and informal presentation or the more sophisticated and highly formal one, according to his personal taste.

3

The Characteristics of American Folk Song

American folk songs are one of our most precious national treasures. Even a cursory glance at American folk music will reveal that each song is like a thread woven into the fabric of American history. The songs that our nation has produced closely reflect its struggles, aspirations, major events, and changing moods, manners, and morals. More than any other nation, America has had the fertile soil from which the seeds of "people music" could grow in abundance. America was the new land, replete with natural resources, unscathed by political turmoil and unexploited by the masses—a virgin land ready for those peoples of the world with the necessary courage and initiative to seek a new beginning. As such, it became the crossroads for a multiplicity of cultures, nationalities, and human aspirations.

In addition to its material wealth, America offered the promise of freedom of expression and its guarantee of the pursuit of happiness—both noble, humanistic goals. Within such a framework, people not only had a natural arena for singing, but more important, they could sing in an unrestrained manner. It is important to keep this in mind as we begin to unlock the wealth of songs contributed by the American public.

In addition to the large volume of American folk songs, we can also boast of their diversity and uniqueness. There are the songs of the American pioneers, cowboys, gold miners, blacks, and the host of songs contributed by our transplanted European nationals. The rich variety of these contributing factors make the study of American folk music a fascinating subject.

American folk music was strongly influenced by the music of the Anglo-Saxons, minimally by the American Indians, and interestingly, by the contributions of the European nationals who emigrated to our shores during the nineteenth century. Therefore, it is safe to say that American folk music is made up of many "flavors," just as are so many other aspects of our culture. Based on a number of pluralistic sources, a new American sound emerged as a result of our unique quality of life and shaped by the events and happenings of our evolving history. Suffice it to say that our collection of American folk songs is unparalleled in its variety and unique sounds.

Each group of settlers who came to our shores tenaciously held on to their way of life and to the culture to which they were born. The early years were ones of major concern for survival, so the early settlers gained some measure of security by surrounding themselves with things from their native culture. Their quest to maintain their own way of life manifested itself in the food they ate, the homes they built and furnished, the clothes they wore, and the songs they sang. Each of the national groups who settled later also tended to preserve those things from their native culture that brought them security and a degree of satisfaction. Beyond this, they made the best of life through gradual adaptation to their new environment.

The early settlers performed the songs of their native homeland as the opportunity presented itself, thereby preserving them. They sang as they worked, prayed, or indulged in leisure-time activities. The songs they sang were their favorites of old. They sang them individually, in family or church groups, and with persons of the same cultural backgrounds. The inspiration and need for new and original American songs did not surface until the days of the Revolutionary War. During this time, however, the acculturation process took place. People took the best of their old cultures and adapted these things to their new way of life. In keeping with this, people took their favorite "old world" songs and changed them to serve a new purpose in their new way of life. As a consequence, these songs actually became American songs "by adoption." This Americanization of songs became a popular practice and resulted in a wealth of songs that were eventually shared among Americans of differing cultures.

It is surprising for one to learn that songs such as "Yankee Doodle" or "On Top of Old Smokey" are not originally American, but rather, American by adoption and adaptation. This should not be at all surprising because it is part and parcel of the folk process where the best and most pleasing songs are borrowed, shaped, and made the property of the adopting group, all without legal sanction. Throughout this book, we will look at a number of such songs and give their musical "genealogy" when it is available and can be somewhat authenticated.

Americans began to create original songs as a consequence of inspiration gained from the events and happenings of the times. This process actually began with the American Revolution when people were emotionally aroused and first began to feel themselves a breed apart, a new people with a common interest. Before proceeding to the musical contributions of the American people, it is necessary that we examine the base roots of that music that was in existence prior to the War for Independence.

Songs of the Pilgrims

The first group of settlers to make a profound effect on the way of music in America were Anglo-Saxons known as Pilgrims. Their music played a dominant role in determining what was to become the basis on which our American music would eventually be structured. The Pilgrims brought along their own collection of "approved" music; they encouraged singing and were instrumental in establishing what kind of music was to be used and how it should be distributed. They believed that the singing voice was a gift of God and should be used exclusively to praise him. The settlements of the southern seaboard were also made up primarily of those of Anglo-Saxon heritage. By the time some of the other nationals came to our shores and began sharing their cultural wares, the foundations for the new emerging American music had already been established.

The Pilgrims were a religious group who had separated from the Church of England in order to pursue their own method of worship. They had fled first to Amsterdam in 1593 because in Holland they found freedom to worship God in their own way. The Pilgrims were singers of psalms. They sang from an exclusive collection known as the Ainsworth Psalter prepared by one of the most musically learned men of their sect, Henry Ainsworth. The collection was prepared in Amsterdam in 1612. The psalms were a most interesting type of song. The lyrics for the songs came directly from the Bible. Because they were "purists," the Pilgrims could not accept man-made adaptations of Biblical teachings when there already existed authentic words that could be reinforced with musical sounds. The psalms, that portion of the Bible that most nearly resembles poetry, and as such, the most easily adaptable to musical treatment, were the obvious perfect choice for the Pilgrims to use.

Music for these psalms came from a variety of sources. The Pilgrims were ordinary folk, and therefore untrained in the art and science of music. Necessarily, then, they retained in their Psalter those English psalms (songs) that they already knew and still found to be acceptable; beyond this, they added psalms for which they could find suitable songs. Interestingly enough, these songs came literally from anywhere, even from sources that the Pilgrims considered morally objectionable. The important objective was to expand their psalter with the best suitable songs.

The practice of borrowing and adapting songs for use in worship went back to Martin Luther, the Father of Protestantism and the rejuvenator of congregational singing. The promotion of congregational singing came directly from Scriptures. ["Make a joyful noise unto the Lord all ye lands." (Psalm 97, v. 6) "Serve the Lord with gladness: come before his presence with singing." (Psalm 99, v. 2)] Luther was musically perceptive enough to know that he had to select songs for his congregation that would be easy to learn and retain. As a result, he borrowed songs from any source if he felt they would serve his purpose. On occasion, Luther was criticized for using songs that were sung by heathens, drunks, and sinners. He responded, "Why should the devil have all the best tunes?" He was very successful in his plight. A contemporary Catholic bishop was reputed to have said: "His songs do us far greater injury than his sermons."

Henry Ainsworth followed in the footsteps of Martin Luther. He wrote, "Tunes for the Psalms I find none set of God: so that each people is to use the most grave, decent and comfortable manner of singing that they know. . . . The singing notes, therefore, I have taken from our former English Psalms when they will fit the measure or verse." Ainsworth adapted a number of English and Dutch folk songs, which enabled him to expand the collection; these were songs that would fit the meter of the lyrics and be pleasing to sing.

Psalm singing in the Pilgrim congregation was performed in unison, which was done for two reasons. First, they believed that singing in harmony was too suggestive and detracted from the importance of the words; second, given their limited musical ability, to be able to learn the melody and sing it acceptably well was in and of itself a major accomplishment.

The Pilgrims sang in a free-flowing style reminiscent of Gregorian chant, which is understandable given that the psalms were not highly rhythmic in basic structure and that the words had only the slightest resemblance to metric poetry. Because the words moved freely, the music also had to move freely. Just as in Gregorian chant, the words were considered to be far more important than the music. Despite this fact, the music that they selected, simple and folklike, was worthy in itself. Together, words and music made some interesting songs, and even today there are some groups who sing these psalms and enjoy them fully.

In addition to those criteria mentioned above, the Pilgrims also looked for versatility when selecting songs to accompany psalms. The struggle involved in learning a particular song was well rewarded when the same tune could be used with more than one psalm. This was not as difficult as would appear because the psalms employed only a limited number of "poetic" structures. The following song illustrates this. It can be used for Psalms 17, 23, 25, 77, 85, 92, and 124 because in each of them the "poetic" structure is composed of five lines of ten syllables each.

PSALM 23

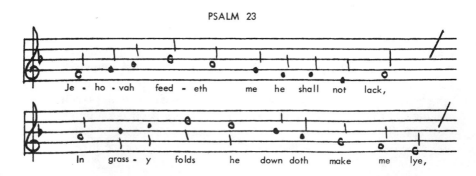

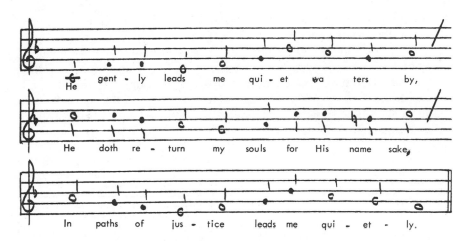

He gent - ly leads me qui - et wa ters by,

He doth re - turn my souls for His name sake,

In paths of jus - tice leads me qui - et - ly.

2. Yea, though I walk in dale of deadly shade
   He fear none ill, for with me thou wilt be,
   Thy rod they staff else they shall comfort me
   For me, a table thou has ready-made
   In their presence that my distressers be.

3. Thou makes fat mine head with anointing oil
   My cup abounds, doubtless, good and mercie
   Shall all the days of my life follow me;
   Also within Jehovah's howse I shall
   To Length of dayse repose me quiet lie.

The Pilgrims used no accompaniment with their congregational singing. Although considered a useful tool in helping to teach songs and maintain musical order, the popular organ was disallowed in Pilgrim worship. For one reason, this instrument would produce harmony and therefore detract from the preeminence of the words. The organ was also a percussive-type instrument and would deter from helping to maintain the fluidity of the presentation. As a matter of fact, the Pilgrims hated the organ so much that they referred to the instrument as "a kist (chest) of whistles."

The teaching of new tunes to accompany the psalms or the adaptation of familiar Psalm tunes to yet other psalms was accomplished by a process known as "lining out."* The person teaching the tune, or more correctly, the psalm, be he minister or song leader, would actually line out the tune line by line. He would sing the first line to the congregation, then have them repeat it with him until the line was satisfactorily committed. Then the same process would be used for each subsequent line through the remainder of the song. Eventually everyone would join together in the singing of the entire psalm.

The song materials used in conjunction with the psalms favored the major scale over the minor scale, a practice that has become a hallmark of American music down to the present. The minor scale was not excluded from

*This same process is used in our elementary schools today. We call it learning new songs via the "rote process."

the song repertoire; however, it was not held in as great favor as those tunes based on the major scale.

The ever popular "Old Hundreth" is presented here in what might be described as its Pilgrim Psalter setting, and then, in its more modern setting. Other than that the words are different, one should notice that as a psalm it is written to be sung as a free-flowing, nonmetric song. In the more modern setting it should be sung giving attention to a definite beat and perhaps with an accompaning harmonization.

OLD HUNDRETH

2. It's He that made us, not wee,
   His folk and sheep of His feeding,
   O with confession inter yee
   His gates, His courtyards with
   praising.

3. Confess to Him bless ye His name
   Because Jehovah He good is.
   His mercy ever is the same
   And His faith into all ages.

DOXOLOGY

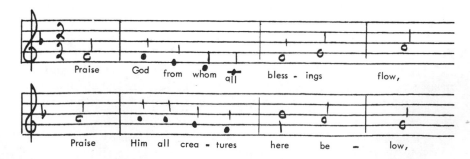

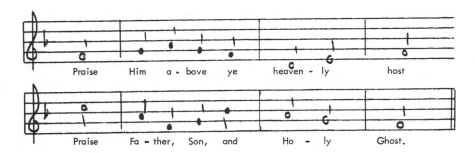

Praise Him a - bove ye heaven - ly host
Praise Fa - ther, Son, and Ho - ly Ghost.

The Pilgrims not only sang psalms in religious worship but also during their leisure hours. Indeed, psalm singing was one of their favorite pastimes. They frequently met with psalters in hand as a family, or at particular homes, or with larger gatherings of friends to indulge in the joy of singing.

It is interesting to note that the very first book printed on American soil was the Bay Psalm Book (1698). This particular collection was considered to be of lesser quality than the original Ainsworth Psalter; however, it was this collection that received broader use with the larger populace known as the Puritan people. The Bay Psalm Book catered to singers of even less musical ability than the Pilgrims. It did, nevertheless, continue in the same musical vein as the original Ainsworth Psalter.

Before leaving this discussion of psalm singing, it should be noted that these psalms and even the processes used in their performance were "folk-like" in the very real sense. The tunes employed were basically folk tunes, and the process involved in learning and sharing them was equally "folk-like." Even the people who collected and used them were ordinary folk. Psalm singing was strongly identified with the New England settlements; the settlements to the south went in another direction.

Hymnody came to America around 1725 through the influence of Charles and John Wesley who first heard the music sung by a group of German Moravians aboard a ship bound for America. Hymn tunes were folk-like in character and had tremendous personal appeal because they had more rhythmic verve than the more complacent psalms. Therefore, they could generate a greater emotional response from their performers, and as a result, people could become more emotionally involved in religious worship.

Whereas psalms had words taken directly from the Bible, hymns were based on poems inspired from Biblical messages. Although psalms were free-flowing and more fluid in rhythmic structure, hymns were in strict metered rhythm. Psalms were sung in unison, without harmony or accompaniment; hymns, on the other hand, were more often harmonized and provided for accompaniment. Finally, the singing or performance of psalms, if handled in the "right" manner, would be on a serious, controlled, and musically correct basis; hymn singing, on the other hand, encouraged the addition of harmonic sounds, embellishments, and the freer use of the expressive elements of music (volume, tempo, style, and so on).

Enthusiasm for hymn singing was so great that Singing Societies were established and many new methods for the easy learning of the "scientific" aspects of music reading were promoted (shaped notes, fa–so–la systems, and so on). Itinerant song masters roamed the countryside bringing the latest in hymns to the rural folk, and periodically big Sing-ins were conducted. New singing hymnals began to appear everywhere, and everyone was into the joy of hymn singing.

It would be correct to say that the art of hymn singing was part of the folk process and, as such, strongly influenced the later creation of folk songs that became staples of American folk music. The musical materials used in the early hymns of the south were very similar to the materials employed in the psalms sung in the north. Again, they were predominantly based on the musical practices of the Anglo-Saxons.

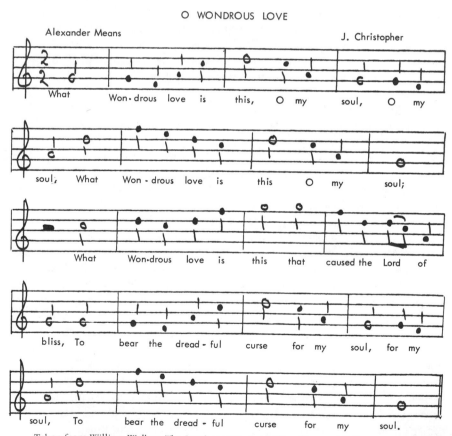

O WONDROUS LOVE

Taken from William Walker, *The Southern Harmony* (New Haven, 1835).

AMAZING GRACE

John Newton   Traditional

A - maz - ing   grace   how   s weet   the   sound,   That

saved   a   wretch   like   me;   I   once   was   lost   but

now   am   found,   Was   blind   but   now   I   see.

Music of the American Indian

In any discussion of American folk music it would be unfair to omit the music of the American Indian, even though (in the final analysis) it did not play a significant role in determining the way of American folk music. Nevertheless, it is American "people" music, and therefore merits our consideration.

The early colonists were intrigued with the music of the Indians; however, they soon came to the conclusion that their own music was far more advanced, culturally speaking, than that of the Indians. It is speculated that the music of the Indians was based on a different system of sounds and that the colonists made the necessary adjustments to accommodate these tones into their sound system.

Indian music was primarily vocal music with some instrumental accompaniment. The singing was done in unison and always by groups rather than by individuals. Women may have sung on their own, but only men participated in the more important events where singing was a part of the ceremony or ritual. What made the singing of the males most intriguing was their extensive use of falsetto or the false voice.

Indian music was based on the pentatonic or five-tone scale, a system normally associated with primitive cultures and especially with Oriental music. All songs were meticulously rehearsed because any flaw in performance would, in effect, nullify the purpose for singing. Indian music was performed almost exclusively for functional purposes. It is unfortunate that the popular impression we have of Indian music is that which we have heard as background music in movies dealing with Indian subjects. The music used in such films is usually war-like in character, and to the average listener it sounds very much the same. The Indian, however, created music about the seasons of the year, sunset and sunrise, mountains, lakes, harvest, and so on. Music, then, served a functional rather than an entertainment role in his way of life. He thought of his music as being "good" or "powerful"; beautiful music or artistic quality were not his chief concerns.

There was no "leader" involved in the proper presentation of their music. Usually, the group began by establishing an appropriate tonal center. Once it had been established, the group proceeded to a series of melodic ideas or phrases in between which they returned to the original tonal center before going off again. The Indian would not tolerate any deviation from the correct conception of the music; indeed, this was frowned upon. There was no place for personal interpretation or improvisation in their music.

The words in their songs were, for the most part, what we would consider nonsense syllables. Each song had an explicit message to convey and the mood expressed in the total effort was sufficient. Therefore, a series of words was not needed to get the message across. However, there are examples of Indian songs that contain pure lyrics.

Indian music was rhythmic in that it had a steady underlying beat that was often joined with bodily movements and percussive effects performed on rather crude instruments. Over and above this steady beat were metric divisions of groups that could best be described as heterometric in nature. One might hear a group of four beats, followed by two groups of three beats, followed by one group of five beats. Even though this phase of musical rhythm is both difficult to respond to and considered to be advanced by Western cultural standards, the Indian performed them with ease and proficiency.

In addition to their collection of drums, sticks, beads, and rattles, the Indians had an impressive instrument known as the end-blown notched flute, which was capable of playing melodic tunes. Carved from wood, this instrument was able to produce a very pleasing, haunting sound.

During the early nineteenth century, when our first breed of American composers was being accused of producing mere European imitations in their artistic endeavors, some of them turned to Indian musical devices in an attempt at originality. This trend did produce some interesting works and helped brand its practitioners as "Indianist composers" (page 33). It soon became the consensus of opinion within musical circles that Indian music was pure ethnic music, and as such, had little potential for determining an American symphonic tradition.

The songs of the Irish, Africans, Germans, Poles, French, Spaniards, Italians, and other nationals who later arrived at our shores were either held intact or absorbed into American folk songs via the assimilation process. Many of their songs were given new lyrics and "Americanized" just as the people who brought them were. These songs have taken on a new identifica-

NA NA HE NA HA HA

Ojibway Indian Song

Na na he na   ha ha,   Na na he na   ha ha,   Na na he na

ha ha,   Na na he na   ha ha,   ha .....   ha....

MOOJE MOCCASIN

Ojibway Indian Song

Moo - je   moc - ca - sin,   O   jah   jah,

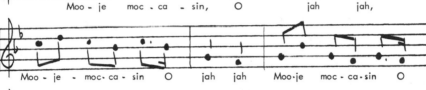

Moo - je - moc- ca - sin   O   jah   jah   Moo·je   moc - ca· sin   O

jah   jah   Moo - je   moc - ca - sin   O   jah   jah.

Translation: "I am wearing wornout moccasins."

tion and have lost their original cultural stamp. Many of the national songs that were considered dear to their people were held intact and can often be heard at weddings, festivals, and other kinds of social gatherings where people in attendance wish to emphasize their ethnic backgrounds. The long-held theory that America is a "melting pot" is now being challenged by sociologists as we evidence groups who prefer to identify themselves as Irish-Americans, Jewish-Americans, or Italian-Americans. Their allegiance to America is never in question; their desire to hold on to their ethnic origins is commendable. America, rather than being a "melting pot" is, in essence, a "Nation from Nations"!

American folk music is pluralistic. Its dominant influence has been exerted by the Anglo-Saxons, with some contributions by other nationals. Be it "Americanized" or original, it is the music that Americans have sung from the Atlantic to the Pacific, from the days of Bunker Hill to the present. It is represented by a fascinating collection of songs. Let us now take a closer look at the various groups of Americans who provided us with their musical heritage and mention the particular events in their lives that served as their sources of inspiration and need. Their contributions contain delightful gems of humor, wit, and wisdom.

4

Songs of the American Revolution

Before proceeding to the songs associated with the American Revolution, mention should be made of a popular type of song, secular in nature as compared with the sacred psalms and hymns, that occupied the attention of the colonists. These songs were called Broadside Ballads. The art of balladry had a long and well-established tradition in the British isles. The joy of singing ballads, both traditional and new, was an integral part of the heritage that the early colonists brought with them from the "mother country." As has already been mentioned, ballads were a special type of solo song in which the singer recounted events connected with a myriad of situations ranging from simple romances to great acts of heroism. The lyrics were usually vignettes from dramatic literature that helped provide the listener with a realistic scenario for an eventful happening. Like a good story, they would keep the listener in complete suspense until the final verse.

Early on, the term *broadside* was connected with the word *ballad;* later, it was used independently—the word *ballad* being held implicit in the one word. A broadside referred to a single sheet of paper on which ballads were printed and distributed. It was of sizable dimensions for a handbill and usually was printed on only one side and from side-to-side across the folds. Sometimes, especially in the colonies, these broadsides were used to editorialize current events. They were "for sale" on the streets and, in effect, functioned as singing newspapers. Broadsides were an important and powerful vehicle for the efficient and widespread dissemination of news through balladry and comment. Suffice it to say that the art of British balladry was a way of life, a vital part of the heritage that all British colonists delighted in and were accustomed to.

One of the most popular of the old British ballads and one that was known to be a favorite of General George Washington was the ballad "Barbara Allen." Surprisingly enough, this ballad has surfaced in several strange places all across the United States. Typically, there are a variety of melodies connected with it; however, the words are in conformity with the general story line. The title appears in some versions as "Bawbree Allen" (Scottish) and, in the particular version to come down from the Southern Mountains, as "Barbry Ellen." By 1776, the ballad was already several centuries old. Most often, the singing of the ballad drew tears from its listeners, especially the ladies of genteel background. The ballad tells of a powerful romance and a man called Sweet William who actually died from a broken heart over his cruel treatment by the hard-hearted Barbara Allen. The song is just as easy to listen to as it is to sing. No wonder it has withstood the test of time and remained forever popular.

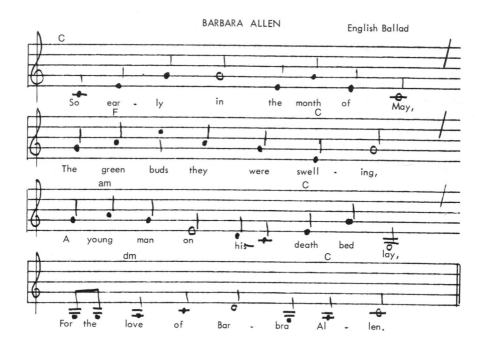

BARBARA ALLEN   English Ballad

So early in the month of May,
The green buds they were swelling,
A young man on his death bed lay,
For the love of Barbra Allen.

He called his servant to his bed,
And lowly he said to him;
"Go bring the one that I love best,
And that is Barbara Allen."

Slowly, slowly he got up,
And went to the dwelling;
Saying, "I'm sent for the one that he
    loves best,
And that is Barbara Allen."

Slowly, slowly she got up,
And slowly she went to him;
The very first word when she got there,
"Young man, I'm afraid you're dying."

"Do you remember the other day,
When we were at the tavern;
You drank a health to the ladies all,
And you slighted Barbara Allen."

"Yes, I remember the other day,
When we were at the tavern;
I drank a health to the ladies all,
And three to Barbara Allen."

"Do you remember the other night,
When we were at the ballroom
dancing?
You gave your hand to the ladies all,
And slighted Barbara Allen."

"Yes, I remember the other night,
When we were at the ballroom dancing;
I gave my hand to the ladies all,
And my heart to Barbara Allen."

He turned his pale face to the wall,
His back upon the dwelling;
And all his friends cried out, "For
shame,
Hard-hearted Barbara Allen."

She hadn't got more than a mile from
town,
'Til she heard some death bell ringing.
And every knock it seemed to say,
"Hard-hearted Barbara Allen."

She hadn't gone more than another
mile
'Til she spied his corpse a-coming,

"Lie down, lie down that cold pale
corpse
And let me gaze upon him."

The longer she gazed, the louder she
cried,
And all of his friends a-telling,
"The loss of your Sweet William dear,
Was the loving of Barbara Allen."

Sweet William he died like it might be
today,
And Barbara died tomorrow;
Sweet William he died out of pure,
pure love,
And Barbara died for sorrow.

Sweet William was buried in the new
church yard,
And Barbara in another;
And out of his grave there grew a red
rose,
From Barbara's grew a briar.

The briar and the rose they grew
together,
'Til they could not grow any higher;
They wrapped and they tied in a true
lover's knot,
For all true lovers to admire.

"The Death of General Wolfe" best illustrates the true function of the broadside ballad as a dramatic–musical vehicle for the dissemination of newsworthy information. The hero of the siege of Quebec on September 13, 1759 was a brave young commander who died during his great moment of triumph. The events surrounding the occasion are retold in literary splendor. The ballad is considered to be among the first created on American soil.

THE DEATH OF GENERAL WOLFE

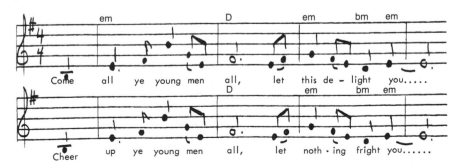

Ne - ver   let your cour - age   fall,   when you're brought to tri - al.........

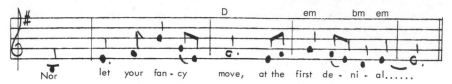

Nor   let your fan - cy   move, at the first de - ni - al......

Lyrics taken from John Anthony Scott, *The Ballad of America: The History of the United States in Song and Story.* Carbondale: Southern Illinois University Press, 1983. 2nd edition, p. 36. Used by permission.

2. Bad news is come to town, bad
   news is carried,
   Bad news is whispered 'round, my
   love is married.
   Bad news is come to town, I fell a-
   weeping
   They stole my love from me while
   I lay sleeping.

3. Love, here's a diamond ring, if
   you'll accept it,
   'Tis for your sake alone, long time
   I've kept it.
   When you this posy read, think on
   the giver,
   Madam, remember me, or I'm
   undone forever.

4. So then this gallant youth did cross
   the ocean,
   To free America from her invasion;
   He landed at Quebec with all his
   party,
   The city to attack, being brave and
   hearty.

5. Brave Wolfe drew up his men, in a
   line so pretty,
   On the plains of Abraham before
   the city;
   A distance from the town the
   French did meet him,
   With a double number they
   resolved to beat him.

6. The French drew up their men, for
   death prepared,
   In one another's face the armies
   stared,
   While Wolfe and Montcalm
   together walked,
   Between their armies they like
   brothers talked.

7. Each man then took this post at
   their retire,
   So then these numerous hosts
   began to fire,
   The cannon on each side did roar
   like thunder,
   And youths in all their pride were
   torn asunder.

8. The drums did loudly beat, colors
   were flying,
   The purple gore did stream, and
   men lay dying;
   When shot off from his horse fell
   this brave hero,
   And we lament his loss in weeds of
   sorrow.

9. The French began to break, their
   ranks were flying,
   Wolfe seemed to revive while he
   lay dying;
   He lifted up his head while guns
   did rattle,
   And to his army said, "How goes
   the battle?"

10. His aide-de-camp replied, "'Tis in
     our favor";
     Quebec with all her pride, nothing
     can save her;
     She falls into our hands with all
     her treasure."
     "O then," brave Wolfe replied, "I
     die with pleasure."

11. Bad news is come to town, bad
     news is carried,
     Some say my love is dead, some
     say he's married;
     As I was a-pondering on this, I fell
     a-weeping,
     They stole my love from me, while
     I lay sleeping.

War is a time when human emotions run their highest. Every man, woman, and child in some way is affected by this extraordinary and abrupt change in lifestyle. Thoughts of death, which could possibly rob you of your loved one, destruction of property, which could possibly be your own, and the inevitability of the displacement of family members to places where they would never travel under normal conditions, are mind shattering. For these reasons people become more emotional and more vocal, and they do not hesitate to make their feelings known. They express them through conversations, articles, pictures, poems, demonstrations—and songs. The songs they sing are often familiar ones to which they add timely lyrics; if the inspiration is great and some degree of musical talent is in evidence, then an entirely new and original song has been created.

One type of song is directly connected with the persons involved in the conflict. These songs are written to cheer on the troops, build their morale, rekindle their patriotism, help them to march, or to think about as they rest and reflect. Commanders of military units have always understood this need for music. Napoleon was one of the first generals in history to realize the importance of establishing military bands, and a considerable amount of patriotic and inspirational music of quality was composed for his bands to perform. General Robert E. Lee was reported to have said "An army cannot win without good music."

There are also songs about the people who are affected by war, those who are back home, well behind the battle lines. These songs are reflective, sentimental songs that deal with departed loved ones.

There are even some war songs that are humorous in nature because it is vitally important at such times to be able to forget reality momentarily and look at the lighter and brighter side of life. Each war has produced its share of songs, songs that help describe the relevant events pertaining to their conflict and their times. The Revolutionary War was no exception in this respect. It was, however, unique in that this was the first conflict in which the new emerging nation, America, was participating. The colonists dared to challenge one of the world's greatest empires, one that had just successfully fought a battle with France for complete control of the North American continent, and indeed, for world supremacy. Persons having only a superficial understanding of American history hold the notion that the entire colonial population was united in their determination to become an independent nation, even to making the supreme sacrifice in order to attain freedom. This was not the case. Actually, only about one third of the population supported the cause for freedom. Another third was passionately loyal to the crown, whereas the remaining third did not care one way or the other. These were perilous times and each of the Founding Fathers, along with their compatriots, was risking treason with every spoken word and deed.

The British crown should never have had any doubt regarding the eventual desire on the part of the colonists to rebel. The new world was a refuge for all those who had the courage to depart from all the things of the old world that they had found objectionable. Additionally, the mere physical separation of the British isles and the colonies provided the right ingredients for the nurturing of rebellion. As more and more rumblings of dissent emerged from the New World, the British leadership retaliated with a strengthening and reaffirmation of their empire-building policies. They decreed that their colonies existed for the sole purpose of rendering to the crown strategic military bases, markets for goods, access for raw materials, manpower, and gold for their coffers. The American colonists, who were just beginning to sense a commonality of culture and a zest for freedom responded with bitter opposition and rebellion.

A number of interesting songs contributed by the rebellious colonists helped to call attention to the injustices being inflicted upon them by the British government. These songs served to spread the word concerning the wrongdoings and tried to enlist the support of others to join in the opposition. This they accomplished by creating new verses to old, well-known songs; more interestingly, however, they prepared new verses to songs that were highly revered by the "opposition." This would be the ultimate insult. The following sets of lyrics dramatically illustrate this practice. These words were penned to accompany the tune of the British national anthem, "God Save the King."

GOD SAVE THE THIRTEEN STATES

God save the thir - teen states, Long rule the Un - i - ted States, God save our states; Make us vic - tor - i - ous Hap - py and glor - i - ous, No ty - rants o - ver us God Save Our States.

GOD SAVE GREAT WASHINGTON
(same tune)

God save Great Washington,
His worth from every tongue
Demands applause.
Ye tuneful pow'rs combine,
And each true Whig now joins,
Whose heart did ne'er resign
The glorious cause.

The 1784 version of the song, credited to Samuel F. Smith, carefully sums up the grand purpose of the conflict and the hope for the new land of freedom. This is the version that Americans sing today.

AMERICA

My country 'tis of thee, Sweet land of liberty,
Of thee I sing; Land where my fathers died,
Land of the Pilgrim's pride, from ev'ry mountainside
Let freedom ring!

Our fathers' God to Thee, Author of liberty,
To thee we sing: Long may our land be bright
With freedom's holy light; Protect us by Thy might,
Great God, our King!

The New Massachusetts Liberty Song (dated around 1770) first appeared as a broadside out of Boston. It is yet another example of a song based on a tune held in high esteem by the "enemy." The message contained in these lyrics laid the groundwork for rebellion and attempted to muster support for the cause of liberty. It is based on the "British Grenadiers," a tune that British soldiers marched to with great pride. The practice of taking the best of the opposing side's songs and making them your own became popular during the Revolutionary War. We will see the reappearance of this practice in subsequent conflicts in which the United States has participated.

THE NEW MASSACHUSETTS LIBERTY SONG

Traditional

That seat of Sci - ence Ath - ens, and Earth's proud Mis - tress Rome,

Where now are all their Glo - ries, We scarce can find their Tomb;

Then guard your rights A - mer - i - cans Nor stoop to law - less Sway....

Op - pose, Op - pose, Op - pose....... My brave A - mer - i - ca.

Music and lyrics from John Anthony Scott, *The Ballad of America: The History of the United States in Song and Story.* Carbondale: Southern Illinois University Press, 1983. 2nd edition, p. 56. Used by permission.

The next selection represents a highly imaginative way of using the vehicle of song to secure support for the cause. With the Townshend Act of 1767 England decreed that a duty would be placed on all tea, glass, paint, and other goods imported by the colonies. This, as we know, made the colonists furious. They retaliated with the Boston Tea Party, but also by asking their people to boycott all textiles imported from Great Britain. To be sure, the boycott had a devastating effect on British trade. A careful scrutiny of the words contained in the song "Young Ladies in Town" will reveal the true genius of the creators in their pleading to women to set their own fashions and place love of country above that of high fashion.

YOUNG LADIES IN TOWN

Colonial Song

Young la - dies in town and those that live 'round, Wear none but your own country

lin - en, Of e - con - o - my boast, let your pride be the most, To show

42

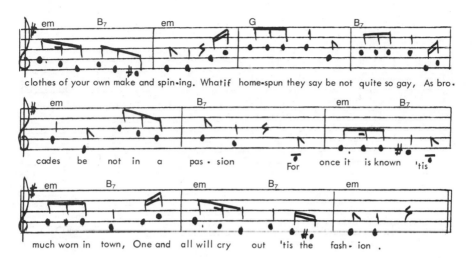

clothes of your own make and spin•ing. What if home•spun they say be not quite so gay, As bro•

cades be not in a pas • sion For once it is known 'tis

much worn in town, One and all will cry out 'tis the fash• ion .

2. And as one all agree, that you'll not married be,
To such as will wear London factory;
But at first sight refuse, tell 'em you will choose,
As encourage our own manufactory.
No more ribbons wear, nor in rich silks appear,
Love your country much better than fine things,
Begin without passion 'twill soon be the fashion,
To grace your smooth locks with a twine string.

3. Throw away your bohea, and your green hyson tea,
And all things of a new fashioned duty;
Get in a good store of the choice Labrador,
There'll soon be enough here to suit ye.
These do without fear and to all you'll appear,
Fair charming, true, lovely and clever,
Though the times remain darkish, young men will be sparkish,
And love you most stronger than ever.

William Billings, a self-styled New England "composer" of psalm and hymn tunes, was a passionate supporter of the American cause of liberty. He took steps to prepare some "revolutionary" lyrics to one of his best-loved hymns in an effort to solicit new supporters. Being physically handicapped, he felt his best contribution was through the writing of inspirational music. Billings' "Chester" received an unprecedented number of performances during the nation's recent bicentennial celebrations in 1976. It should be noted, tangentially, that songs like "Chester," whose titles are the name of a town, city, or area, were the type to which other sets of words could easily be adapted. People could immediately identify the tune by name and sing a different set of words to it. This concept of song versatility and adaptability, which was discussed earlier, is firmly entrenched in the folk process. Carefully scrutinize the words of this martial tune and think of the great inspiration it gave our troops as they marched confidently onward to victory.

43

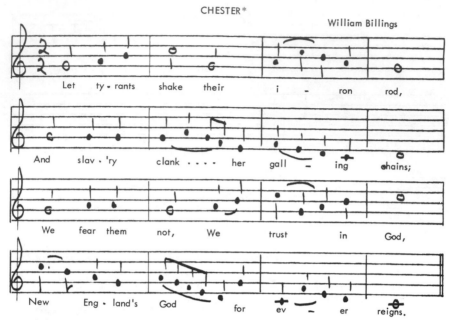

CHESTER*

William Billings

Let ty-rants shake their i - ron rod,
And slav-'ry clank . . . . her gall - ing chains;
We fear them not, We trust in God,
New Eng-land's God for ev - er reigns.

*The Singing Master's Assistant (Boston 1778).

2. Howe and Burgoyne and Clinton too,
   With Prescot and Cornwallis join'd
   Together plot our Overthrow
   In one Infernal league combin'd.

3. When God inspir'd us for the fight
   Their ranks were broke, their lines were forc'd
   Their ships were shatter'd in our sight
   Or swiftly driven from our coast.

4. The Foe comes on with haughty stride
   Our troops advance with martial noise
   Their Vet'runs flee before our Youth
   And Gen'rals yield to beardless boys.

5. What grateful Off'rings shall we bring,
   What shall we render to the Lord?
   Loud Hallelujahs let us sing
   And praise his name on ev'ry Chord.

Without exception, the song "Yankee Doodle" should appear on everyone's list of top ten best American folk songs. However, as was mentioned earlier, it was a song that became American through the process of adoption and total assimilation. As a matter of fact, prior to the Revolutionary War it had been well known both in England and the European mainland as well. There is no question about its tunefulness and immediate appeal. The events connected with its American appeal and eventual adoption as an informal national anthem are fascinating. Reportedly, a British surgeon, Dr. Richard Shackburg, used the song during the early days of conflict to mock the appearance of the American militiamen. Compared to the polished, splendidly outfitted British soldiers, the bumpkin colonials looked anything but

44

professional. After careful scrutiny of the song's title and lyrics, one can fully appreciate their satiric wit.

Yankee is said to be an Indian corruption or derogatory term used to identify the colonial settlers. *Doodle* is a term that was rather liberally used to call attention to a trifling fool. Thus, the title pointedly served to identify exactly what the surgeon was describing. The word *macaroni* as it is used in the lyrics does not, as one might assume, refer to Italian pasta. Rather, the term was meant to describe an overdressed, perhaps even flamboyantly dressed, person. Macaroni is somewhat synonymous with the term *dandy,* which appears later in the lyric. In a very subtle way, then, the lyrics poke fun at the poorly clad colonial soldiers and their chances of winning the girls.

The song became an instant "hit" with the British troops and was used at every opportunity to mock the American militiamen. Months later, however, as American forces were beginning to savor victory, the song was literally taken up by the American militiamen in the British version and, in turn, used to mock them. Without a doubt, this was the supreme insult. New sets of verses were added to this fine, jaunty song, many of which made their sudden appearance and disappearance. The versions handed down and preserved to this day still retain the original first verse along with some descriptive verses connected with the war. "Yankee Doodle" was played by the victorious troops at the ceremonies connected with Cornwallis's surrender at Yorktown on October 9, 1781. Ironically enough, the British chose to play "The World Turned Upside Down"!

YANKEE DOODLE

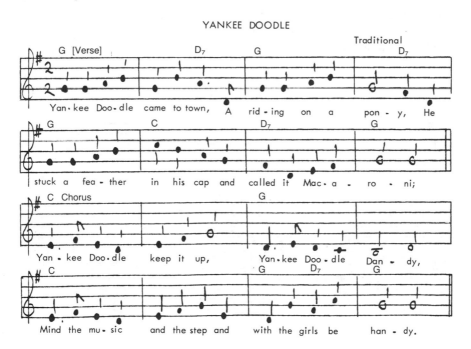

2. Father and I went down to camp
   Along with Captain Gooding
   And there we saw the men and boys
   As thick as hasty pudding.
   (*Chorus*)

3. There was Captain Washington
   Upon a slapping stallion
   A-giving orders to his men
   I guess there was a million.
   (*Chorus*)

4. The troopers they would gallop up
   And fire right in our faces
   It scared me almost half to death
   To see them run such races.
   (*Chorus*)

5. We saw a little barrel, too
   The heads were made of leather,
   They knocked on it with little clubs
   And called the folks together.
   (*Chorus*)

6. And then we saw a giant run
   Large as a log of maple
   Upon a deuced little cart
   A load for father's cattle.
   (*Chorus*)

7. And every time they shoot it off
   It takes a horn of powder
   It makes a noise like father's gun
   Only a nation louder.
   (*Chorus*)

8. I can't tell you half I see
   They kept up such a smother
   So I took my hat off, made a bow
   And scampered home to mother.
   (*Chorus*)

9. Yankee Doodle is the tune
   Americans delight in
   'Twill do to whistle, sing or play
   And just the thing for fightin'.
   (*Chorus*)

Another song that alludes to the ill-clad colonial soldier and his resourcefulness in acquiring a "complete" uniform is the delightful and humorous "Soldier, Soldier Will You Marry Me." There are differences of opinion regarding the origin of the song. Some would claim that it is an adopted song containing few changes, if any; others would suggest that it is an original song shaped from the events surrounding the war. The song has remained mostly intact, except for the final verse where the punch line becomes the property of the singer.

SOLDIER, SOLDIER WILL YOU MARRY ME

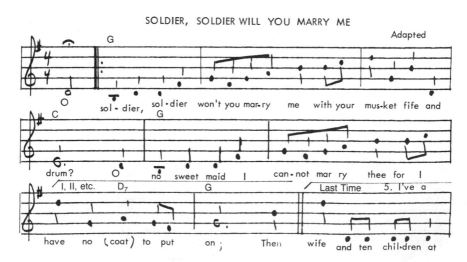

home.　Off she went to her grand fath.ers chest And got him a (coat) of the ver-y, ver - y best, She got him a (coat) of the ver-y, ver - y best, And the sol - dier put it on;

2. hat　　3. gloves　　4. boots

One of the loveliest songs sung during the American Revolution was "Johnny Has Gone for a Soldier." This song is based on an old Irish tune entitled "Shoon Aroon." It tells about a girl who waits longingly at home for her lover who is off to war. The song is hauntingly beautiful and musically perfect; the words describe the situation with marvelous sensitivity.

JOHNNY HAS GONE FOR A SOLDIER

Irish Tune

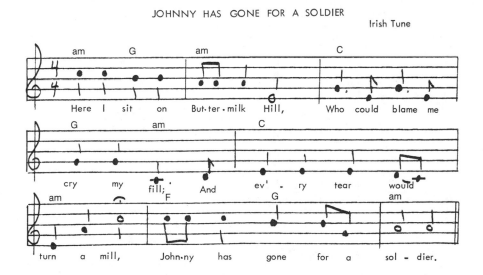

Here I sit on But-ter-milk Hill, Who could blame me cry my fill; And ev' - ry tear would turn a mill, John-ny has gone for a sol - dier.

2. Me oh my, I loved him so,
   Broke my heart to see him go
   And only time will heal my woe,
   Johnny has gone for a soldier.

3. I'll sell my flax, I'll sell my wheel,
   Buy my love a sword of steel
   So it in battle he may wield,
   Johnny has gone for a soldier.

4. (*Repeat first verse*)

   The events that surrounded the stunning American victory at Bennington were the source of inspiration for "The Riflemen of Bennington." General Stark, who had fought at Bunker Hill and with Washington at Trenton, commanded a contingent of Mountain Boys who repelled an attempt by Burgoyne's troops to seek some important stores stockpiled outside Bennington. This defeat at the hands of the sharpshooters not only made the surrender of Burgoyne at Saratoga probable, but also inevitable. The song made its first appearance as a broadside, and in a very short time it was sung by the supporters of the cause all up and down the eastern seaboard. American militiamen and other volunteers were expert sharpshooters. They had perfected their skill while living on the frontiers where they had to rely on their marksmanship to supply their dinner table with fresh meat. Americans used this ability in a most unorthodox method while fighting the British. Traditionally, wars had been fought by both armies advancing to a locale conducive for battle. Once the battle lines were drawn, they would advance by columns and ranks firing by platoons. Not so with the American forces; they hid behind trees and barricades and "picked off" the enemy one by one. Americans had every right to boast about their riflemen, as was done so well in this broadside.

THE RIFLEMEN OF BENNINGTON

Revolutionary War Song

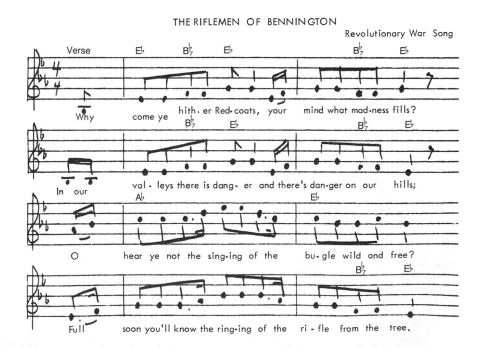

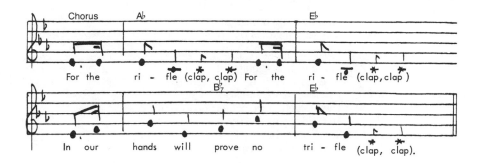

For the ri - fle (clap, clap) For the ri - fle (clap, clap)
In our hands will prove no tri - fle (clap, clap).

2. Ye ride a goodly steed, ye may know another master;
   Ye forward come with speed, but ye'll learn to back much faster.
   When ye meet our mountain boys, and their leader Johnny Stark
   Lads who make but little noise, lads who always hit the mark.
   (*Chorus*)

The broadside ballad that best illustrates the functional use to which these singing newspapers were aimed was "Lord Cornwallis's Surrender." As in the New Massachusetts Liberty Song cited above, the words of this song were prepared to accompany the much revered British marching song, "The British Grenadiers," thus making the humiliation all the more complete. The ballad helps dramatize the events of the surrender and ends with a note of hope for the future of the new nation.

"LORD CORNWALLIS'S SURRENDER"

1. Come all you brave Americans,
   The truth to you I'll tell,
   'Tis of sad misfortune,
   To Britain late befell;
   'Twas all in the heights of Yorktown,
   Where cannons loud did roar,
   They summoned Lord Cornwallis,
   To fight or else give o'er.

2. The summons then to be served,
   Was sent unto my Lord,
   Which made him feel like poor Burgoyne,
   And quickly draw his sword;
   Say must I give these glittering troops,
   These ships and Hessians too,
   And yield to General Washington,
   And his bold rebel crew?

3. A grand council then was called,
   His Lordship gave command,
   Say what think you now my heroes,
   To yield you may depend.
   For don't you see the bombshells fly,
   And cannons loud do roar,

Count de Grasse lies in the harbour,
And Washington's on shore.

4. 'Twas the nineteenth of October,
   In the year of eighty-one,
   Lord Cornwallis he surrendered,
   To General Washington.
   They marched from their posts brave boys,
   And quickly grounded arms.
   Rejoice you brave Americans,
   With music's sweetest charms.

5. Six thousand chosen British troops
   To Washington resigned,
   Besides some ships and Hessians,
   That could not stay behind;
   With refugees and blackamores,
   Oh what a direful crew,
   It was then he had some thousands,
   But now he's got but few.

6. Here's a health to great Washington,
   And his brave army too,
   And likewise to our worthy Greene,
   To him much honor's due;
   May we subdue those English troops,
   And clear the eastern shore,
   That we may live in peace, my boys,
   While wars they are no more.

The song that appropriately serves to close this chapter on the songs of the American Revolution is "In the Good Old Colony Days." The tune itself is considered to be an old one and a good one. The new words were added around the year 1780, just prior to the surrender. The song is unique because it is reflective, already asking its presenters and listeners to begin to think back to the good old days. It is very British in style, with its fa-la-la's from the old English madrigals. The song is best appreciated for its bouncy beat and delightful humor.

IN THE GOOD OLD COLONY DAYS

Colonial Song

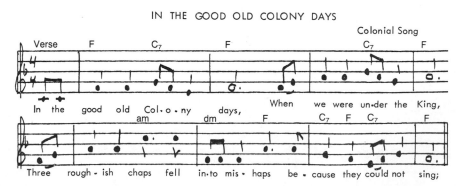

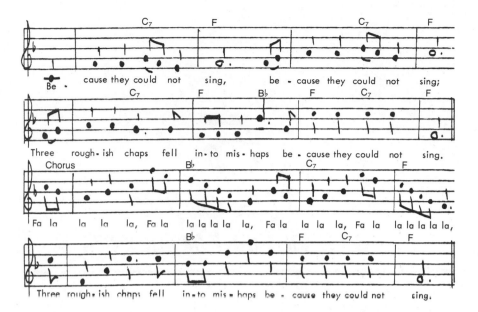

(with chords: C₇, F, C₇, F)
Be- cause they could not sing, be - cause they could not sing;

(C₇, F, B♭, F, C₇, F)
Three rough-ish chaps fell in-to mis-haps be - cause they could not sing.

Chorus (B♭, C₇, F)
Fa la la la la, Fa la la la la la la, Fa la la la la, Fa la la la la la la,

(B♭, F, C₇, F)
Three rough-ish chaps fell in-to mis-haps be - cause they could not sing.

(*Verse*)
2. The first one he was a miller
And the second he was a weaver
The third one was a little tailor
Three jolly roughs together.

(*Chorus*)
But they could not sing (fa, la, la, la, la, la, la)
No, they could not sing (fa, la, la, la, la, la, la)
The miller, the weaver, the little tailor
Three jolly roughs together.

(*Verse*)
3. Well the miller, he stole corn
The weaver, he stole yarn
And the tailor he stole yarn to keep him warm
Because they could not sing.

(*Chorus*)
Fa, la, la, la, la (fa, la, la, la, la, la, la, la)

Fa, la, la, la, la (fa, la, la, la, la, la, la, la)
Three rougish chaps fell into mishaps
Because they could not sing. (tra, la, la)

(*Verse*)
4. Now the miller drowned in his dam (poor thing)
And the weaver hung in his yarn (poor thing)
And the devil kept his eye on the little tailor
With his broadcloth under his arm.

(*Verse*)
Because they could not sing
Because they could not sing
Three rougish chaps fell into mishaps
Because they could not sing. (tra, la, la)

51

5

Songs of the American Pioneers

George Washington was inaugurated first President of the United States in New York City in 1789. The period from 1790 through 1810 was a time when the American people were deeply involved in the establishment of a new nation. Very soon, however, the fledgling nation was once again engaged in a conflict to reaffirm its independence. With the end of the War of 1812, Americans began to devote their full energies toward the renewal of their goal to build a new nation, under God, with liberty and justice for all. This was the beginning of a period of unprecedented expansion. The northeastern section of the nation was boldly moving in the direction of industrialization with the building of new factories, canals, and roads, all of which were a blanket invitation to a whole new contingent of immigrants to come seek a better livelihood. New construction and new methods of manufacturing products demanded laborers; equally, American soil that was both plentiful and fertile beckoned to those who were adept at farming. Immigrants began flooding into the nation, especially now that it was a secure and independent one. The guarantee of freedom and the promise of opportunities for better living were great incentives.

Up to this time, only a small number of people had dared to venture into the central and western parts of the continent. Most of these were men who were not out seeking to build homesteads; rather, they were out trapping for furs or involved with some other money-making projects. Most of them were loners. They became friendly with the Indians and many even married into the tribes and became blood brothers.

With the great influx of immigrants, land along the eastern seaboard became scarce and expensive. As a result, a movement toward the west was initiated. A new breed of American came into being—the pioneer, an individual unlike any other in the history of modern civilization. In large swarms these pioneers moved toward the Mississippi, setting up homesteads, tilling the soil, starting whole communities, and forming new states all in rapid succession. The trek westward did not stop at the Mississippi; many pushed on to the western plains and even to California and the great Oregon territory. As the pioneers ventured west, they began to infringe on those lands that had been the sole possession of the Indian tribes. The Plains Indians had wandered on these lands as the seasons changed and as their needs demanded. They became angered at being pushed out and deprived of what was theirs; obviously, they rebelled and life on the frontier became extremely hazardous.

The American pioneers have given us a huge storehouse of songs. They are quite original and, like other folk songs, they are musical vehicles through which the pioneers tell about themselves and their lives. Significantly, these songs were the first that introduced a non-European character into American folk music. Americans were beginning to develop their own original sound; to be sure, it was a kind of rural sound, but America at that time was essentially an agrarian nation.

The songs of the American pioneers are varied, span various age groups, and are unique in character. The lyrics to these songs are both true and somewhat exaggerated. Some are brief and relate only the highlights of certain events; others are lengthy, elaborate, and seemingly exaggerated. These songs tell of the hazards of wilderness travel, the extreme weather, the rugged country, problems with hostile Indians, the strange new animals that they encountered, the sicknesses they experienced, and even about such new methods of travel as the covered wagon or prairie schooner. Suffice it to say, they were a tough lot, a people who had already crossed a large and awesome ocean and who now were off once again into a land only superficially explored—rugged, wild, yet highly promising.

Musically, it should be noted that these songs were most frequently structured in the verse–chorus mold. Thus, anyone in the group could avail himself of the opportunity to add his contribution to the total effort. The pioneers sang by wagon trains, families, church groups, or in whole communities. Indeed, these songs presented them with one of the few opportunities for recreation and social interaction.

One of their most telling songs is "Pretty Saro." It beautifully portrays a young man in love, out in the wilderness building a homestead so that he might be able to provide the basic necessities preliminary to marriage. He is lonesome, reflective, somewhat discouraged, yet hopeful. The music itself is highly expressive and mirrors the mood portrayed in the words. One can easily empathize with the fine young man's difficult plight to establish himself in this frustrating world.

PRETTY SARO

Traditional

2. My love, she won't have me, so I understand,
   She wants a freeholder who owns house and land;
   I cannot maintain her with silver and gold,
   Nor buy all the fine things that a big house can hold.

3. If I were a merchant and I could write a fine book,
   I'd write my love a letter that she'd understand;
   I'd write it by the river where the waters e'er flow,
   And I'll dream of Pretty Saro wherever I go.

"The Sioux Indians" is a song that best describes the hardships experienced in traveling west by wagon train, especially the encounters with hostile Indians. The song is quite revealing. It may be accurate in its account of the wagon train's skirmish with the Sioux; on the other hand, it may have been grossly exaggerated to make it worth retelling. The song did, however, prove to be one that people on similar journeys could identify with and also occupy themselves with during the evening hours as they sat around the campfires. The song gave them hope because the group described in the song did reach their destination despite their trials; moreover, the land that they sought was everything they dreamed about and more. The chorus section of this song repeats the last line of each verse. It is brief compared to the chorus section found in other pioneer songs.

THE SIOUX INDIANS

Pioneer Song

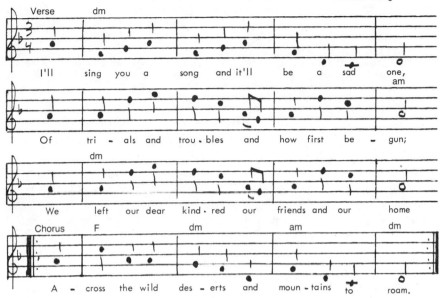

I'll sing you a song and it'll be a sad one, am
Of tri - als and trou - bles and how first be - gun;
We left our dear kind - red our friends and our home
A - cross the wild des - erts and moun - tains to roam.

2. We crossed the Missouri and joined
   a large train,
   Which bore us o'er mountains and
   valleys and plains;
   And often of an evening out hunting
   we'd go,
   To shoot the fleet antelope and the
   wild buffalo.

3. We heard of Sioux Indians all out on
   the plains,
   A-killing poor drivers and burning
   their trains;
   A-killing poor drivers with arrows
   and bows,
   When captured by Indians, no mercy
   they'd show.

4. We traveled three weeks till we
   came to the Platte,
   We set up our camp at the head of
   the flat;
   We spread down our blankets on
   the green grassy ground
   While our mules and our horses
   were grazing around.

5. While taking refreshment we heard a
   low yell;
   The whoop of Sioux Indians coming
   out of the dell;
   We sprang to our rifles with a flash
   in each eye,
   "Boys," said our brave leader, "we'll
   fight till we die."

6. They made a bold dash and came
   near to our train,
   The arrows fell round us like
   showers of rain;
   But with our long rifles we fed them
   hot lead,
   Till many a brave warrior around us
   lay dead.

7. In our little band there were just
   twenty-four,
   And of the Sioux Indians, five
   hundred or more;
   We fought them with courage, we
   said not a word,
   The whoop of the Indians was all
   could be heard.

8. We shot their bold chief at the head
 of his band,
 He died like a warrior with his bow
 in his hand;
 When they saw their brave chief
 lying dead in his gore,
 They whooped and they yelled and
 we saw them no more.

9. We traveled by day, guarded camp
 in the night,
 Till Oregon's mountains look'd high
 in their might;
 Now in a green valley, beside a clear
 stream,
 Our journey has ended in the land
 of our dream.

Wagon trains were made up of whole families. Songs that were intended for the adults have been handed down to us; similarly, there are many outstanding songs created and adapted specifically for children. These songs are very simple both in words and music, and are ideally suited for a child's voice, with its limited range. These songs have continued to remain on the best song list down to our day. "Skip To My Lou" was a favorite play song. The word "lou" meant sweetheart and perhaps derived from the Scottish *lou*, which was a shortened form of the word for love. In the game the person who is "it" skips around and stops in front of his "lou."

SKIP TO MY LOU

2. I'll get another purtier'n you

3. Can't get a red bird, a blue-bird'll do

4. Little red wagon, painted blue

5. Fly in the sugar bowl, shoo fly shoo

6. Gone again, what'll I do

7. Hair in the butterdish, six feet long

8. Goin' to Texas, two by two

   (*Repeat chorus after each verse*)

Play-party songs continued to be popular long after the wagon trains had reached their destinations and whole communities had been formed. Church groups encouraged social interaction as a spinoff of their religious services and rural schools needed games to help children find a constructive outlet for their pent up energies; as a result, these songs were preserved and remained favorites among our children. Many of the same songs were also enjoyed by adults and used as background music for square dancing.

A song that was used exclusively for the purpose of lulling children to sleep is "Hush, Little Baby." It is short, contains many verses, and its lyric repetitions present a pleasant alternative to counting sheep. It is a charming song with endless opportunities for lyric variations.

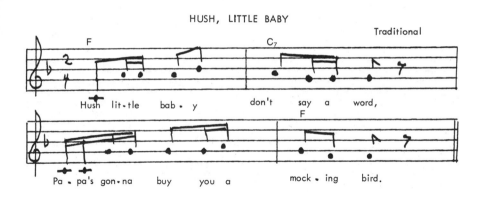

HUSH, LITTLE BABY

Traditional

If that mocking bird won't sing,
Papa's gonna buy you a diamond ring.

If that diamond ring turns brass,
Papa's gonna buy you a looking glass.

If that looking glass gets broke,
Papa's gonna buy you a billy goat.

If that billy goat won't pull,
Papa's gonna buy you a cart and bull.

If that cart and bull turn over,

Papa's gonna buy you a dog named Rover.

If that dog named Rover won't bark,
Papa's gonna buy you a horse and cart.

If that horse and cart fall down,
You'll still be the sweetest little baby in town.

Hush, little baby, don't say a word,
Papa's gonna buy you a mocking bird.

In an effort to make the frontier a safer place for homesteaders, the United States government declared a bounty on buffalo hides. The Plains Indians were a nomadic people who moved from place to place following the buffalo, their principle source for food. It has been reported that the buffalo was so plentiful that it staggered the imagination. The rationale behind the declaration was one of curbing the ready supply of buffalo in order to force the Indian to retreat to a designated place and remain there. The declaration gave rise to the creation of the bounty hunter, in this instance known as a buffalo skinner, thus raising the curtain on one of the most savage and inhumane undertakings in the history of our young nation. (Americans were reminded of this criminal act in the song "Now That the Buffalo's Gone" [page 249] by Buffy Sainte-Marie, an Indian woman of unusual musical talent and sensitivity.) "Buffalo Skinner," sometimes known as "The Range of the Buffalo," masterfully describes the events connected with this horrible enterprise, the kinds of people engaged in the mass slaughtering of the docile animals, and the futility of their immoral acts.

THE BUFFALO SKINNER

Pioneer Song

On the range of the Buf. fa - lo

It's me being out of employment, boys,
   to old Crego I did say:
"This going out on the buffalo range
   depends upon the pay;
But if you will pay good wages, give
   transportation too,
I think, sir, I will go with you to the
   range of the buffalo."

It's now our outfit was complete, seven
   able-bodied men,
With navy six and needle gun our
   troubles did begin;
Our way, it was a pleasant one, the
   route we had to go,
Until we crossed Pease River on the
   range of the buffalo.

It's now we've crossed Pease River, our
   troubles have begun,
The first damned tail I went to rip, it's
   how I cut my thumb;
The water was salty as hell-fire, the beef
   I could not go,
And the Indians waited to pick us off,
   while skinning buffalo.

Our hearts were cased with buffalo
   hocks, our souls were cased with
   steel,
And the hardships of that summer
   would nearly make us reel.
While skinning the damned old
   stinkers, our lives they had no show,
For the Indians waited to pick us off on
   the hills of Mexico.

The season being near over, boys, old
   Crego he did say,
The crowd had been extravagant, was
   in debt to him that day;
We coaxed him and we begged him,
   but still it was no go,
So we left his damned old bones to
   bleach on the range of the buffalo.

Oh it's now we've crossed Pease River
   and homeward we are bound,
No more in that hell-fired country shall
   ever we be found;
Go home to our wives and sweethearts,
   tell others not to go,
For God's forsaken the buffalo range
   and the damned old buffalo.

Without a doubt, the most interesting of American pioneers were the forty-niners. The discovery of gold in California resulted in a maniacal desire for sudden wealth and a wild race for the west. For the most part, the overnight miners were bachelors, willing to gamble everything they had, including their lives, on the prospect of becoming instant millionaires. Some came by ship, taking the long and treacherous route around Cape Horn. Some journeyed via the swamp-laden route across Central America; still others took the wagon trails across the North American continent. Of the thousands who scampered for gold, many died in shipwrecks, from fever and disease, gun battles, starvation, or accident. Very few found the answer to their dreams.

The songs of the forty-niners describe all aspects of their adventure, from accounts of their travels, to the kind of lives they led while seeking their fortune, even to their eventual wake-up to reality and subsequent attempt at establishing a normal life in the west. Their songs were mostly adaptations of

favorite familiar songs. They made up parodies on the songs as they journeyed the long hours en route to their destinations; other songs were prepared for them by itinerant entertainers who performed in the saloons, trying
to skim off easy money from those few who had been lucky at gold mining.
The miners were, in essence, workers or laborers. Our nation's workers, such
as the sailors or cowboys, have produced hundreds of work songs that they
created to accompany their labors and make the work less burdensome.
Unlike his counterpart in the labor field, the gold miner did not sing while he
was engaged in the monotonous job of panning for gold. He had to give full
attention and careful concentration to each panning. The thought that the
next scoop would be the answer to his quest for glory was foremost in his
thoughts. The forty-niner, however, did frolic on weekends or whenever he
came to town.

"Oh Susanna" was everybody's favorite song at that time and one that
was used to accommodate literally hundreds of parodies. The version that
follows, entitled "Oh California," perhaps best describes those who took the
ocean route to their land of destiny.

OH CALIFORNIA
(Oh Susanna)

Stephen Foster

Oh Cal - i - forn - ia......... That's the land for me,

I'm bound for San Fran - cis - co with my wash -bowl on my knee.

2. I jumped aboard the Liza ship
   And traveled on the sea,
   And every time I thought of home
   I wished it wasn't me;
   The vessel reared like any horse,
   That had of oats and wealth
   I found it wouldn't throw me so
   I thought I'd throw myself.
   (*Chorus*)

3. I thought of all the pleasant times
   We've had together here,
   I thought I ought to cry a bit
   But couldn't find a tear;
   The pilot's bread was in my mouth
   The gold dust in my eye

And though I'm going far away
Dear brothers, don't you cry.
(*Chorus*)

4. I soon shall be in Frisco,
   And there I'll look around,
   And when I see the gold lumps
     there,
   I'll pick them off the ground;
   I'll scrape the mountains clean, my
     boys,
   I'll drain the rivers dry,
   A pocket full of rocks bring home,
   So brothers, don't you cry.
   (*Chorus*)

One of the songs that best represents the gold miners who chose the land route across the United States is the beautiful "Sweet Betsy from Pike," which is based on an old English ballad. This is a true folk song, with its multiplicity of available musical and verbal versions. It vividly describes the kind of person who ventured in search of gold. The forty-niners were adventuresome, fatalistic, and fun-loving; every day for them was a gamble and every night could very well have been their last. A number of treatments of the song follow. The words in the chorus change with the particular group that was using it. The first version reaffirms the sense of the ballad. In another, we have some frontier-like nonsense words. In still another version, the words are Irish in nature. In the popular version sung today, Ike is characterized as stronger and more determined than Betsy as they journey to Placerville. The set of lyrics found at the end of the song presentation comes from a version that portrays Betsy as the stronger of the two. At any rate, the final outcome of their adventure is joyful, for Betsy has fully adjusted to her new environment and is having the time of her life!

SWEET BETSY FROM PIKE

Traditional

Verse

Did you ev-er hear of Sweet Bet-sy from Pike, Who crossed the wide prair-ies with her lov-er Ike, With two yoke of ox-en and one spot-ted hog, A tall Shang-hai roost-er and one yal-ler dog.

Chorus

Say-ing "Good-bye Pike coun-ty fare-well for a while, We'll come back a-gain when we've panned out our pile.

They swam the wild rivers and
  climbed the tall peaks,
And camped on the prairies for
  weeks upon weeks,
Starvation and cholera, hard work
  and slaughter,
They reached Californy, spite of hell
  and high water.
(*Chorus*)

They soon reached the desert where
  Betsy gave out,
And down in the sand she lay rolling
  about,
While Ike in great wonder looked
  on in surprise,
Sayin' "Get up now Betsy, you'll get
  sand in your eyes."
(*Chorus*)

The Indians come down in a wild
  yelling horde,

And Betsy got skeered they would
  scalp her adored,
So behind the front wagon wheel
  Betsy did crawl,
And fought off the Indians with
  musket and ball.
(*Chorus*)

They stopped off at Salt Lake to
  inquire the way,
And Brigham declared that sweet
  Betsy should stay,
But Betsy got frightened and ran like
  a deer,
While Brigham stood pawing the
  ground like a steer.
(*Chorus*)

One morning they climbed up a
  very high peak,
And with wonder looked down
  upon old Placerville,

Ike shouted and said as he cast his eyes down,
"Sweet Betsy, my darlin', we've got to Hangtown."
(*Chorus*)

Long Ike and Sweet Betsy attended a dance,
Where Ike wore a pair of his Pike County pants,
And Betsy was covered with ribbons and rings,
Quoth Ike, "You're an angel, but where are your wings?"
(*Chorus*)

A miner said, "Betsy, will you dance with me?"

"I will, you old hoss, if you don't make too free,
But don't dance me hard, do you want to know why?
Doggone ye, I'm chock full of strong alkali!"
(*Chorus*)

Long Ike and sweet Betsy got married, of course,
But Ike, getting jealous, obtained a divorce,
While Betsy, well satisfied, said with a shout,
"Goodbye, you big lummox, I'm glad you backed out!"
(*Chorus*)

Chorus with frontier-like words:

Hoodle dang fol di dye do, hoodle dang fol di day,
Hoodle dang fol di dye do, hoodle dang fol di day.

Chorus with Irish-like words:

Sing too ra li oo ra li oo ra li aye,
Sing too ra li oo ra li oo ra li aye.

Verses in which Betsy is portrayed as the bolder of the two:

'Twas out on the prairie one bright starry night,
They broke out the whiskey and Betsy got tight,
She sang and she howled and she danced o'er the plain,
And showed her bare legs to the whole wagon train.

The terrible desert was burning and bare,
And Isaac he shrank from the death lurkin' there,
"Dear old Pike County, I'll come back to you."
Says Betsy, "You'll go by yourself if you do!"

"Clementine" is a staple among American folk songs. One need only examine closely the lyrics of this song to draw a stereotype for the typical forty-niner. In the version presented here there are three additional verses added that rarely appear in song books. The song is very singable and is structured like most of the songs of the American pioneer. One should note that the music for the chorus is identical to that of the verse. This makes it all the easier to learn. "Clementine" was a favorite among the miners because they could easily identify with it. The fatalistic attitude of the adventuresome miner is beautifully portrayed in his reaction to his daughter's drowning and in the carefree manner in which he treats the whole incident.

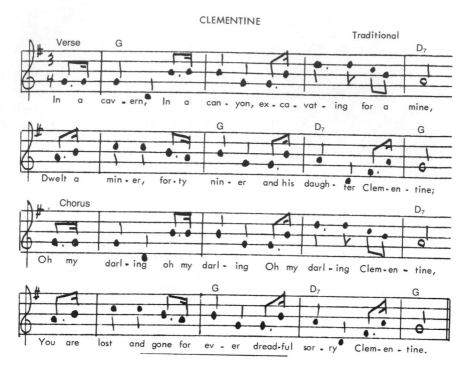

CLEMENTINE

Traditional

In a cav - ern, In a can - yon, ex - ca - vat - ing for a mine,

Dwelt a min - er, for - ty nin - er and his daugh - ter Clem - en - tine;

Chorus

Oh my darl - ing oh my darl - ing Oh my darl - ing Clem - en - tine,

You are lost and gone for ev - er dread-ful sor - ry Clem - en - tine.

Light she was and like a fairy, And her
  shoes were number nine;
Herring boxes without topses, Sandals
  were for Clementine.
(*Chorus*)

Drove she duckling to the water, Every
  morning just at nine,
Hit her foot against a splinter, Fell into
  the foaming brine.
(*Chorus*)

Ruby lips above the water, Blowing
  bubbles soft and fine,
Alas for me, I was no swimmer, So I
  lost my Clementine.
(*Chorus*)

In a churchyard near the canyon,
  Where the myrtle doth entwine,
There grow roses and other posies,
  Fertilized by Clementine.
(*Chorus*)

In my dreams she oft doth haunt me,
  With her garments soaked in brine;
Though in life I used to hug her, Now
  she's dead I draw the line.
(*Chorus*)

Then the miner, forty-niner, Soon
  began to peak and pine;
Thought he 'oughter jin'e his daughter,
  Now he's with his Clementine.
(*Chorus*)

"Joe Bowers" became the folk hero of the gold miners. The origin of
the song is attributed to a saloon entertainer whose name is unknown. Some
even claim that there once was a Joe Bowers and that this represents his
musical autobiography. We do know that many a miner enjoyed singing this
song or had it sung for him during a nostalgic moment. It certainly tells the
whole story.

JOE BOWERS

Traditional

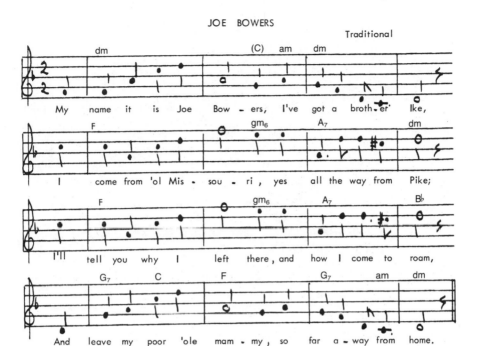

My name it is Joe Bow - ers, I've got a broth-er Ike,
I come from 'ol Mis - sou - ri, yes all the way from Pike;
I'll tell you why I left there, and how I come to roam,
And leave my poor 'ole mam - my, so far a - way from home.

I used to love a gal there, they called
her Sally Black,
I axed her to marry me, she said it was
a whack,
Says she to me, "Joe Bowers, before we
hitch for life
You'd orter have a little house to keep
your little wife."

Says I, "My dearest Sally, oh Sally for
your sake
I'll go to Californy, and try to raise a
stake."
Says she to me, "Joe Bowers, oh you're
the chap to win
Give me a buss to seal the bargain,"
and she threw a dozen in.

I shall ne'er forgit my feelin's when I
bid adieu to all,
Sally catched me round the neck then I
began to bawl.
When I sat in they all commenced, you
ne'er did hear the like,
How they all took on and cried, the day
I left old Pike.

When I got to this 'ere country, I hadn't
nary a red.
I had such walfish feelin's I wished
myself most dead.
But thoughts of my dear Sally soon
made them feelins' git
And whispered hopes to
Bowers . . . Lord, I wish I had 'em yit.

At length I went to mining, put in my
biggest licks,
Come down upon the boulders just like
a thousand bricks.
I worked both late and early, in rain
and sun and snow,
But I was working for my Sally, so 'twas
all the same to Joe.

I made a very lucky strike, as the gold
itself did tell,
And saved it for my Sally, the gal I
loved so well.
I saved it for my Sally, that I might pour
it at her feet,
That she might kiss and hug me, and
call me something sweet.

65

But one day I got a letter from my dear
  kind brother Ike.
It came from old Missouri, sent all the
  way from Pike.
It brought me the gol-darn'dest news as
  ever you did hear.
My heart is almost bustin', so pray
  excuse this tear.

It said my Sal was fickle, that her love
  for me had fled.
That she'd married with a butcher
  whose hair was awful red.

It told me more than that . . . Oh it's
  enough to make one swear.
It said Sally had a baby and the baby
  had red hair.

Now, I've told you all I could tell about
  this sad affair.
'Bout Sally marryin' the butcher and the
  butcher had red hair.
Whether 'twas a boy or girl child the
  letter never said.
It only said its' cussed hair was inclined
  to be red!

The final song in this series, "The Old Settler's Song," comes once again from an old Irish air. It tells of the many prospectors who finally gave up searching for their instant fortune and decided to settle down to a more stable and socially acceptable life.

THE OLD SETTLER'S SONG

Old Irish Air

2. For each man who got rich by
   mining,
   Perceiving that hundreds grew poor;
   I made up my mind to try farming,
   The only pursuit that was sure.

   (*The choruses are formed by
   repetition of the fourth and third
   lines*)

3. So rolling my grub in my blanket,
   I left all my tools on the ground;
   I started one morning to shank it,
   For the country they called Puget
   Sound.

4. Arriving flat broke in midwinter,
   I found it enveloped in fog;
   And covered all over with timber,
   Thick as hair on the back of a dog.

5. When I looked on the prospects so
   gloomy,
   The tears trickled over my face;
   And I thought that my travels had
   brought me,
   To the end of that jumping off place.

6. I staked me a claim in the forest,
   And sat myself down to hard toil;
   For two years I chopped and I
   niggered,
   But I never got down to the soil.

7. I tried to get out of the country,
   But poverty forced me to stay;
   Until I became an old settler,
   Then nothing could drive me away.

8. And now that I'm used to the
   climate,
   I think that if a man ever found
   A place to live easy and happy,
   That Eden is on Puget Sound.

9. No longer the slave of ambition,
   I laugh at the world and its shams;
   As I think of my pleasant condition,
   Surrounded by acres of clams.

   Last Refrain:
   Surrounded by acres of cla-a-ams,
   Surrounded by acres of clams;
   As I think of my happy condition,
   Surrounded by acres of clams.

6

Songs of the Southern Mountains

The Southern Appalachian Mountains lie just behind the southeastern coastline of the United States, running north and south. They trail the western borders of Virginia and North Carolina, the eastern borders of Kentucky and Tennessee, and even touch parts of Georgia and Alabama. So much rich, flat land was available for the early colonists that only trappers and curious explorers like Daniel Boone even bothered with the mountain territory. However, as land became less plentiful along the eastern seaboard and as people attempted to escape the tax programs of King George, the ravages of war, the demands of the newly formed churches, and the aristocratic aura developing in the south, they had but two options before them from which to choose. Either they joined the wagon trains heading west or took their chances in the mountains. For hundreds of folks the mountain range known as the Appalachians presented the better choice. These people were of English, Scots-Irish, and German extraction and were associated with a variety of Protestant faiths. They were kind, gentle folk who wished nothing more than the opportunity to till the soil and live and let live. For them, money and the manifestations of wealth meant little; they would be content with personal freedom and independence. The hassles of war and the problems connected with the nurturing of an advancing society were not to their liking. Accordingly, they chose to settle apart from the emerging mainstream of American society in an effort to carry on their easy, simplistic, rural way of life.

In order to secure the hills for themselves and their posterity, they had to ward off the Cherokee Indians, a very formidable group. This they accomplished within the life span of one generation. Once the hill country became secure, they let it be known far and near that the hills belonged to them and no one was to trespass without their expressed consent. Their policy of complete isolation remained in effect for more than one hundred years. As a matter of record, these hills were not opened to the "public" until around the 1930s. Many folks made attempts to transgress, including government officials, known as "revenuers" by the mountaineers. They invaded the mountains in an effort to collect taxes and legalize the making of moonshine. They were chased off or summarily killed.

As a consequence of their long isolation, a whole segment of American society was allowed to flourish apart from the mainstream of American life. Held almost intact, this particular group actually preserved their Elizabethan culture as if they had been in a deep freeze or deep sleep like Rip Van Winkle. Curiously enough, the renowned English folklorist Cecil Sharp was able to unearth more examples of old English folk songs in their original settings in the Appalachian Mountains than he was able to collect back home in England.

Even though the Americans of Appalachia belong chronologically to that period just prior to the Revolutionary War and perhaps some years shortly after, the folk culture of the mountaineers was not revealed to the general public until around the 1930s. To use their own expression, they were "holed up" in those hills to create and foster their own kind of society.

The mountain folk were a very interesting group. In modern parlance we might best describe them as a counterculture cult or even as America's first breed of "hippies." With their rejection of war and their hang-up on the accumulation of material wealth as a hallmark of success, they overwhelmingly chose a free, easygoing type of living. The mountaineers clung on to their philosophy of living and asked little more than the opportunity to obtain the basic necessities for living.

After examining the base roots of their language, their knowledge of cultural music, along with a number of other societal factors, we can conclude that they initially must have been people of good breeding. Because of their long isolation, along with their quest for the easygoing life, their cultural level, as measured against general standards, actually deteriorated in quality. Perhaps one of the most significant factors that contributed to this down turn was their almost total lack of interest in providing a formal educational system for their offspring. Human values were taught at home or within the larger family group; reading and writing and the other components of a formal education were given practically no attention.

The mountaineer's language was based on a rich vocabulary, one that is directly related to the great literary works of Shakespeare, Chaucer, and Milton. Such terms as *feisty, courting, e'er* and *ne'er, sevigrous,* and so on, are not a part of the vocabulary that Americans normally use in their every day conversations. These words, however, were very much a part of the vocabulary of the mountaineers. As with so many things connected with their culture, they chose to preserve the best from their Elizabethan heritage, yet in their use of these things they allowed them to deteriorate in quality. A case in point is their flagrant use of double and triple negatives, an almost unpardonable sin in American schools. Such an expression as, "I don't never want no revenuers 'round here," is a common example of their use of language.

Another interesting trait connected with their culture was the long-standing hatred between the English and the Scots (even the Irish) that had festered for generations back in the British isles. With all of their hatred for war and their strong commitment to human life, they would fight even to the death to keep their blood lines free from the other "nationality." Feuding between families in the hills was notorious. Even when periods of truce or amnesty were declared by the feuding families, the peace would be suddenly broken by the itching few who would jump at the slightest provocation to renew the fighting. As a result, intermarriage between closely related members of the same family was allowed, which resulted in imbecilic children. Still, the sacredness of the blood line had to be preserved even though young people within feuding families fell in love and desired to marry.

The skills required to produce alcohol that had been learned in the old world were openly practiced by members of the mountain society. They built their own stills and in due course perfected the quality of their good old mountain "dew." Their love and reverence for this liquor is in evidence even today when one visits this region of the country. People there are allowed to "brown bag it," that is, they may legally bring their own liquor into nightclubs and taverns. More often than not, the brown bags contain some form of mountain moonshine.

The exceptional romance with music that mountaineers exhibited is phenomenal. These folk not only sought to retain their potpourri of ancient songs, especially ballads, but they also continued to contribute to the song well in unbelievable numbers. Music, especially singing, was a major part of their way of life. They would gather together every day of the week to play their instruments, exchange songs, and create new ones. Suffice it to say they spent many hours of each day happily engaged in making music. Their love for music was so great that they would even put aside their shotguns and petty hatreds for just about any chance to make music. During their "big sing-in's" they would show off their abilities at playing instruments, display their family-styled musical performances or renditions, and even showcase their newly created tunes. A major part of the courting process included songs appropriate to the occasion.

To know their songs is to know the people. The rural quality of the music perfectly reflects the value systems of the hills. The fractured use of Elizabethan language is prominently displayed in the lyrics of their songs. Their great love for and ability to play their instruments is evident in the exciting rhythms and technical aspects of their music. Their music is unique and highly representative of their lifestyle, and its output is enormous and musically appealing.

The beautiful ballads of old were held in high esteem by the mountaineers. These songs were an integral part of their heritage and the one thing that they elected to preserve and point to with great pride. Ironically, these ballads did not suffer as much in the cultural deterioration process as compared with their language and other habits. Perhaps their great respect for the songs dictated their attention toward presenting them as traditionally perfect as possible. Although there is some evidence that some old ballads were transformed (such as "Barbara Allen" having become "Barbry Ellen"), the hill folk so loved the ballad-type song that they created several and patterned them after the models that they had so carefully learned while in the British isles.

The most significant characteristic connected with Southern Mountain music is the conversational element. Generally, their songs involve the question–answer or dialogue format. For example, a song might involve a boy who was courtin' a girl, or an individual or series of individuals engaged in conversation within a group situation. We identify mountain songs primarily as being "answering back songs." This differs from the solo songs or the verse–chorus songs discussed in Chapter 5, that were so popular with the pioneers. Mountain songs involve questions or statements that are answered almost immediately.

As was mentioned earlier, the mountaineers had a great interest in playing their instruments, and they developed a phenomenal technique and distinctive style accordingly. The violin was one of the instruments popularly associated with them. Back in the British isles this instrument was primarily associated with the more cultured society. It was, however, being played more and more by members of the lower classes. The early mountaineers brought their violins with them into the hills. Interestingly enough, during their period of isolation the name of the instrument along with its method of play was changed. Indeed, it is more appropriate to refer to the instrument as played by a mountaineer as a fiddle rather than a violin. It is also interesting to note that the approach to the playing of the instrument went from placing it properly underneath the chin to resting it on the upper chest. More importantly, the whole technique involved in the playing of the instrument was changed, as is easily evidenced when one compares the literature created for the instrument by the mountaineer with that composed by Beethoven, for example. Fiddlin', hillbilly style, is novel, exciting, and just plain fun! There is nothing else like it in the field of violin music.

The dulcimer is yet another instrument of high cultural status that is associated with mountain music. The dulcimer, taken from the Italian words, *dulce melos* (of sweet song), is a kind of lap lyre that cultured ladies and gentlemen strummed as accompaniment while they sang such pieces as ballads. They would strum the instrument, usually not in the rhythm of the piece but more often at certain choice places in the music to give a kind of harmonic base to their singing. The dulcimer may also be used as a solo instrument capable of playing both melody and harmony. The sound of a dulcimer makes a truly tasteful companion to the singing of a beautiful ballad. The instruments that the first generations of mountaineers used soon wore out with the result that the mountaineers had to construct their own. They perfected the art of dulcimer construction, and many of them are still in existence; these instruments are original in design and most expressive in their musical quality.

The guitar was an ideal instrument for the Southern Mountain folk. The interest they had in the instrument and the level of proficiency they attained in its playing are noteworthy. Nevertheless, when they were introduced to the banjo, a fretted instrument associated with the American blacks and later with minstrelsy, they quickly became intrigued with it and set out to acquire the necessary skill needed for playing. It is safe to say that the Southern Mountain "pickers" on both guitar and banjo rank among the very best from any geographical area, and the Appalachian fiddlers can be said to be among the finest.

As is typical of folk music, none of the huge repertoire of songs contributed by the Southern Mountain folk was ever written down; rather, they were handed down orally from one generation to the next. These songs underwent considerable modification as each group had a "crack" at them. What we have today is actually a distillation of their work. Because whole family groups remained detached from other family groups on other hills within the mountain range, there developed some quasi-provincialisms, as in ancient times, in their musical and verbal treatments of songs. In less than one hundred years the Southern Mountain folk compiled an impressive repertoire of songs and ballads that have become staples in folk literature. They are fun to listen to and perform.

The joy of singing and listening to the standard ballads was commonplace in the mountaineer's society. One of the most delightful of the old world ballads and one that has surfaced in many places around the United States, especially the Southern Mountains, is one known simply as the "Riddle Song." This ballad is a little unusual in that the singer speaks in the first person. It is a piece of sculptured beauty and so perfect unto itself that few if any singers have taken liberties with it by altering its tune or its lyrics. It is loved not only because of its sheer musical beauty but also for the wisdom expressed in its verbal message.

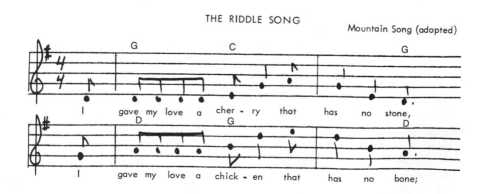

THE RIDDLE SONG

Mountain Song (adapted)

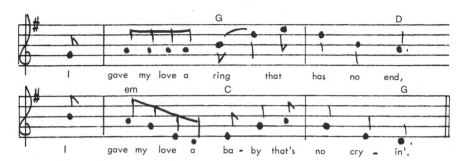

How can there be a cherry that has no stone?
How can there be a chicken that has no bone?
How can there be a ring that has no end?
How can there be a baby that's no cryin'?

Another of the old ballads that deserves to be included in our discussion of Southern Mountain ballads is a very ancient one. "The Farmer's Curst Wife" has always evoked laughter from its listeners. Mountaineers had a penchant for boy–girl songs. Add to this their genuine love for ballads and "The Farmer's Curst Wife" became one of their most popular songs. This number can also be sung as a group song because it has what might be loosely identified as a chorus section. As a solo song the section with the nonsense syllables actually serves to give the singer time to think of the next phase of the song story.

THE FARMER'S CURST WIFE

Mountain Song

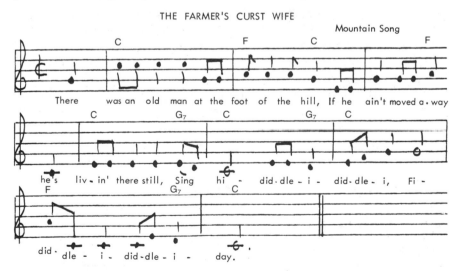

2. He hitched up his horse and he went out to plough,
But how to get around he didn't know how.

3. The devil come to his house one day,
Says, "One of your family I'm gonna take away."

(Repeat chorus after each verse)

4. "Take her, take her with all of my heart,
And I hope, by gollie, you never part."

5. The devil put her up on his back,
And off to Hell he went, clickity-clack.

6. When he got her down to the gates of hell,
He says, "Punch up the fire, we'll scorch her well."

7. Ten little devils came rushing with the chains,
She upped with her foot and kicked out their brains.

8. Ten little devils called her a liar,
She upped with her foot and kicked nine in the fire.

9. The odd little devil peeped over the wall,
Take her daddy, she'll kill us all!

10. The old man was a-peepin' out of a crack,
And saw the old devil come draggin' her back.

11. She found the old man sick in his bed,
She upped with a butter stick and paddled his head.

12. The old woman went whistlin' over the hill,
"The devil won't have me, I wonder who will."

13. There's one advantage women have over men,
They can go to hell and come back again.

Romance, or as the mountaineers preferred to call it, courtin', was a popular activity, especially after a hard day's work at finding the bare necessities for survival. They not only relished this kind of activity, but created music to be used as a major part of the courtship process. As a result, literally hundreds of courtin' songs were handed down to us. These songs beautifully illustrated their unique "answering-back" song structure. The courtin' songs are most enjoyable and filled with subtle humor. They talk of the boy or girl in love while at the same time they warn of the miserable life ahead when the courtship ends and the marriage begins. "Billy Boy" gives us a setting for a young boy who has found his true love and is answering some final questions being posed by (perhaps) his mother. From the text one can assume that the "formal engagement" has already taken place and the last minute questions regarding her suitability as a wife are under discussion.

BILLY BOY

Mountain Song

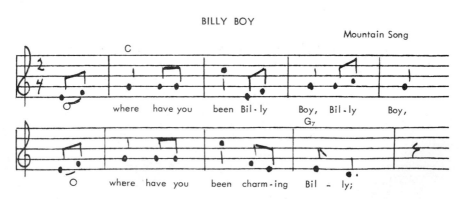

I have gone to seek a wife, She's the darl-ing of my life,

She's a young thing that can-not leave her moth-er.

"Did she ask you to come in? (etc.)
Did she ask you to come in?" (etc.)
"Yes, she asked me to come in,
And she bit me on the chin." (etc.)

"Did she take your hat?"
"Yes, she took my hat,
And she threw it at the cat."

"How old is she?"
"Twice six, 'twice seven,
Forty-eight and eleven."

"How tall is she?"
"She's tall as a pine
Straight as a pumpkin vine."

"Can she bake a cherry pie?"
"She can bake a cherry pie
Quick as a cat can wink its eye."

"Can she make a pair of britches?"
"She can make a pair of britches
Quick as you can count the stitches."

"Did she sit close to you?"
"Yes, she sat close to me
As the back upon the tree."

"Is she fitted for your wife?"
"Yes, she's fitted for my wife
As my pocket for my knife."

"The Deaf Woman's Courtship" is one of the more humorous songs in the courtin' category. It wonderfully illustrates in a most clever way that one can hear only what one wants to hear. As is true for most of these songs, they can be performed either as solo songs or group songs. They take on a whole new dimension, however, when they are given a more dramatic treatment, such as having the boy sing his part and the girl sing her part or even with boys and girls singing their respective parts.

THE DEAF WOMAN'S COURTSHIP

Mountain Song

Old wom-an, Old wom-an, are you fond of smok-ing?

Old wom-an, Old wom-an are you fond of smok-ing?

Speak a lit-tle loud-er sir, I'm rath-er hard of hear-ing,

Speak a lit-tle loud-er sir, I'm rath-er hard of hear-ing.

Old woman, old woman, are you
  fond of carding?
Old woman, old woman, are you
  fond of carding?
Speak a little louder, sir, I'm rather
  hard of hearing;
Speak a little louder, sir, I'm rather
  hard of hearing.

Old woman, old woman, will you let
  me court you?
Old woman, old woman, will you let
  me court you?

Speak a little louder, sir, I just begin
  to hear you,
Speak a little louder, sir, I just begin
  to hear you.

Old woman, old woman, don't you
  want to marry me?
Old woman, old woman, don't you
  want to marry me?
Lord have mercy on my soul, I think
  that now I hear you,
Lord have mercy on my soul, I think
  that now I hear you.

"Paper of Pins" is a short song with many verses. It is another of the boy–girl or "answering-back" songs. This one, again, is a humorous one; nonetheless, like so many of the mountain songs it also contains a subtle message. The moral in this song is that money really means everything to girls. The young lover offers his sweetheart a number of precious gifts both material and personal and yet cannot win her over. Just as soon as he mentions money in great supply, she quickly changes her mind and decides to marry him. The song does not stop there, however. Learning of her lust for money, he begins to question her priorities and then changes his mind, withdrawing his offer of love and marriage. The song ends with the girl realizing she messed up a good offer of marriage and resigns herself to be an old maid.

PAPER OF PINS

Traditional

I'll give to you this pa-per of pins, And that's the way our love a-gins,

If you will mar-ry me, me, me; If you will mar-ry me.....

76

No, I'll not accept your paper of pins
If that's the way your love a-gins.
And I'll not marry you, you, you,
And I'll not marry you.

I'll give to you this blue silk gown
With golden tassels all around.
If you will marry me, me, me,
If you will marry me.

(*Repeat chorus*)

I'll give to you this old big horse
That paced these hills from cross to
    cross.
(etc.)

(*Repeat chorus*)

I'll give to you my hand and my
    heart
That we may marry and never part.
(etc.)

(*Repeat chorus*)

I'll give to you the key to my chest
That you may have gold at your
    request.
(etc.)

Yes, I'll accept the key to your chest,
That I may have gold at my request.
And I will marry you, you, you,
And I will marry you.

You would not accept my hand and
    my heart,
That we might marry and never part.
So I'll not marry you, you, you,
So I'll not marry you.

For now I see that money is all
That woman's love is nothing at all.
So I'll not marry you, you, you,
So I'll not marry you.

Now I'm resolved to be an old maid
To take my stool and sit in the shade.
If you won't marry me, me, me,
If you won't marry me.

"Buffalo Boy" also puts the girls in a bad light concerning their sincere interest in marriage. The young lady in this song asks questions relative to her wedding plans. In the course of the questioning she learns, to her surprise, that her future husband is already a father of five children plus one other "if the weather is dry" on the day of their proposed wedding. Unlike "Paper of Pins," in this song the girl changes her mind and calls the wedding off.

BUFFALO BOY

Mountain Song

I guess we'll marry in a week, in a
    week, in a week,
I guess we'll marry in a week,
That is, if the weather be good.

How're you gonna come to the
    wedding, wedding, wedding,
How're you gonna come to the
    wedding, dear old Buffalo Boy?

I guess I'll come in my ox cart, ox
    cart, ox cart,
I guess I'll come in my ox cart,
That is, if the weather be good.

Why don't you come in your buggy,
    buggy, buggy,
Why don't you come in your buggy,
    dear old Buffalo Boy?

My ox won't fit in the buggy, buggy,
    buggy,
My ox won't fit in the buggy,
Not even if the weather be good.

Who you gonna bring to the
    wedding, wedding, wedding,
Who you gonna bring to the
    wedding, dear old Buffalo Boy?

I guess I'll bring the children,
    children, children,
I guess I'll bring the children,
That is, if the weather be good.

I didn't know you had any children,
    children, children,
I didn't know you had any children,
    dear old Buffalo Boy.

Oh yes, I have five children,
    children, children,
Oh yes, I have five children,
Six if the weather be good.

There ain't gonna be no wedding,
    wedding, wedding,
There ain't gonna be no wedding,
Not even if the weather be good!

Should you have formed the impression that all mountain boys were great romantic lovers and anything but shy, the following lyrics will dispel that belief. In this song, the girls are discussing the "Johnson Boys," calling them hopeless cases at the art of romance who will undoubtedly end up as bachelors.

JOHNSON BOYS

Johnson boys were raised in the ashes,
Didn't know how to court a maid;
Turn their backs and hide their faces,
Sight of a pretty girl makes 'em afraid.

Johnson boys, they went a courtin',
Coon creek girls so pretty and sweet;
They couldn't make no conversation,
They didn't know where to put their feet.

Johnson boys'll never get married,
They'll stay single all their life;
They're too scared to pop the question,
Ain't no woman that'll be their wife.

Courtin' songs provided young ones with a perfect vehicle to cover up their shyness, allowing them the opportunity to court right out in the open without once overstepping the bounds of propriety. Through these dialogue songs one could express one's mind without having to create one's own words to do it. In "Jennie Jenkins," sometimes called the Color Song, a boy can get to know something about his girl simply by soliciting some information about her color preferences. (People of that day placed a great deal of stock in the particular colors women chose to wear.) The following folk poem of the period beautifully illustrates color symbolism as these folk defined it:

Blue is true,
Yeller's jealous,
Green's forsaken,
Red is brazen,
White is love, and
Black is death.

But all mountain courtin' songs were not light and humorous, as the following song demonstrates. "Pretty Polly," which is cast in the minor mode to give it a somber musical setting, involves a gruesome dialogue between a man named Willie and his Polly. Just based on its violent content, this song would receive an "R" rating by today's standards.

PRETTY POLLY

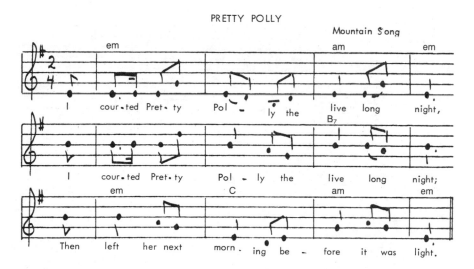

O Polly, pretty Polly, come away
  with me (*repeat two times*)
Before we get married, some
  pleasure to see.

He led her over the fields and the
  valleys so wide
Until pretty Polly, she fell by his
  side.

Oh Willie, oh Willie, I'm afraid of
  your ways,
I'm afraid you will lead my poor
  body astray.

Polly, pretty Polly, you're guessin'
  just right.
I dug on your grave the best part of
  last night.

She threw her arms around him and
  trembled with fear
How can you kill the poor girl that
  loves you so dear?

There's no time to talk and there's
  no time to stand,
Then he drew his knife all in his
  right hand.

He stabbed her to the heart and her
  heart's blood did flow
And into the grave pretty Polly did
  go.

Then he threw a little dirt over her
  and started for home,
Leavin' no one behind but the wild
  birds to moan.

The quintessential courtin' song is "Black is the Color of My True Love's Hair." The song is cast in the mold of the great English ballads. It is based on a haunting melody of exquisite line and beauty, one that is far more vocally demanding on the singer than the usual folk song. One cannot help but visualize a lovesick boy, perhaps out in the woods sitting on a log, telling the whole world about the girl he loves so dearly. He describes her in the most tender of ways so that there is no doubt that she has won him over. This song is often sung by female singers with, of course, some appropriate alterations in the lyrics; it is, however, best performed in its original setting. The song is so outstanding that it is no wonder it has survived the test of time.

BLACK IS THE COLOR OF MY TRUE LOVE'S HAIR

Even though courtin' was generally looked on by mountain folk as a cruel comedy, marriage, on the other hand, was considered as something to be feared and forewarned. Songs dealing with the married life are full of warnings, citing the unification of man and wife as a dangerous and explosive battle. A few of these songs deal with the economics of marriage, that is, the responsibilities of a wife and a huge brood of children to feed and clothe. Many more of the songs address themselves to the ways in which girls change from courtship to marriage, from being a sweetheart to being a wife. Young men are warned that the "kitten" they court will turn into a "bear" once the marriage vows are sealed. A couple of stanzas from the mountain song "Devilish Mary" (note the use of the word *devilish* to describe Mary) sum up their philosophy of marriage.

DEVILISH MARY

She washed my clothes in live soap suds,
She peeled my back with switches,
She let me know right up to date
She's gonna wear my britches.

If I ever marry the second time,
It'll be for love not riches,
I'll marry a little girl 'bout two feet tall,
So she can't wear my britches.

"Old Joe Clark" was a favorite song of the Southern Mountain folk. Legend has it that there really was a man named Joe Clark, a moonshiner who lived in the Virginia hills. The song is based on the ancient modes of Elizabethan times. Specifically, it is based on the Mixolydian mode. There is no end to the number of verses connected with this song.

OLD JOE CLARK

Fare you well, old Joe Clark, For I'm a go-in' a - way.

Had a banjo made of gold,
Strings were made of twine;
Only tune that I could play,
Wish that gal were mine.
(*Chorus*)

Old Joe Clark he had a dog,
Blind as he could be;
Run a possum up a log,
You'd swear that dog could see.

I went down to Lexington,
Didn't know the route;
Put me in a coffee pot,
And poured me out the spout.

I went down to old Joe's house,
Old Joe wasn't home;
Jumped in bed with old Joe's wife,
And broke her tuckin' comb.

Met a possum in the road,
Mean as he could be;
Jumped the fence and whopped my
        dog,
And bristled up to me.

I wish I was an apple,
A-hangin' on a tree;
Ev'ry time that pretty gal passed,
She'd take a bite of me.

I wish I had a muley cow,
Corn to feed it on;

Pretty little girl to stay at home,
And feed it while I'm gone.

If I had a sweetheart,
I'd set her on the shelf;
Ev'ry time she smiled at me,
I'd get up there myself.

I wish I had a lariat rope,
Long as I could throw;
Throw it 'round my sweetheart's
        waist,
And down the road we'd go.

Peaches in the summertime,
Apples in the fall;
If I can't get the girl I want,
I won't have none at all.

Old Joe Clark, he's killed a man,
Throwed him in the branch;
Now Old Joe's a-goin' ta hang,
Ain't no other chance.

Never got no money,
Got no place to stay;
Got no place to lay my head,
With the chickin's a-crowin' for day

Final Chorus:
Fare you well, Old Joe Clark,
Fare you well, good-bye;
Fare you well, Old Joe Clark,
I hate to see you die.

As has been mentioned, the mountaineer became quite adept at the art of brewing hard liquor, better known as mountain dew, moonshine, or just plain booze. Indeed, then, drinking songs are some of the funniest mountain songs. "Real Old Mountain Dew" gives us some indication of where this art originated; it goes on to describe the still where the liquor is made, and finally, it beckons everyone who is listening to join in on the joy! Interestingly, this melody is more characteristic of music to be fiddled rather than sung. Nonetheless, it is a good melody and a highly singable one.

REAL OLD MOUNTAIN DEW

Mountain Song

At the foot of the hill there's a neat
   little still,
Where the smoke curls up to the
   sky;
By the smoke and the smell you can
   plainly tell,
That there's whiskey brewin' by.
(*Chorus*)

For it fills the air with odor rare,
And betwixt both me and you,
When home you roll you can take a
   bowl
Or a bucket of the Mountain Dew.
(*Chorus*)

Now learned men who use the pen,
Who've wrote your praises high;
This sweet 'pocheen (potion) from
   Ireland's green,
Distilled from wheat and rye.
(*Chorus*)

Throw away your pills, it'll cure all
   ills,
Of pagan or Christian or Jew;
Take off your coat and free your
   throat,
With the real old Mountain Dew.
(*Chorus*)

"Rye Whiskey" came directly to us from the Southern Mountains, yet it was sung by Confederate soldiers and even found its way westward to cowboy towns. The song vividly tells of a man's love for the bottle and the many problems it has given him in return. The bottle has, in the end, become his mistress and the wager is on to see which of the two will win in the end.

83

RYE WHISKEY

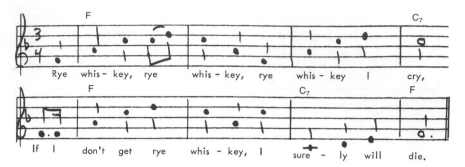

Rye whis - key, rye whis - key, rye whis - key I cry,

If I don't get rye whis - key, I sure - ly will die.

It's whiskey, rye whiskey, I know
you of old,
You robbed my poor pockets of
silver and gold.
(*first verse*)

It's beefsteak when I'm hungry, Rye
Whiskey when I'm dry,
A greenback when I'm hard up, Oh
heaven when I die.
(*first verse*)

I go to yonder holler and I'll build
me a still,
And I'll give you a gallon for a five
dollar bill.
(*first verse*)

If the ocean was whiskey and I was a
duck,

I'd dive to the bottom and never
come up.
(*first verse*)

But the ocean ain't whiskey and I
ain't a duck,
So I'll play Jack o' Diamonds and
trust to my luck.
(*first verse*)

Her parents don't like me, they say
I'm poor,
And I'm unfit, To darken her door.
(*first verse*)

Oh whiskey, you villain, you're no
friend to me,
You killed my poor pappy, God
damn you, try me.
(*first verse*)

The contributions of the Southern Mountain folk represent a unique collection of musical gems. The great love these people had for music is clearly demonstrated both by the quantity and quality of their musical offerings. These songs serve as musical biographies of a most interesting group of people who went through life living free and easy, a society unaffected by outside cultural influences. Indeed, what a pleasure it was for the peoples of the world to suddenly be presented with a huge outpouring of great songs that were perhaps one hundred years in the making. Because of the direct influence of the Southern Mountain folk's musical talents, the areas surrounding these mountains are today the hub of activity in country-western music. Nashville, the Grand Ole Op'ry, blue grass music, and others, are all spinoffs of the music planted by those mountaineers over two hundred years ago.

7

Songs of the American Blacks

One of the greatest blemishes on American democracy, with its promise of individual freedom and the pursuit of happiness, was the taking of black human beings and converting them into profit-making chattel. During a period of one hundred years, hundreds of thousands of black Africans were bartered and stolen from their birth places, bought and sold on the open market, and forced to live first as slaves and then, after the war for their emancipation, as second-class citizens. Whose idea was it to initiate the process that led to this massive exploitation of these primitive African peoples? One theory tells of a missionary who had served in Africa and who was then reassigned to America. He was so taken up with the richness of this country and its great potential for living that, with his love of humanity, he thought America would be an ideal place to relocate those indolent Africans. Here they would find fertile soil, unpolluted water, and the opportunity to work at gainful employment, thus increasing their chances of leading more fulfilling lives. His intentions, however honorable, gave birth to a highly profitable enterprise—one of the most inhumane adventures in American history that snowballed into an almost unstoppable avalanche.

America was the answer to a dream for the thousands of poor and oppressed Europeans who, of their own volition, came to these shores to seek a better life. Africans, on the other hand, although they shared many of the same hardships as the poor whites of Europe, did not voluntarily choose to come here nor did they have the same opportunity once they did arrive to avail themselves of the human freedoms guaranteed in the American Bill of Rights.

Initially, slavery was introduced throughout the entire new nation. The practice was ideally suited to the southern states where the trend toward an

85

aristocratic society was definitely taking hold, where the prevailing climate was more nearly like that of the Africans' homeland, and where huge parcels of lands required large numbers of persons to work them. In the north, however, slavery did not take hold because opposite societal trends prevailed there, but especially because northerners were moving more in the direction of industrialization, under which system persons worked in factories or provided services on an individual basis. The buying and selling of Africans without regard for the breaking up of family units went on unabated for a full century. The practice finally led to a confrontation between the states; yet, even after the emancipation of the slaves, black Americans continued to live in quasi-servitude until the enactment of civil rights legislation in the mid-twentieth century.

The outstanding musical ability of the American black is now a well-documented fact. The blacks' interest and ability in music were well known to their captors, who used this interest and ability in music to help keep them calm or make them excited as the occasion dictated. Similarly, slave owners preyed on this interest and ability in an effort to maintain control over their slaves and increase their productivity. Even the early missionaries and itinerant preachers of the gospel were aware of the blacks' love of music and capitalized on it through the presentation of song fests as an aid in their mission to convert the blacks to Christianity.

The Africans' great interest in music was a well-kept secret, shared only by those persons who directly interacted with them. It was not until the Civil War era that their musical capabilities came to the attention of the public at large, through the publication of the book, *Slave Songs of the United States,* written and compiled in 1861 by a group of agents sent on an educational mission to the Port Royal Islands. These agents were fascinated with the originality and unique sound of the blacks' musical shouts and "sperichels" and felt that it should be shared with the general public.

Thomas Jefferson was unquestionably the most musically gifted and skilled of the Founding Fathers. Whenever the great leaders met, they always set aside time to play chamber music for their own enjoyment and as a change of pace from their trying governmental chores. There was never any doubt about who would play first violin in the ensemble. Thomas Jefferson was the most knowledgeable musician in the group. It was Jefferson who made the first "valid" statement regarding the musicianship of the Africans. He summed up his observations as follows: "They are extremely gifted, with accurate ears for tune and time and quickness in catching a tune." In effect, he was stating that their musicianship was such that they were able to hear music, remember it, and reproduce it with accurate intonation and rhythm. On another occasion Jefferson remarked that their renditions of music showed an uncanny inclination for a strongly pronounced beat and rhythmic verve.

There are several important characteristics connected with the musical contributions of the American blacks that relate directly back to their musical practices in Africa. First, their music is essentially communal, that is, in the process of performing music, whole groups of people are actively and intimately involved. Momentary opportunities for individuals to express personal statements are provided for; however, the group spontaneously and unabashedly reenter the performance until such time as someone else asks to be heard. Second, their music is highly emotional. Deeply engrossed with the subject at hand, they begin on a low level of feeling, and surge at the end to the pinnacle of heightened emotion. Third, and perhaps most directly related to the study of folk music, is their unique use of musical structure, known as call–response. Although somewhat similar to the "answering-back" structure of the Southern Mountain folk, it is structure that is most distinctive and in a class by itself. In the typical black folk song there is usually a place in the music where an individual or even a series of individuals can musically call out to the other members of their group. These individuals are not necessarily tossing out questions, as is the case in the mountain songs. In these songs they are actually calling out important personal pronouncements. The response from the other members of the group is spontaneous, immediate, and usually, supportive. Particular mention is made of this unique aspect of the structure of these songs because, all too often, we do not recognize or even take into consideration this important facet when performing them. Renditions of these songs as often presented today involve whole groups or perhaps single individuals singing the entire song from beginning to end. The proper presentation of these songs, however, should provide for particular individuals to call out their musical statements with members of the group "basing" them with emotionally charged responses. There must be a dialogue between certain callers and members of the listening groups. Additionally, the songs must necessarily surge emotionally from beginning to end. Not all songs are expected to be sung loud and rhythmically fast; there are many songs that should move at a slow, lazy pace and be performed more tastefully on lower levels of volume.

A perfect illustration of this call–response technique in its proper execution can be observed in the black prayer meeting where the minister calls out to his congregation, which responds with Amens, Hallelujahs, and Glory-Glories. The authentic renditions of call–response songs are a joy to experience both as an observer or a participant. It is indeed unfortunate that black American songs are so often sung from beginning to end by single individuals or by whole groups completely disregarding the built-in dialogue between individual and group.

Another of the misconceptions, or better, abuses connected with the modern performance of American black songs is in their elaborately harmonized settings. We must remember that Africans were a very primitive people when they first arrived here. Rhythm and melody are always in evidence in music of primitive people; however, harmony is a more sophisticated element. Only advanced cultures have addressed themselves to this element, and that only after hundreds of years of serious experimentation. Admittedly, black American songs beautifully lend themselves to elaborate harmonizations, and skilled musical arrangers find they simply cannot resist the temptation to "over-harmonize" them. Expressly for this reason, we today hear these great songs wonderously arranged for choirs or instrumental organizations. The final product is most impressive, in which members of both the performing groups and audience experience music on the highest of expressive levels. The early Africans sang only in unison. Smatterings of harmony were realized accidentally as caller and respondents musically bumped into one another, causing more than one sound or tone to be sounded simultaneously. The practice of harmonizing black American songs is not being condemned. However, it would be a misconception to think that the original utterances of the blacks were presented in harmonized settings.

Musical instruments were used in the early performance of these songs; for the most part, these instruments were percussive in nature. The early blacks habitually picked up just about anything that would produce a rhythmic sound—from sticks and rattles to anything that even remotely resembled a drum. Even today, one can walk the streets of a southern (or northern) city and witness the musical ingenuity of young black children who have used their creativity to bring together various materials, even including some "junk" materials, to make their musical instruments.

The early Africans were quick to take up the guitar and employ it to accompany their songs. Because of their natural musical talents they soon became quite proficient in playing this instrument. Their single most significant contribution in the area of musical instruments was the *banjar,* a fretted instrument that, in principle, plays much like a guitar. It is unique, however, because something resembling a drum serves as its belly. We can only speculate on the theory that Africans were exposed to the use of tuned strings via the violin or lap harps as played by European missionaries who worked among them. With their deep interest in percussion instruments they ingeniously combined the best of stringed sounds along with percussive sounds, thus creating the new instrument. The crude banjars of the early Africans became an instant hit here in America. The original four-string model was given a fifth string to expand its musical capabilities. The name of the instrument was changed from banjar to banjo. Obviously, during the great days of minstrelsy it was essential for the black man's instrument to be used in order that proper settings for the music be included. The sounds that came from the banjo were enthusiastically received by the listening public and many a banjoist learned to play the instrument with great flair and deftness. Even today, the banjo continues to be a popular folk-type instrument.

Folk music of black Americans falls neatly into three categories: religious music, work music, and leisure or recreational music, and are made solely for purposes of study and for drawing certain commonalities of style and intent. By far, the religious music is the most appealing, exciting, and representative of the songs that have been handed down and preserved. The early Africans had a considerable number of work songs that they used to accompany their burdensome labors; however, they were careful not to share these songs with outsiders. Partly, this was because of the teachings of their church, which looked upon nonreligious songs as products of the devil. They also felt that these songs were personal, belonged to them, and not to be used for anything other than their labors.

Similarly, they were reluctant to share their leisure or play songs. These songs occupied their time during those few moments they had to frolic just before bedtime. They were always hesitant to perform these songs for outsiders. They strongly felt that the songs not only belonged to them but that they should only be sung within the confines of their living quarters.

Religious Songs

In the early years of colonization, black Africans were considered to be heathens. Southerners were deeply engrossed in the establishment of new and more satisfying methods of religious worship. Many dissenters actively advocated more spirited approaches for Christian worship. New Baptist and Methodist church groups were formed by folks who wanted their religion heated up with the power of the holy spirit. Black people, at the outset, were content merely to observe the conduct of these worship services; however, as more and more of the religionists sought to bring their redemptive messages to more and more of God's people, they began to include the blacks within the realm of their missionary practices. Slave owners found no cause for alarm over the Christianizing of their properties; however, as their slaves began participating in unbelievable numbers and with great intensity, they found the practice most difficult to terminate. It has been reported that between 1780 and 1800, membership in the Baptist church in the south alone increased fourfold. Many of the new converts who helped swell the numbers were blacks.

The Christian ethic as purported by the spirited Protestant sects of the south had a tremendous effect on the African slave. They found the promise of eternal glory in heaven in return for their suffering through bondage here on earth to be the answer to their prayers. Additionally, they found the communal-style worship service with the preacher's hellfire and damnation sermons and the emotional carrying-on (such as being "possessed," getting happy, dancing, and hollering) to be most inviting. They listened intently to the telling of stories from the Bible and found that great Hebrew leaders such as David, Moses, Daniel, and Joshua, who fought courageously against great odds, to be heroes with whom they could identify and find comfort.

As with everything else, black Americans personalized their newly found religion and adapted it to their own way of life. Back in Africa, the high leader was reputed to have mystical powers and was acclaimed king. Accordingly, they chose to identify Jesus Christ not by his full name but as King Jesus. The heroes of the ancient Bible were identified as ole Jonah and ole Moses. Even the devil was casually called ole Satan. The black Christians loved terms of jubilation, such as Hallelujah, Glory, and especially, Amen, with which they could respond in their customary call–response deliberations. Christianity preached earthly sin and suffering along with forgiveness, resurrection, and eternal life in heaven. Black Americans found great comfort in talking and meditating about heaven, referring to it as the Promised Land or the Good Life. Heaven carried the message of redemption from the sins of this world and freedom from slavery where all God's children would be happy and equal. Symbolism meant a great deal to them and they were quick to symbolically associate the teachings of the Bible to their own earthly lives. For example, every river symbolically became for them the River Jordan with its promise of better things on the other side.

From their attendance at so many hellfire and damnation sermons, the blacks developed an obsession with the sins of mankind and his affinity for sinning. This became a major issue because they knew that sin would deprive them of their ultimate goal of becoming free and happy in God's Promised Land. In their everyday living they tried to abide by the laws of God and took every opportunity to warn others of the occasions of sin and the penalties pertaining thereto. The following lyrics excerpted from one of their songs wonderfully illustrates this:

> See that woman all dressed so fine,
> She ain't got Jesus on her mind.
>
> See that woman all dressed in red,
> She's gonna get herself in bed.

The lion's share of their religious songs are more commonly known as spirituals. The hymns of the more established Protestant churches in the south were a far cry from the more doleful psalms as sung by members of the northern churches. However, as more and more churchgoers found hymn singing too confining for demonstrating the inner joy that they were experiencing, they began to create their own type of religious songs, called spirituals. As their name suggests, these songs were emotionally conceived and delivered because the singers were actually invoking the holy spirit. The new black converts were accustomed to hearing spirituals as sung by their white Christian brethren. They were aware of the emotional content and the surging techniques employed in the singing of spirituals. Through their creative musical gifts they were able to add literally hundreds of spirituals to the grand collection, spirituals of uncommon sincerity and beauty. One of the finest "white" spirituals popular at the time was "Poor Wayfaring Stranger." This song was the product of the Revivalist movement that Baptists and Methodists initiated as they wandered in search of greater religious excitement. It is a song of unusual beauty, based on low levels of emotion; nonetheless, it is an authentic spiritual.

POOR WAYFARING STRANGER

White Spiritual

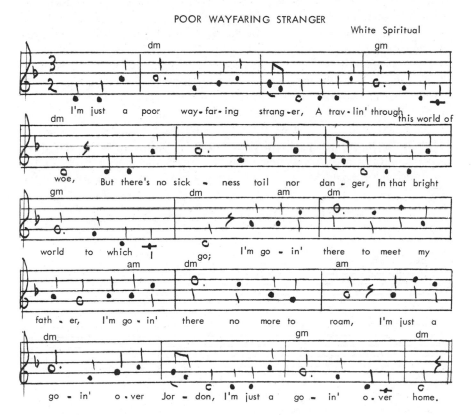

I know dark clouds will gather
round me,
I know my way is steep and rough,
But beauteous fields lie just beyond
me,
Where souls redeemed their vigil
keep;
I'm goin' there to meet my mother,
She said she'd meet me when I
come,
I'm only goin' over Jordan,
I'm only goin' over home.

I want to wear a crown of glory,
When I get home to that bright land,
I want to shout Salvation's story,
In concert with that bloodwashed
band;
I'm goin' there to meet my Saviour,
To sing his praise forever more,
I'm only goin' over Jordan,
I'm only goin' over home.

Most of the black spirituals were spontaneously conceived. Just as soon as the preacher was finished delivering his sermon, and perhaps even before, the preacher or a member of the congregation would break out in song and call out some aspect of the message of the day. Members of the congregation would respond. Before you knew it a whole, beautiful new spiritual would be carved out. If it was a good song, it would be remembered and sung again and again as the occasion called for it. In essence, then, the spiritual was the black man's way of retelling Biblical stories or of relating moral messages in his own words and in his own way through song.

To better understand the process involved in giving birth to a spiritual we need only turn to the spiritual "Michael Row de Boat Ashore." Visualize a group of blacks who were given the task of rowing a boat from one shore to the other. They would naturally engage in singing as they went about the boring job of rowing and, even more, in an effort to coordinate their strokes. As they sang, they would create new lyrics spontaneously with their typical symbolic associations. What would eventually result would be a whole new spiritual, beautifully shaped and completed, by the time they reached the opposite shore. In this particular song they used Michael the Archangel as their hero figure, connecting him with their labors and longing for the other side.

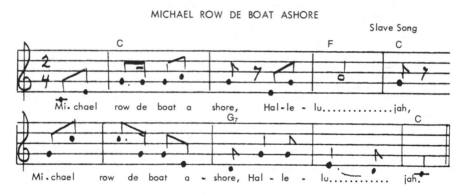

MICHAEL ROW DE BOAT ASHORE

2. Gabriel blow de trumpet horn

3. Jordan stream am wide and deep

4. Jesus stand on d' other side

5. Lordy plants his garden there

6. He raise fruit for you to eat

7. He dat eat shall never die

8. Sinner row to save your soul

Musically speaking, the spirituals of the American blacks are wholly original in sound and tremendously exciting in rhythm. The slow songs are simplistic, yet express a soul-searching, deeply emotional, hauntingly beautiful message. In their up-tempo songs we find ourselves instinctively responding to the hand-clapping, toe-tapping beat of the music. To perform these songs correctly one must put aside some of the niceties required in the presentation of ordinary songs and do as the songs' originators say—"Go with the flow!"

The spiritual that best illustrates what might be considered a stereotypical black spiritual is "Set Down Servant." This song admirably reveals the call–response structure. The calling out is done in a slow, rhythmically free manner after which the tempo picks up and the whole group joins in with a pronounced beat. In this song we not only have the petitioner calling to God for certain promised favors but we also have the added voice of God granting the petitioner's prayers. Several outstanding choral arrangements of this spiritual are available.

SET DOWN SERVANT

"My Lawd, you know
That you promise me,
Promise me a long white robe,
An' a starry crown."

"Go yonder angel,
Fetch me a starry crown,
Place it on-a my servant's head
Now servant, pleast set down."
(*Chorus*)

"My Lawd, you know
That you promise me,
Promise me a long white robe,
An' a golden waistband."

"Go yonder angel,
Fetch me a golden waistband,
Place it round my servant's waist,
Now servant, pleast set down."
(*Chorus*)

"Didn't My Lord Deliver Daniel?" is a spiritual that illustrates the black man's practice of taking a Biblical tale and relating it to his own desperate life. In this spiritual one hears the caller's plea for freedom as he reminds his listeners of a crisis situation that faced Daniel in the lion's den and the Lord's intervention in delivering him from harm. The song is full of hope and comfort in the knowledge that God in his own time will punish the wicked and bring justice to his suffering people just as he did with Daniel, Jonah, and the Hebrew people. This is another of the up-tempo, rhythmically strong spirituals.

DIDN'T MY LORD DELIVER DANIEL ?

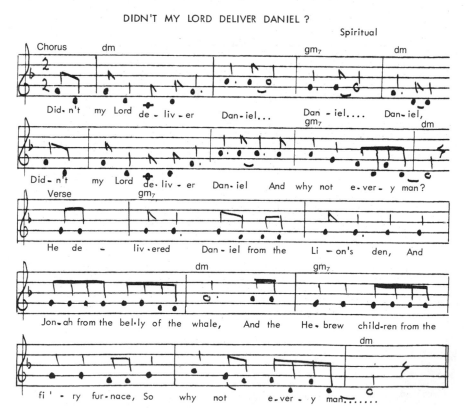

The wind blows east, the wind blows west,
It blows like judgment day;
And ev'ry soul that never did pray,
Will be glad to pray that day.
(*Chorus*)

The moon run down in a purple stream,
The sun refuse to shine;
And every star will disappear,
King Jesus will be mine.
(*Chorus*)

The story of the Hebrews held in bondage in Egypt was one with which the American black could easily identify and empathize. They saw themselves in the same situation. They found new hope in the fact that these people were eventually granted their freedom and given the opportunity, with the help of God, to return to their homeland. "Go Down, Moses" is one of the slow-tempo spirituals that should move as the spirit moves the singers. It is mournful, labored, and even has places for the singers to insert deep wailing and harsh scolding sounds.

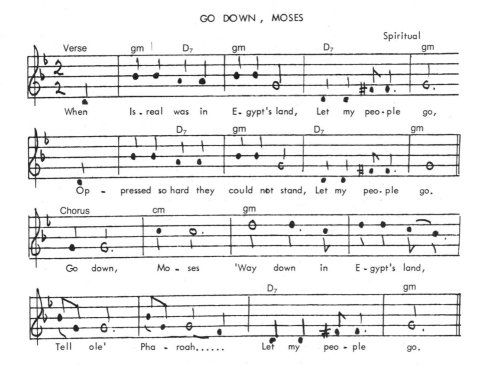

GO DOWN, MOSES

Thus saith the Lord, bold Moses said
Let my People go,
If not, I'll smite your first-born dead,
Let my people go.
(*Chorus*)

No more shall they in bondage toil,
Let my People go,
Let them come out with Egypt's spoil,
Let my People go.
(*Chorus*)

Religious meetings meant a great deal to the early Christianized Africans. It provided them with opportunities to congregate in large groups as allowed by their slave owners. They found temporary comfort during these times to unload their burdens and gain renewed hope. The number of approved prayer meetings never were sufficient to satisfy their wants and so they frequently called for secret meetings through the singing of the spiritual "Steal Away." This is another slow-tempoed spiritual. It should be sung in a rhythmically free manner to depict people with heavy burdens dragging themselves off to some secret destination to pray.

STEAL AWAY

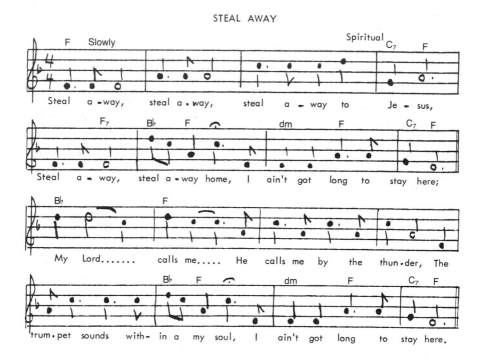

My Lord calls me,
He calls me by the lightning.

The American blacks created spirituals that coincided with important events in the Christian calendar, that is, they produced songs for such Christian holidays as Christmas, Easter, and so forth. "Were You There," is an Easter (Holy Week) spiritual of consummate beauty that depicts the pain and suffering connected with the crucifixion of Christ. What makes it special is the naïve, yet sincere manner in which the caller asks his followers to relive the event with him. Musically, it depicts the scene far more dramatically than even the most gifted preacher could using speech and gestures.

WERE YOU THERE

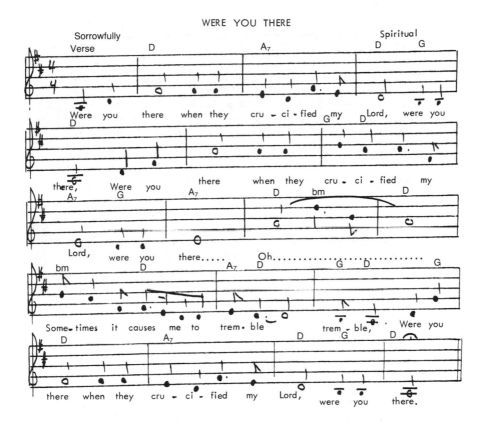

Were you there when they nailed Him to the cross?
Were you there when they laid Him in the tomb?

"What You Gonna Call Your Pretty Little Baby?" is a poignant, beautiful Christmas spiritual that depicts the nativity scene. It has many of the fine qualities contained in "Were You There?" The qualities of simplicity, sincerity, and even naïveté are all very much in evidence.

WHAT YOU GONNA CALL YOUR PRETTY LITTLE BABY ?

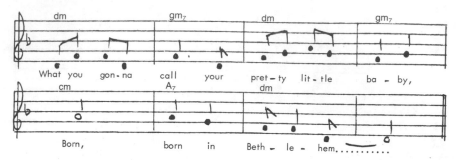

What you gon-na call your pret-ty lit-tle ba - by, Born, born in Beth - le - hem..........

I'm a-gonna call the little baby Jesus.
Who's a-gonna come to see the baby Jesus?
I'm a-gonna come to see the baby Jesus.

One of the lesser known of the slow, soulful spirituals is "Balm in Gilead." It would be a mistake not to bring this great spiritual to the attention of the general public. The melody is soul-searching and deeply moving; the lyrics are soothing, comforting, and ringing with hope. Like so many of the other fine spirituals, arrangers of choral music have produced a number of impressive arrangements of this song. If sung properly, this spiritual can move even the most despondent person to positive heights.

BALM IN GILEAD

There is a balm in Gil. e - ad to make the wound. ed whole............. There is a balm in Gil. e - ad to heal the sin - sick soul.

Some - times I feel dis - cour. aged and think my work's in vain, But then the Ho. ly Spir - it re - vives my soul a - gain..... al Fine

Don't ever feel discouraged,
Your Father is your friend,
And if you lack for knowledge,
He'll not refuse to lend.

Work Songs

The work songs of the American blacks available today are few in number simply because the slaves were reluctant to share them with outsiders. Southern slave owners regarded singing at work to be a harmless activity, and indeed, they even encouraged it by singling out certain of the better singers and assigning them the easy task of singing out in the open fields. The workers would join in the singing in an effort to pass the time away at their monotonous labors and make the whole affair more bearable. Certain chores demanded a concerted effort, so appropriate songs were sung to allow the team of workers to pull their energies together with the rhythm of the song. It is interesting to note, however, that the Negro churches frowned upon the practice of singing at work because they considered it to be a product of the devil. Like the early Pilgrims, they shared the notion that the singing voice should be used solely to praise God. Those work songs that were sung in the cotton or peanut fields, in the prisons, and on the river docks and boats were heard and have been remembered; but when asked face to face, a black man would have been quick to state that he didn't know any work songs and would substitute a spiritual in its place.

"Pick a Bale of Cotton" is a work song full of bouncy rhythms and is just plain fun to sing. Unlike the spirituals, the jazzy rhythms of these songs almost force one to let go. One can easily understand what the singing of this song would do in the open cotton fields to help build morale and increase productivity. Even though the song is basically a work or secular song, the black man typically interjected religious items into it. Again, this was part of his habit of relating religious teachings into his everyday life or it may have been his inability to think up totally nonreligious lyrics. Incidentally, the picking of a whole bale of cotton in one day by one person doing it by hand was a totally unreachable goal at the time. It may have been selected as a target toward which they should aspire.

PICK A BALE OF COTTON

Traditional

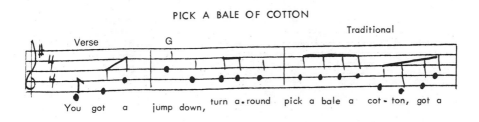

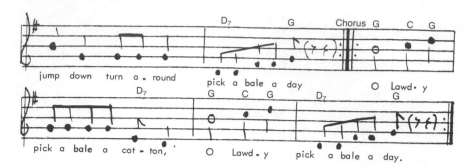

jump down turn a - round pick a bale a day O Lawd - y
pick a bale a cot - ton, O Lawd - y pick a bale a day.

Me an' my pardner can
Pick a bale of cotton.
Me an' my pardner can
Pick a bale a day.

Had a little woman could
Pick a bale 'a cotton.

Had a little woman could
Pick a bale a day.

I b'lieve to my soul I can
Pick a bale 'a cotton.
I b'lieve to my soul I can
Pick a bale a day.

The boll weevil is a parasite that raises havoc with cotton ready for harvesting. It is much feared because it can send even the most successful farmer into bankruptcy in a single growing season. "The Ballad of the Boll Weevil" is a story-telling song that humorously relates the events connected with an epidemic that began in Texas in the 1890s and then spread eastward like wildfire. After the emancipation, many of the more enterprising blacks wandered from farm to farm seeking employment. In this song the black man identifies himself with the boll weevil as they both go a-wandering, "just a-lookin' for a home." One cannot help but take notice of the subtle satire contained in the telling of this tale.

BALLAD OF THE BOLL WEEVIL

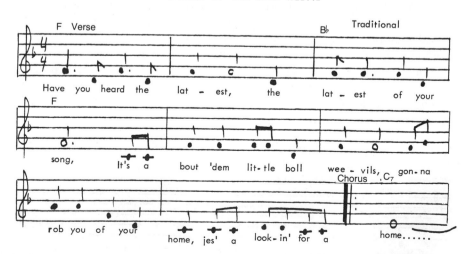

Have you heard the lat - est, the lat - est of your
song, It's a bout 'dem lit - tle boll wee - vils, gon - na
rob you of your home, jes' a look - in' for a home......

jes' a look-in' for a home....... jes' a look-in' for a home.

The boll weevil is a little black bug
Come from Mexico they tell.
Come to eat our cotton up
And raise pertic'ler hell.

The farmer ask the boll weevil
"What makes your head so red?"
"I've been traveling this wide world
    over
It's a wonder I ain't dead."

The first time I seen the boll weevil
He was on that western plain.
The next time I seen the boll weevil
He had hopped that Memphis train.

The next time I seen the boll weevil
He was runnin' a spinning wheel.
The last time I seen him
He was ridin' a new machine.

The farmer said to the merchant
"I'm in an awful fix.
The boll weevil ate all my cotton up
And left me only sticks."

The farmer said to the banker
"I ain't got but one bale.

And before you take that one
I'll suffer and die in jail."

Then the farmer taken the boll weevil
And buried him down in ice.
The boll weevil tell the farmer, "Lawd,
That's mighty cool and nice."

Then the farmer taken the boll weevil
And put him in Paris Green.
The boll weevil tell the farmer, "Lawd,
That's the best I ever seen."

Boll weevil say to the lightin' bug
"I wish I could be you.
With that little tail light of yours
I could work the whole night through."

Boll weevil say to the doctor
"Better pour out all your pills.
When I get through with the farmer
He won't pay no doctor bills."

The merchant got half the cotton,
Boll weevil got the rest.
Didn't leave the poor farmer's wife
But one ole cotton dress.

Leisure Songs

As with their work songs, the American blacks shared very few of their leisure or play songs with outsiders. As a consequence only a small number of these songs exist. Slaves would gather together in a particular section of their living compound to sing songs and pass the time away. This was one of the few recreational activities that they could enjoy in their restrictive quarters. There are written accounts by slave owners reporting their surprise at finding their slaves completely sapped of energy as they left the fields from the long day's work and then suddenly change as they appeared charged with renewed energy as they frolicked at night entertaining each other. If psychologists were in operation at that time they would have had little difficulty in explaining that freedom to choose. Joy, happiness, interest, incentive, attitude, and motivation have everything to do with pumping up one's energy to do anything.

"Shortnin' Bread" is a song that attests to the miraculous powers of Mammy's shortnin' bread to cure just about any malady. It may have been created by a black mammy while she cared for a sick child. It was such a good song that it ultimately became a popular song to sing at any social occasion.

SHORTNIN' BREAD

Went to de kitchin, kicked off the lead,
Filled my pockets full with shortnin'
    bread.
Shortnin' bread an' it baked so thin,
That's what it takes to make 'em grin.
(*Chorus*)

One little baby lyin' in bed
When he hear tell of shortnin' bread.
Popped up so quick an' he dance and
    sing
Almos' cut him de pigeon's wing.
(*Chorus*)

"Hushaby," sometimes known as "All the Pretty Little Horses," is certainly one of the songs that mammys sang to comfort the children they had in their care. This one has survived because it may have been remembered by those children who were the recipients of the comforting qualities of the song. It is a lovely lullaby and ranks with the very best.

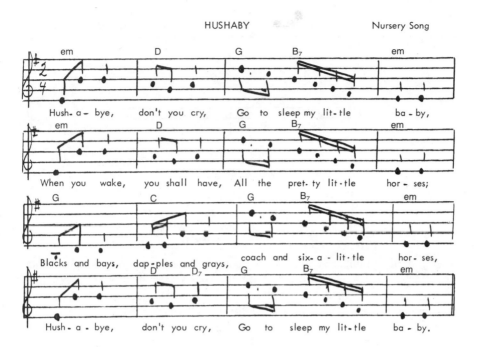

Hushabye, don't you cry,
Go to sleep my little baby,
Way down yonder, in de medder
Lies a po' l'il bambie;
De bees an' de butterflies,
Pickin' out its eyes
De po' l'il thing cried, "mammy!"
Hushabye, don't you cry
Go to sleepy, little baby.

On the lighter side, one of the easiest and most singable of the leisure songs is "L'il Liza Jane." The call—response element is there, along with a section that could conceivably be interpreted as a chorus.

L'IL LIZA JANE

Traditional

I got a house in Baltimo',
L'il Liza Jane;
Street cars runnin' by my do',
L'il Liza Jane.
(*Chorus*)

Come my love an' be with me,
L'il Liza Jane;
I'll take very good care of thee,
L'il Liza Jane.
(*Chorus*)

Not all the leisure songs are light in nature nor necessarily happy and gay. "Nobody Knows the Trouble 'Ob Seen" has a great deal of the depth and seriousness of the spirituals, yet its text is more on the secular side. One can just picture a group of black slaves after a particularly hard and depressing day sitting on the porches of their shacks lightening their burdens in a kind of group therapy exercise through song.

NOBODY KNOWS THE TROUBLE 'OB SEEN

What makes ole Satan treat me so?
Oh, yes, Lord,
Because he got me once but he let me go.
Oh, yes, Lord.

The great wealth of folk songs contributed by early African Americans are now a mainstay in our collection of American folk songs. They are original, pleasantly profound, and eminently singable. These songs have brought enjoyment to all those who have associated themselves with them. From the songs we have discussed throughout this chapter have flowered the jazz, gospel, and soul music of the twentieth century. We are still too close to this music to accurately assess its true worth and influence. The next century should certainly give us a broader perspective on the cultural influence of the musical contributions of black Americans.

8

Songs of the American Sailors

In its infancy, the American maritime services were a carbon copy of that of the British. Prior to the Revolutionary War, the British mercantile fleets accumulated huge fortunes as they transported large amounts of raw materials to England and returned to the American colonies with immigrants and finished goods. The cycle was repeated over and over again with little delay, bringing fat profits to the fleet merchants as well as to the crown. The need for the maintenance and building of new vessels was so great that shipbuilding yards were established in a number of the larger seaports up and down the eastern seaboard of the colonies. There were two reasons for this: first, labor was both available and cheap; second, the required raw materials, such as lumber, were readily available. At that time, the decision to establish shipbuilding yards in the colonies was a wise idea; however, the plan backfired when the Revolutionary War broke out. Americans not only took immediate possession of the yards, but more important, demonstrated that they had mastered the art of shipbuilding and could manage well on their own. As a result, in both of our early conflicts with the British, including the War of 1812, the American Navy proved itself to be a very formidable opponent. It should be noted, nonetheless, that the Americans had learned everything they knew about sailing and about ships from their British mentors and had completely patterned every practice after them.

The new breed of American naval officer had not had the luxury of a formal education in a school of navigation as had their esteemed British counterparts. They had to learn their craft the hard way—and while at sea. This, in a sense, would constitute a definite deficiency regarding their ability to manage and maneuver their ships in both war and peace. As it turned out, it actually became a very positive factor for the Americans. Records indicate that American ships ran circles around the fleets of the other sailing nations. In accordance with the old saying, "Fools rush in where wise men fear to tread," American ships became notorious for their unbelievable speed and recklessness and were feared by all who sailed the high seas. Even in a storm with winds reaching gale levels, American ships were sighted with all sails set and catching the full powers of the wind. Although on the one hand, American ships had the reputation for sailing at full speed and with real daring, on the other hand, they also had the reputation for running ships aground, breaking them in two, and even having some sink.

From about 1815 to 1860 American sailing practices began to break away from their British model and started to develop their own types of vessels and sailing techniques. With the close of the War of 1812 came the establishment of the American mercantile fleet, which went on to become one of the most successful businesses in America. One of the most important factors that contributed to this success was the development of an outstanding ship, the "Yankee Clipper." American shipbuilders designed ships with keener, sharper lines that sat higher in the water, thus cutting a narrow swath in the ocean and placing less resistance against the water. The Yankee clippers were streamlined, slim, sleek, fast, and truly seaworthy. As a matter of fact, the Yankee clipper reigned as Queen of the Seas for almost one hundred years; thereafter, steam- and diesel-powered ships supplanted less reliable wind-powered vessels.

In addition to their recklessness, American sailors were also known for their hard, back-breaking approach to sailing. American naval officers were notorious for driving their crews to the utmost. It is no wonder they were able to get their jobs done in record time. In short, American sailing established a reputation for itself in a very brief span of time, under circumstances that had provided little or no formal schooling for its officers and crews.

The life of a sailor was not an easy one, spent enjoying the magic of the sea, the excitement of foreign shores, or any of the other fringe benefits one might associate with such a life. Rather, it was a life filled with exhausting work, long hours of daily labor, voyages that lasted months, even years, and that, at times, were filled with danger. Sailors had to cope with boredom, despair, homesickness, and monotony. Work aboard ship involved the continual process of loading cargo, watching over it en route, unloading it, weighing anchor, and so forth. The ship's rigging demanded constant attention in response to changing sailing conditions. Sails had to be set, reefed, furled, and bunted. Decks has to be scrubbed clean each day. Pumps in the bilge had to be operated in fair weather or foul because wooden ships continually seeped water. Sailors had a tour of work duty as well as two tours of watch duty, one in which they were actively on watch and the other in which they were constantly on call. The job was physically exhausting, difficult, and dangerous. The dangers involved in sailing during those years were not so much from the threat of swashbuckling pirates as from the usual emergencies created by extremes in weather conditions. Manning sails atop a mast during a gale storm or risking being washed overboard during a wind and rain storm somehow presented more than the usual bundle of occupational hazards. Perhaps the most dangerous phase of sailing was experienced by the whalermen. These men sailed the treacherous northern Atlantic and Pacific oceans in pursuit of their prey, which, once spotted, had to be dealt with. This was not an easy task, since these creatures were both enormous and dangerous.

As with the British fleets before them, the American mercantile companies thrived on their wildly expanding business and its resultant fat profits. They supplied the world markets with raw materials, then brought millions of immigrants (as well as tons of needed manufactured products) back to the United States. American sailing, then, had created its own unique image; however, the British influence still remained in subtle evidence. And this influence can clearly be seen in the music of the American sailor.

It is common knowledge that a song is as important to a sailor as a military band is to a soldier. For sailors, singing is rooted in ancient times, when boats were powered by wind and man and when voyages lasted for many months, even years. Singing was a sailor's way to counteract boredom as he momentarily reflected on his home, loved ones, and great exploits in an attempt to maintain his sanity. Sailors also used singing as a way of helping them coordinate their strokes as oarsmen on both sides of the ship, setting up a rhythm in their pulls on the oars through the use of music. More than this, many of the so-called chores aboard ship were better executed if sailors combined their efforts in the rhythm of a song. The art of singing was developed over many hundreds of years by sailors sailing all over the world and under all kinds of flags. The practice resulted in a huge collection of marvelous, engaging songs and in a style of singing that is both unique and exciting.

The sailor sang in a most uninhibited manner. He sang this way while sailing on the high seas; he sang this way while ashore because this was the only way he knew how to sing. The sailor always sang with a full voice and with large volume. This is understandable because singing on the open sea with a spanking breeze at one's back, one had to sing with full power simply in order to be heard. Similarly, he sang in an uninhibited manner because he lived, to a great extent, solely in male company. The sailor has been characterized as a "natural singer" both on land and on sea. His songs were sturdy and strong, full of boasting and bragging, relating adventures, good times, hard times, and the rigors of his work; at no time did they express boredom, human weaknesses, or complaints. Many of their songs could be classified as profane, especially those versions reserved for the open seas. In modern jargon, we would describe them as "macho" songs (in the most extreme sense of the word).

On a comparative basis, sailor songs are the most cosmopolitan or multinational of all American folk songs. The obvious reason for this, of course, was that sailors were more often in touch with peoples from other cultures. As they visited foreign shores and became accquainted with other ways of life they could not help but be influenced, even if indirectly, by significant aspects of these foreign cultures. Along with actual visits to other lands, American ships often took on sailors from other nations either to replace members of their crew who had jumped ship or had died on the high seas, or else because they needed some additional hands on board. These foreign sailors interacted closely with the Americans and shared their customs with them, especially their music. Even a cursory glance at the music literature of the American sailor will reveal the influence of other cultures. For example, on a percentage basis, there are more songs based on minor scales in the sailor's repertoire than in any other group of American folk songs. Most of the nations bordering the Mediterranean Sea base their songs on the minor scale as compared to the American preference for the major scale. Even the melodic tone clusters and the rhythmic patterns display a more cosmopolitan air. Many of the traditional American sailor songs are strict adaptations of songs that originated in the British isles; others come from such countries as France, Germany, Spain, and Italy.

A sailor's song is distinguished from all other folk songs in its identification as a *chantey* or *shantey*. It is speculated that the word is derived from the French *chantez* (to sing). Further speculation suggests that the alliteration "sea shantey" sounded so good that it was maintained as a most compatible combination. And so, we refer to sailors' songs as sea shanteys, or simply shanteys. The narrow use of the term restricts it to those songs that were devised to accompany particular types of labors; accordingly, those songs intended for use during leisure time would be called forecastle (or fo'c's'le) songs because they were usually sung in and around the living quarters in the forward section of the ship called the forecastle or fo'c's'le. Today the term *shantey* is used very generally to include any and all sailor songs, thus distinguishing them from all other folk songs.

In addition to the work shanteys and the leisure shanteys, there are two other types of shanteys, the outbound and homebound shanteys. These sailor songs are usually identified by their lyrics. An outbound shantey's lyrics describe a sailor's departure from his loved ones and home. Homebound shanteys have lyrics that deal with a sailor's leaving port and heading for home. Although sailors created and adapted songs for particular occasions, there were no hard and fast rules or regulations to prohibit their use in other situations, especially when the sailors were on land and showing off their repertoire of special songs.

The sea shantey is immediately identified with the sea; thus, the sailor is described as a shanteyman. In reality, this title was reserved for a very special singing sailor. The shanteyman was a crew leader with exceptional musical skills and talent. In addition to his ability to take charge of his crew and get the job done, he also had to have musical abilities. This fact alone attests to the high esteem that music and singing held among sailors. A shanteyman had to have a loud, bellowing voice that could be heard and that could maintain the music as it was intended to be sung. He had to have a good memory for songs as well. This would include a large repertoire of songs, as well as the several verses that went with each of the songs. His reputation as a competent shanteyman also rested on his wit and his ability to spontaneously create new verses according to the situation at hand. Crewmen had to respect and admire their leader if they were to work to their best capacity; therefore, the burden of success lay with the shanteyman to come up with the right song at the right time and to present verses that would be received enthusiastically by the crewmen. The more boastful and bawdy the lyrics, the better they were received. A shanteyman was not always fortunate enough to come up with the right song for each given task. If he observed that the crew was not responding to their fullest capacity, he would quickly shift to another shantey or to a third or even a fourth.

The shanteyman had to select the songs, establish the keys, and set the rhythmic pulse. On the first few days at sea, he would sing both his part of the songs (the verse) and also the crew's section (the chorus). Because there were so many versions of each song, the shanteyman wisely elected to present "his version" to his crewmen. Once his version had been learned they would sing the song as it had been intended to be sung. The exchange of parts between the shanteyman and his crew would sound like a well-rehearsed concert when they reached their destination. While the crewmen sang their part, the shanteyman had the opportunity to rest his voice and to prepare the next verse of the song. At the same time, the shanteyman would check to make certain that the music was in concert with the rhythm of the work at hand; if it wasn't, it was his responsibility to make the necessary musical adjustments. A good shanteyman could meet or even surpass the minimum musical requirements of the job; but only a great shanteyman could also add all kinds of vocal ornamentations to the song fest.

An example of the shanteyman's wit and humor is found in the following lyrics taken from the shantey, "Haul Away Joe":

> Oh, once I had a German gal,
> But she was fat and lazy;
> And then I had an Irish gal,
> She nigh drove me crazy;
> But now I've got a Yankee gal,
> And she is just a daisy!

Shanteys sung to accompany an act of labor were always sung unaccompanied; those songs sung as the sailors sat or laid around the fo'c's'le were ordinarily accompanied. This brings us to a discussion of the instruments sailors used. Because of the limited living space aboard ship and because sailors were actually itinerant workers, those who wanted to play musical instruments could only carry portable instruments. Thus, the guitar was at the top of their list, along with the accordion and its smaller version, the concertina. All three of these instruments have a Mediterranean, or at least a European connection, thus affirming the cosmopolitan influence of the music on the American sailor. These instruments could play both melody and harmony, which greatly contributed to the overall presentation of the song. It is said that sailors loved to sing to the accompaniment of these instruments. The mouth organ, another portable instrument, was popular with the ordinary seaman who could carry it in his pocket for easy retrieval. Instruments that resemble the flute, piccolo, and finger whistle were also used. The more exotic the song, the more necessary it was to use such instruments as the accordion in order to provide the requisite colorful harmonies.

There are three kinds of work shanteys. The first and simplest of these is the *short drag shantey*. Not many of these have survived because they were extremely brief and never were given the chance to develop to the point where they constituted a pleasing and memorable melody. Short drag shanteys were used essentially for chores that required one concerted pull. The song would open with a section sung by the shanteyman as the crew prepared themselves for the big pull. The crew would then join in the song and take it to its grand conclusion—the one giant pull. If the end result was not achieved, the shanteyman would begin another shantey or use the same one with a different verse until the job was accomplished.

"Haul On the Bowline" is one of the few short drag shanteys still remembered. A close examination of the song reveals its inherent structure. The goal of the song is found on the final tone and the word "haul." Additional verses are included for use if there were a number of other jobs that required one big pull to accomplish the assigned task.

HAUL ON THE BOWLINE

Short Drag Chantey

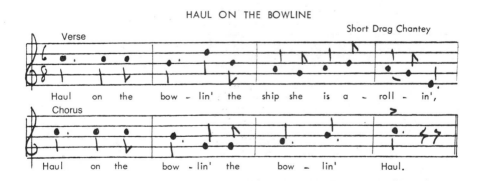

Haul on the bowlin', The bosun is a growlin'.
(*Chorus*)

Haul on the bowlin', So early in the mornin'.
(*Chorus*)

Haul on the bowlin', Haul for better weather.
(*Chorus*)

Haul on the bowlin', The bully ship's a-rollin'.
(*Chorus*)

Haul on the bowlin', A long time 'til pay day.
(*Chorus*)

Haul on the bowlin', Susie is my darling.
(*Chorus*)

Haul on the bowlin', Susie comes from Boston.
(*Chorus*)

Haul on the bowlin', We'll either break or bend her.
(*Chorus*)

There are many more of the second type of work shanteys, called *halyard* of *halliard shanteys,* that have been remembered and preserved. Haulyards, as they were known originally, were ropes used to hoist or lower large spars slung across the masts supporting the sails. Halyard shanteys are longer in length and structured to accommodate a recurring series of concerted pulls. While singing these songs it was extremely important for a unanimity of pull to be established and for the pace to be steadily maintained, otherwise the whole process would serve for naught. Picture, if you will, a small crew of men with their shanteyman standing off to one side, involved in the hoisting or lowering of a sail that required a series of punctuated pulls all rhythmically joined with the singing of a halyard shantey. "Blow the Man Down" is understandably one of the favorite halyard shanteys. It has a good melody and all the swashbuckling flavor of a bold, robust sailor song. Note the parts that are to be sung by the shanteyman and the parts to be sung by the crew.

BLOW THE MAN DOWN

Sea Chantey

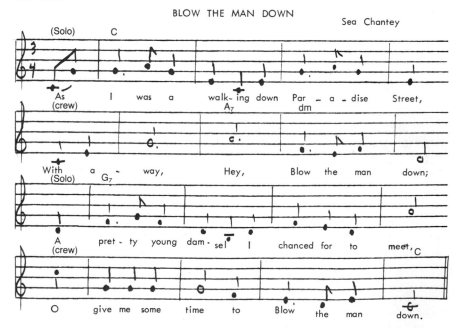

So I threw her my flipper and took her in tow,
With a way, hey, blow the man down;
And yardarm to yardarm away we did go.
Oh give me some time to blow the man down.

Come all you young fellows that follow the sea,
With a way, hey, blow the man down;
Now pray pay attention and listen to me.
Oh give me some time to blow the man down.

Come tinkers and tailors and soldiers and all,
With a way, hey, blow the man down;
For you'll seldom find sailors aboard a Black Ball.
Oh give me some time to blow the man down.

'Tis when the Black Baller is clear of the land,
With a way, hey, blow the man down;
The crew musters aft at the word of command.
Oh give me some time to blow the man down.

Pay attention to orders now you one and all,
With a way, hey, blow the man down;
For see right above you there flies the Black Ball.
Oh give me some time to blow the man down.

On board the Black Baller I served in my prime,
With a way, hey, blow the man down;
And in the Black Baller I wasted my time.
Oh give me some time to blow the man down.

With "larboard" and "starboard" we jumped to the call,
With a way, hey, blow the man down;
The skipper's commands we obeyed, one and all.
Oh give me some time to blow the man down.

The third type of work shantey, the *capstan shantey,* was sung in marching rhythm as the crew walked around and "wound the capstan." The capstan was a vertical, drum-like cylinder around which was attached a heavy rope or cable. The object to be moved to some place on deck or in or out of the hold was bound by a rope that was attached on the other end to the capstan. On top of the capstan there were afixed from four to six poles. Crewmen would get behind these poles in groups of twos or threes and wind up the capstan as they pushed and walked along. This, like the handling of the halyards, had to be done in perfect rhythm or in perfect sync, as we would say today. The ship's anchor, for example, was lifted out of the water with the use of the capstan.

Capstan shanteys were more numerous in number perhaps because they were more fully developed melodies, and hence, more easily remembered. The task of winding up the capstan took longer, so as a result capstan shanteys have many more verses to their credit. "A-Roving" was a great favorite of the sailors. They enjoyed singing songs about girls whom they had met while a-roving. In this song, they have finally found the real one and vow to go no more a-roving.

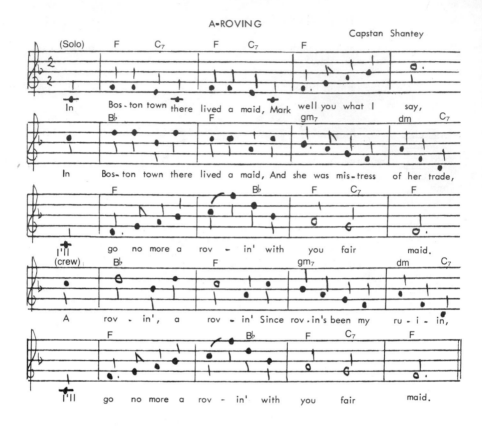

A-ROVING

Capstan Shantey

(Solo) ... In Bos-ton town there lived a maid, Mark well you what I say,

In Bos-ton town there lived a maid, And she was mis-tress of her trade,

(crew) I'll go no more a rov - in' with you fair maid.

A rov - in', a rov - in' Since rov-in's been my ru-i-in,

I'll go no more a rov - in' with you fair maid.

I took this fair maid for a walk,
Mark well you what I say;
I took this fair maid for a walk,
And we had some pleasant talk.
I'll go no more a-rovin' with you, fair
    maid.
(*Chorus*)

I took her hand and she took mine,
Mark well you what I say;
I took her hand and she took mine,
And said, "I'm bound for my home
    town."
I'll go no more a-rovin' with you, fair
    maid.
(*Chorus*)

One of the more demanding chores at sea was working in the ship's bilge, the lowest portion of the interior. No matter how expertly the ship's hull was structured and prepared or how water soaked its bottom, wooden ships would always take on water. Therefore, the ship's bilge had to be emptied each day. The bilge was not only the darkest place on the ship but also the most foul smelling. This duty, then, was often given to those sailors who stood in bad company with their superiors. To counteract their depression and yet engage in a song appropriate to the task at hand, the crew would elect to sing a beautiful song such as "Lowlands" while they worked in the bilge. This song is said to have had its origins in England and Scotland and was well known by almost every sailor. A song of haunting beauty, it is structured as a ballad. Even though this is a work song, it was sung unlike other shanteys. Sailors would sing it in a free rhythmic style, because although emptying the bilge required organization, it was not necessary for the sailors to work to the same rhythmic pulse as the music being sung.

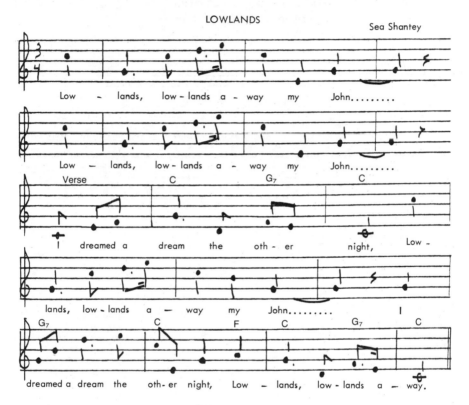

LOWLANDS

Sea Shantey

Low — lands, low-lands a - way my John.........

Low — lands, low-lands a - way my John.........

Verse   C   G₇   C

I dreamed a dream the oth - er night, Low -

lands, low - lands a — way my John......... I

G₇   C   F   C   G₇   C

dreamed a dream the oth- er night, Low — lands, low - lands a — way.

2. Lowlands, lowlands, away, my John,
   Lowlands, lowlands, away, my John,
   I dreamed I saw my own true love,
   Lowlands, lowlands, away, my John,
   I dreamed I saw my own true love,
   Lowlands, lowlands, away.

3. Lowlands, lowlands, away, my John,
   Lowlands, lowlands, away, my John,
   She came to me all in my sleep,
   Lowlands, lowlands, away, my John,
   She came to me all in my sleep,
   Lowlands, lowlands, away.

4. Lowlands, lowlands, away, my John,
   Lowlands, lowlands, away, my John,
   'Twas then I knew my love was
       dead,
   Lowlands, lowlands, away, my John,
   'Twas then I knew my love was
       dead,
   Lowlands, lowlands, away.

The *forecastle* or *fo'c's'le shantey* was named after the area on the forward deck where the sailors lived and spent their leisure time singing, dancing, and spinning yarns. These shanteys could be ballads, national folk songs, or almost anything else. For the most part, they were long songs with many verses. Sometimes they were songs sung as solos by one sailor; other times they were sung by a number of solo singers with the whole group coming in on the chorus section. "Blow Ye Winds" was the type of fo'c's'le shantey in which crewmen "took their crack" at the several solo parts, each offering one of his favorite verses or even making one up on the spot. This song has all the characteristics of a fine shantey.

BLOW YE WINDS

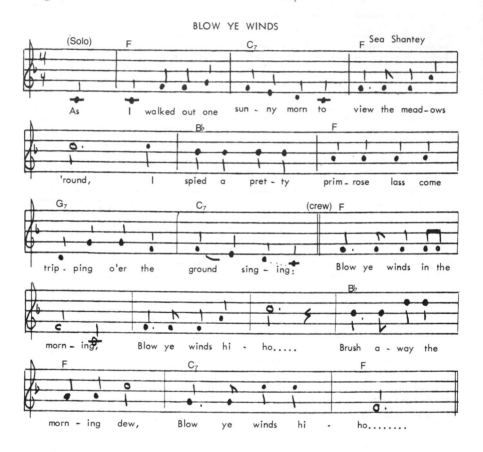

I saddled me an Arab steed and saddled her another,.
And off we rode together just like sister and like brother.
(*Chorus*)

'Tis advertised in Boston town, New York, and Buffalo,
Five hundred brave Americans a-whaling for to go.
(*Chorus*)

They tell you of the clipper ships a-going in and out.
They say you'll take five hundred sperm before you're six months out.
(*Chorus*)

It's now we're out to sea, my boys, the winds begin to blow,
One half the watch is sick as hell, the other half below.
(*Chorus*)

Then comes the running riggin' which
you're supposed to know,
It's lay aloft you son-of-a-gun or
overboard you'll go.
(*Chorus*)

The skipper's on the quarterdeck, a-
lookin' at the sails,
When up aloft the lookout sights a
helluva school of whales.
(*Chorus*)

So clear away the boats, me boys, and
after them we'll travel.
But if you git too near his flukes, he'll
kick you to the devil.
(*Chorus*)

Now we've got him turned up and
towin' alongside,

We're over him with our blubber hooks
and we'll rob him of his hide.
(*Chorus*)

Next comes the stowing down, me lads,
it takes both night and day.
And you'll get fifty cents apiece if ever
there's a pay day.
(*Chorus*)

And when the ship is full of oil and we
don't give a damn,
We'll bend on all our biggest sails and
head for Yankee land.
(*Chorus*)

When we get home our ship made fast
and we are through our sailin',
A winding glass around we'll pass and
damn this blubber whalin'.
(*Chorus*)

The following song, "The Maid on the Shore," is a typical example of a
fo'c's'le shantey. These songs were sung by individuals and more closely cast
in the form of a ballad. In their leisure time, sailors would reflect on life
ashore, especially back home, and listen intently to a singing sailor as he
presented a tale about a serious or humorous event on shore. "The Maid on
the Shore," a prize song full of wit, wisdom, and satire, is the product of a
highly imaginative person who tells a tall tale about how an enterprising maid
outwitted both captain and crew and robbed them of their wealth. Hearing
this song, one cannot help but picture a group of sailors milling around the
deck listening to a tale about a captain who was so enamored by a beautiful
maid that he relinquished both fortune and better judgment to have her. The
events that took place are masterfully dramatized and end in disappointment
over the beautiful maid who got away.

THE MAID ON THE SHORE

Sea Shantey

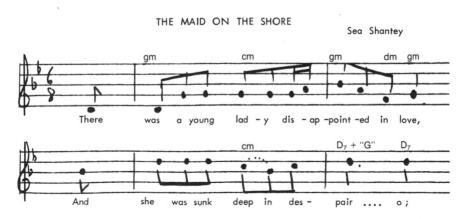

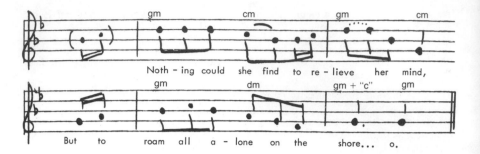

Noth - ing could she find to re - lieve her mind,

But to roam all a - lone on the shore... o.

There was a sea captain that plowed the salt sea,
The sea it ran calm and clear, O;
I shall die, I shall die, this sea captain cried,
If I can't get that young lady fair, O.

Oh, what shall I give you my bonny brave boys,
For all for to fetch her on board, O;
Some magical art has got into her heart,
Makes her roam all alone on the shore, O.

Our captain got pearls and diamonds, and rings,
And he has got costly attire, O;
If you'll get her on board just as quick as you can,
I will give you a run around the shore, O.

With many a persuasion she entered on board,
The captain he used her so fair, O;

He invited her down to his cabin below,
So it's farewell to sorrow and care, O.

I will sing you a song this fair maiden did cry,
So the captain he sat her a chair, O;
She sung him a song so loud and complete,
That the sea boys they all fell asleep, O.

She took all his pearls and diamonds, and rings,
And likewise his costly attire, O;
The captain's broad sword she used for an oar,
And paddled her boat to the shore, O.

Now were my men sober or were my men drunk,
Or were they sunk deep in despair, O;
For to let her get away with her beauty so gay,
For to rove all alone on the shore, O.

As has been stated, the fo'c's'le shanteys were usually accompanied. During such special times, the sailors would take out their guitars, accordions, concertinas, mouth organs, and other instruments and join in on the musical performance. In addition to singing during their leisure-time activities, certain sailors would perform solo dances as part of the entertainment. The sailor developed a style of dancing unlike that of any other dancer. The foot work and the hip movements may have come from their way of mimicking female dancers or perhaps as a result of trying to dance on a ship that was rolling and swaying. These dances were called hornpipes, a term that related to an old English instrument that had a single reed that may at one time have been used to accompany the dance. Today the term is expressly reserved for the sailor's dance itself. Anyone who has seen a Popeye cartoon has heard one of the more popular and better of these hornpipe tunes, a portion of which is presented on page 119.

Before we leave the songs of the high-seas sailor, we must present the song that holds first position in his music literature. This song is considered to be the perfect prototype for all folk songs. "Shenandoah" (or "Shandore" or "Wild Mizzourye") is a song of deep meaning and singular beauty. A solo singer with a great voice, singing unaccompanied, can produce an unforgettable rendition of this song by accenting its supple lines and amazing melodic grace. The song is said to have been the product of French voyageurs or Missouri River boatmen. It was immediately claimed by sailors and considered to be their exclusive property. There are several sets of lyrics based on the melody.

SHENANDOAH

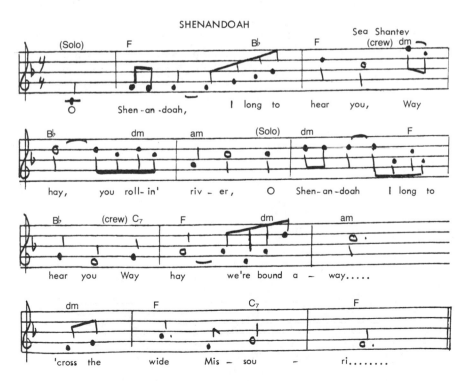

2. Oh Shenandoah, I love your
     daughter,
   Way hey, you rollin' river.
   Oh Shenandoah, I love your
     daughter,
   Way hey, we're bound away
   'Cross the wide Missouri.

3. Oh Shenandoah, I love her truly,
   Way hey, you rollin' river.
   Oh Shenandoah, I love her truly,
   Way hey, we're bound away
   'Cross the wide Missouri.

4. I long to see your fertile valley,
   Way hey, you rollin' river.
   I long to see your fertile valley,
   Way hey, we're bound away
   'Cross the wide Missouri.

5. Oh Shenandoah, I'm bound to leave
     you,
   Way hey, you rollin' river.
   Oh Shenandoah, I'm bound to leave
     you,
   Way hey, we're bound away
   'Cross the wide Missouri.

The Inland Sailors

Sailing on the Great Lakes, the wild rivers, and canals on the mainland was no easy task and sailors who worked these waters would declare war on anyone who would even so much as intimate that they were second-class seamen. Many of the vessels that sailed the Great Lakes were often as large as the sea-going variety; moreover, the Lakes, capable of producing white caps of enormous height, could become as treacherous as the North Atlantic. Similarly, sailing up and down such rivers as the Mississippi, Hudson, Ohio, or Missouri was a tricky kind of business and a sailor had to work just as hard on the job as did the high-seas sailor. There is recorded testimony from sailors who had sailed both the high seas and the inland waterways who rated the two as comparable in many ways. Prior to the coming of the "iron horse," the rivers, lakes, and streams were the principle means for speedy, long-distance delivery of people and goods. For all the same reasons as the high-seas sailor, the inland sailor sang at work and at play, and developed his own appropriate song repertoire.

The Great Lakes provided a series of chain lakes that could move people and goods almost halfway across the continent. One of the main commodities transported by vessel was huge quantities of red iron ore. This material was shipped from Escanaba in the Lake Superior region all the way to Cleveland, Ohio. "Red Iron Ore" describes the sailors engaged in this activity. It has all the same characteristics of the songs of the high-seas sailor that we have already discussed.

RED IRON ORE

Great Lakes Chantey

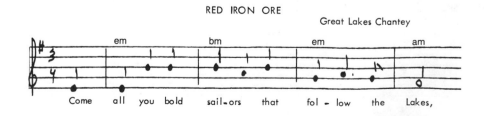

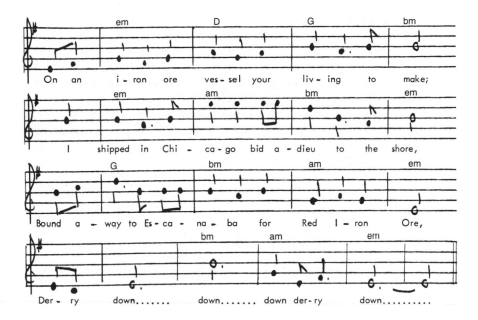

On an i-ron ore ves-sel your liv-ing to make;
I shipped in Chi-ca-go bid a-dieu to the shore,
Bound a-way to Es-ca-na-ba for Red I-ron Ore,
Der-ry down...... down...... down der-ry down.........

In the month of September, the
    seventeenth day,
Two dollars and a quarter is all they
    would pay;
And on Monday morning the
    "Bridgeport" did take,
The "E. C. Roberts" out in the lake.
Derry down, down, down, down derry
    down.

The wind from the south'ard sprang up
    a fresh breeze,
And away through Lake Michigan the
    "Roberts" did sneeze.
Down through Lake Michigan the
    "Roberts" did roar,
And on Friday morning we passed
    through death's door.
Derry down, down, down, down derry
    down.

This packet she howled across the
    Green Bay,
And before the cutwater she dashed the
    white spray;
We rounded the sand point, our anchor
    let go,
We furled in our canvas and the watch
    went below.
Derry down, down, down, down derry
    down.

Next morning we hove alongside the
    "Exile,"
And soon was made fast to an iron ore
    pile;
They lowered their shutes and like
    thunder did roar,
They spouted into us that red iron ore.
Derry down, down, down, down derry
    down.

Some sailors took shovels while others
    got spades,
And some took wheelbarrows, each
    man to his trade;
We looked like red devils, our fingers
    got sore,
We cursed Escanaba and that red iron
    ore.
Derry down, down, down, down derry
    down.

Now the "Roberts" is in Cleveland
    made fast stem and stern,
And with our companions we'll spin a
    big yarn;
Here's a health to the "Roberts," she's
    staunch, strong, and true,
And a health to the bold boys that make
    up her crew.
Derry down, down, down, down derry
    down.

The Mississippi River was a natural divider that broke up the continent into two almost equal parts. More importantly, it was a sizable river that would allow the transport of huge amounts of cargo to be moved deep into the heartland of the nation. Needless to say, New Orleans became a very busy port and boats in large numbers passed back and forth on both sides of the river. Because the river was comparatively shallow and rather calm, the paddle wheel boat was designed and found to be ideal for use on the waterway. With the invention of the steam engine, these boats became the queens of the river and the talk of every observer, passenger, and especially, folk singer. The musical play *Showboat* by Jerome Kern captures the feel of life aboard the riverboat named the "Robert E. Lee." Unfortunately, few people are familiar with a song by Stephen Foster called "Glendy Burk," that perhaps best describes life aboard a riverboat.

GLENDY BURK

De Glendy Burk has a funny old crew
And dey sing de boatman's song,
Day burn de pitch and de pine knot
  too,
For to shove de boat along.
De smoke goes up and de engine roars,
And de wheel goes round and round;
So fare you well for I'll take a little
  ride,
When de Glendy Burk comes down.
(*Chorus*)

I'll work all night in de wind and
  storm,
I'll work all day in de rain;
'Til I find myself on de levy-dock,
In New Orleans again.

Dey make me mow in de hay field
  here,
And knock my head wid de flail;
I'll go wha dey work wid de sugar and
  de cane,
And roll on de cotton bail.
(*Chorus*)

My lady love is as pretty as a pink,
I'll meet her on de way;
I'll take her back to de sunny old south,
And dah I'll make her stay.
So don't you fret my honey, dear,
Oh don't you fret Miss Brown,
I'll take you back 'fore de middle of de
  week,
When de Glendy Burk comes down.
(*Chorus*)

America's booming mercantile business gave rise to consideration of a connecting link between the mighty Hudson River at Albany and the Great Lakes at Buffalo that would provide a direct waterway from the Atlantic into the West. The idea culminated in the Erie Canal, or as it was affectionately called, Governor Clinton's ditch. Eight years of hard work with some rather primitive methods of digging resulted in a 363-mile waterway that not only provided the necessary link to the chain but that also enabled central New York to become one of the busiest and most thriving areas in the East. Just as today a small town can turn into a huge metropolis with the added access of a superhighway, so too the hamlet of Syracuse turned into a bustling city with the advent of the Erie Canal. The canal was completed in 1825 and officially opened with Governor Clinton and his party of friends making the maiden trip from Buffalo to New York City. In its day, the Erie Canal was a truly spectacular development.

The process of moving boats along the canal with its narrow locks and shallow waters demanded a totally new approach in transportation over water. Power to move the barges was supplied by teams of mules walking singly along a towpath running parallel with the canal. A rope from the harness of the mule was strung to the bow of the barge. The crew consisted of a towpath driver, a tiller operator (these two would spell one another), a cook (most often a female), and a captain who sat atop the hut on the barge and gave directions. The barge usually moved around the clock with frequent stops along the way to change mules and spell the towpath driver. The barge floated in about four feet of water and went at an average speed of four miles per hour. Those who worked the barges were called "canawlers."

It is said that life was relatively easy on the old canal boats. There were no sails to hoist, no capstan to march around, and very little deck scrubbing because there was no salt water to contend with. So, a song was a handy thing with which to combat boredom and also for keeping one awake during the wee hours of the morning while driving the mule or manning the tiller. Canawlers were known to sing so lustily during the early morning hours that people who lived within earshot of the canal found it impossible to sleep. The "alma mammy" of this manmade waterway is a song appropriately entitled the "Erie Canal." It perfectly describes life along the route, especially that of going through towns with their low bridges over the canal. Fifteen miles was the usual tour of duty along the towpath for both man and mule. The song is especially noteworthy in its musical content. The verse is in a minor key, the chorus in a relative major key. In addition to this, the song foreshadows the coming of jazz in that it very definitely evokes a jazz beat.

ERIE CANAL

coming to a town, And you'll al-ways know your neighbor, You'll al-ways know your pal, If you've ever nav-i-gat-ed on the E-rie Ca-nal.....

We'd better get along, old pal, fifteen miles on the Erie Canal,
You can bet your life I'll never part from Sal, fifteen miles on the Erie Canal.
Get up there, mule, here comes a lock, we'll make Rome by six o'clock.
One more trip and back we'll go, back we'll go to Buffalo.
(*Chorus*)

One of the more humorous songs to emerge from this waterway life was "E-R-I-E." Just as the high-seas sailors spun yarns and told fantastic tales, the canawlers also exaggerated their stories of trying experiences.

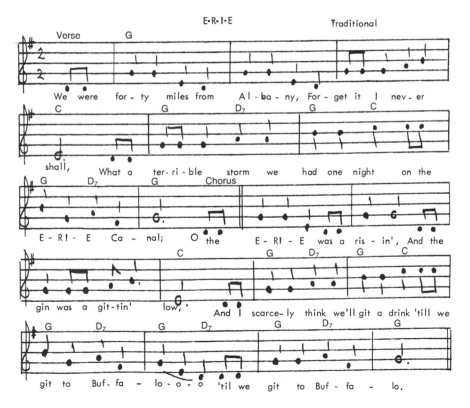

E·R·I·E

Traditional

We were for-ty miles from Al-ba-ny, For-get it I nev-er shall, What a ter-ri-ble storm we had one night on the E-RI-E Ca-nal; O the E-RI-E was a ris-in', And the gin was a git-tin' low, And I scarce-ly think we'll git a drink 'till we git to Buf-fa-lo-o-o 'til we git to Buf-fa-lo.

We were loaded down with barley,
We were chock-up full of rye;
And the captain he looked down on me,
With a gol-durn wicked eye.
(*Chorus*)

Two days out from Syracuse,
The vessel struck a shoal;
And we like to all been foundered,
On a chunk o' Lackawanna coal.
(*Chorus*)

We hollered to the captain,
On the towpath, treadin' dirt;
He jumped on board and stopped the leak,
With his old red flannel shirt.
(*Chorus*)

The cook she was a kind old soul,
She had a ragged dress,

We hoisted her upon a pole
As a signal of distress.
(*Chorus*)

The winds begin to whistle,
And the waves begin to roll;
And we had to reef our royals
On the raging Canawl.
(*Chorus*)

When we got to Syracuse,
The off-mule he was dead;
The nigh mule got blind staggers,
And we cracked him on the head.
(*Chorus*)

The captain, he got married,
The cook, she went to jail;
And I'm the only son-of-a-gun,
That's left to tell the tale.
(*Chorus*)

One of the few serious problems facing canawlers was having to travel on a low level of water. Reducing the depth of water from about four feet to anything less constituted a serious problem. Waters that fed into the Erie Canal came essentially from the Adirondack Mountains to the north. Winters in which the snowfall was below normal would cause havoc with the water level. "We're Going to Pump Out Old Lake Erie" describes this grave situation and also the tremendous pride that the canawlers took in their boats and their vocation.

WE'RE GOING TO PUMP OUT OLD LAKE ERIE

when we are done you can tell by the sun there'll be whisk-ers on the
moon; For the ca - nal needs the wa - ter to keep things all a
float, And I ne-ver will put wheels on my ca - nal boat, For I
love the old tow path and all things that float, So you
can-not make a wag-on of my grand old boat......

The Portage Lakes often fail us (*Yes*)
And often our summit's low;
Oh, then for some rain we would have to wait,
With a load we cannot go. (*So*)
(*Chorus*)

We'll all watch our gates and paddles (*Yes*)
The tumbles and wasteways too;
They'll help us along with their merry song,
And will see that we get through.
(*Chorus*)

The songs of the American sailor have a distinctive quality. The roll of the waves, the sway of the ships, and the openness of the seas are implicitly built into the music. Their boasting and bragging, used to cover up their homesickness and boredom, are wonderfully in evidence. The fact that the American sailor had a long tradition of singing, as well as a great number of songs on which to rely, accounts for his desire to use and replenish this remarkable storehouse of songs. With the coming of steam power and diesel-powered engines, ships were able to dramatically cut down the time involved in their trips. Less time on the high seas meant less time to become dejected; no sails to hoist and a gasoline engine to haul heavy cargo made shanteymen obsolete. As a result, there was less singing on board ship and fewer circumstances to spawn the creation of a new song. We are grateful for the bountiful supply of songs created and accumulated during the short span of time that the Yankee clippers ran rings around the vessels of the world and sailed the seven seas.

9

Songs of the Civil War

Directly or indirectly, everyone is effected by war. As we have said, war is a time when people's emotions run high, when they cannot hesitate to make their feelings known through whatever means of communication best suits them. Songs are a perfect vehicle for expressing a multitude of emotions, ranging from extreme sadness to extreme happiness. No other war in which the United States participated has produced songs in greater abundance than the Civil War. Of course, one of the obvious reasons is that in this particular war there are songs to represent both sides of the conflict—Americans versus Americans. In addition to this, however, there was a greater emphasis placed on the importance of music in recruiting volunteers, mustering support for the cause, preparing the soldiers for battle, and for downgrading the other side. Literally hundreds of anonymous Americans, both Yankees and Rebels, contributed to the huge outpouring of songs that addressed themselves to a multitude of related topics. Many of the songs were passed back and forth through oral communication; many more of the songs appeared as broadsides just as they had during the Revolutionary War and were distributed in the cities, factories, fields, and army camps.

With the advent of the Civil War came the first appearance of professional song writers who, knowing of the intense interest in the war shared by members of both sides, saw the perfect opportunity to garner wealth by producing songs to whet the emotional appetites of the eager consumers. Music publishers, producing songs by the hundreds, searched for the perfect tunes and distributed them for profit in the form of sheet music. The sheet music contained both words and music, unlike the broadsides, thus affording ordinary musicians the opportunity to perform the music on a variety of instruments. Music publishers also marketed low-priced song books, containing only the lyrics, in pocket-sized editions. It is estimated that well over 10,000 songs were both shared and promoted during the course of the war. Interestingly, there were literally over one hundred "Lincoln songs" alone being circulated, some of which were highly complimentary, others of which were downright derogatory. Many of the Civil War songs were parodies on familiar, popular songs, a typical folklike practice. Some of the songs were original and of real musical worth and expressiveness; others were of poor quality and more often than not, the product of the commercialists and profiteers.

It would be fair to say that songs played an important role in the war effort. Written accounts tell of the great emphasis placed on singing, not only by the folks back home, but especially by the troops. Soldiers on both sides were issued pocket songsters and encouraged to sing at every available opportunity. These publications were printed on cheap-quality paper and contained only the words to standard and "approved" songs. Many of the songs were popular, patriotic airs; others were recreational songs added purely for the joy of singing. Both sides of the conflict placed major emphasis on the establishment of military bands whose function it was to play martial music for ceremonies, but also to provide accompaniment for the informal singing of patriotic and recreational music.

Members of both sides of the conflict boasted about the quality and quantity of their collections of war songs. A northerner, for example, was quoted as having said, "Good martial, national music is one of the great advantages we have over the rebels." Sometimes excuses were made suggesting that perhaps the other side had better music; for example, a southern major was reported to have said, "Gentlemen, if we would have had your songs, we would have licked you right out of your boots!" Numerous other statements are on record attesting to the greatness of the music from the southern constituency as well. Persons on the highest eschelons of the war effort, such as Abraham Lincoln and General Robert E. Lee, strongly supported music. As has been stated earlier in this book, General Lee said, "An army cannot win without good music."

The practice of taking a popular song and using it as a sort of dummy upon which to write new sets of appropriate verses was considered common practice and part of the folk process. The Civil War, with its passionate issues, was the source of inspiration for the creation of hundreds of such parodies. It was so convenient (and, in fact, quite easy) to take a well-known song, write a parody based on it, hand it out to the singers, and end up with a guaranteed successful and enjoyable song fest. The two parodies that follow relate to Abraham Lincoln and are good illustrations of this practice.

YANKEE DOODLE FOR LINCOLN

Yankee Doodle does as well
As anybody can, sir;

And like the ladies, he's for Abe,
And Union to a man, sir.

Yankee Doodle never fails,
When he resolves to try, sir;
To elect a man who can't split rails
That's just "all my eye, sir."

Yankee Doodle's come to town,
And on mature reflection;
He's gonna do the Slavites brown,
At the next election.

Yankee Doodle cuts a swell,
Although he will not bet, sir;
Yet he goes in for Abraham
And Hamlin of old Maine, sir.

And he invites you one and all,
No matter what your station;
To vote for Freedom and Free Soil,
And that will save the nation!

LINCOLN
(OLD DAN TUCKER)

Old Abe is coming down to fight,
And put the Democrats to flight;
He's coming with the wedge and maul
And he will split 'em one and all.

Abe, he lives in a big log hut,
Can drive the wedge and use the glut;
He swings the maul and when he hits,
It goes in the ground or else it splits.

Old Abe knows how to drive the team,
Because he never goes by steam;
But now the ox-goad he will use,
And dust the giant in his shoes.

Look, the prairie's all on fire,
If poor Douglas had grown higher;
He might have seen the smoke and stuff,
But his short legs can't run fast enough.

Chorus:
Get out the way, you little giant (*three times*)
You can't come in, you're too short and pliant.

During the course of the war circumstances were often such that soldiers from one side of the conflict were able to hear members of the opposing army sing their songs and vice versa. On an evening before the ensuing day's battle, soldiers would sit around their campfires and sing their songs loudly enough so that members of the opposing forces could hear them.

They were usually camped just over the hill from one another. In rebuttal, the opposing side would offer their songs in kind. The musical fest would not only include their favorite partisan songs but also their song parodies on the favorite tunes from the other side, that is, the Yankees had their parodies based on favorite Rebel songs and vice versa. (Two such sets of parodies will be presented later in this chapter.)

The one significant characteristic that aptly describes the songs from the Civil War is sadness. To be sure, there were a few happy, win-the-war songs as well as a few flippant, satirical songs; however, the great bulk of the songs could best be described as sentimental, solemn, bitter, melodramatic, and even melancholy. Songs such as "Tramp, Tramp, Tramp" or even "The Battle Hymn of the Republic," which are sung today in a bright, robust manner, were sung in a slow, somber way during Civil War years. The conflict was truly shameful—brother fighting against brother, Americans killing Americans. This was bound to have a chilling effect on the people and surface in the music representative of the period. In essence, the music was descriptive of the mood of the people. This was evident in the songs created by the many anonymous contributors; predictably, it was totally exploited in the music produced by the commercialists.

It is interesting to note at this juncture that the songs of Stephen Foster, which were extremely popular at the time and sung by just about everyone, were summarily dismissed from the war-time song repertoires. Northerners were reluctant to sing them because they were primarily about the south and spoke glowingly of the land. On the other hand, southerners were equally apprehensive about singing them, even though they glorified the south, because they were written by a northerner. This was probably one of the factors that contributed to Stephen Foster's excessive drinking and early death.

The one, notable exception to this notion was the song "Dixie." This song was written by Daniel Emmett, a black-faced end man who was considered to be one of the more successful of the minstrel show media. Emmett wrote the song as a walk around to accompany one of his featured numbers. Southerners made the exception in the case of "Dixie" because not only did it glorify the south but, more important, it contained the lines, "In Dixieland I'll take my stand, to live and die in Dixie." These were lines that provided them with an ideal motto for the purposes of defending their lands. "Dixie" became the informal national anthem of the southern confederacy and received an unprecedented number of spirited performances. Emmett, whose allegiance was with the north, was quoted as saying, "If I had known to what use they were going to put my song, I'd be damned if I'd have written it!"

The slavery issue was one that had been building for quite some time and was predictably headed on a collision course. Abolitionists such as Frederick Douglass and Harriet Tubman were soon joined by hosts of supporters who devised means of helping the blacks escape from their enslavement. For the most part, their efforts were nonviolent and conducted "underground."

However, they were soon joined by a tall fiery-haired man named John Brown. With his sons and neighbors, John Brown had carried on a guerrilla war against the "slavers" out in Kansas. John Brown brought his fight eastward. He devised a plan wherein he would seize the arsenal at Harper's Ferry, distribute the captured arms among the slaves, organize his army in the secluded southern mountains, and then proceed to put an end to slavery once and for all. It turned into an abortive mission in which John Brown and his handful of men were captured after only a short skirmish by none other than Colonel Robert E. Lee. John Brown was subsequently hanged for his crime. He died calmly and quietly, yet his sacrifice soon became immortalized in song and became the symbol of the Abolitionists. Persons who wished to rally support for the anti-slavery cause wisely reminded their listeners of John Brown's body, which was "a-mouldering" in the grave.

The tune to "John Brown's Body" was taken from a hymn attributed to William Steffe originally entitled, "Come Brothers, Will You Come and Meet with Us." The song was a good one and perfectly suited for its new purpose. Julia Ward Howe used the same song as a framework for her poem, *The Battle Hymn of the Republic.* At one point during the war Mrs. Howe was visiting the Union forces engaged in battle just outside of Washington, D.C. The position came under attack forcing Mrs. Howe to spend the evening there. The song, "John Brown's Body," which she had heard the troops sing all that day, was still running through her mind as she lay sleeplessly watching the encircling congregation of campfires. The words to her poem, much like those of "The Star Spangled Banner," were inspired by the circumstances of the moment. Ironically, "The Battle Hymn of the Republic" goes on record as being one of those rare songs from the Civil War that was neutral and nonpartisan. It pointed up the futility of the war and trusted in God to put an end to the shameful conflict.

JOHN BROWN'S BODY

William Steffe

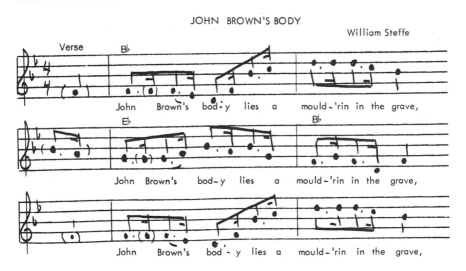

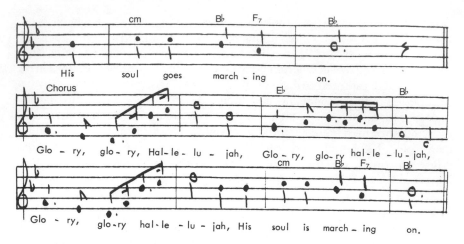

His soul goes march - ing on.

Chorus

Glo - ry, glo - ry, Hal - le - lu - jah, Glo - ry, glo - ry hal - le - lu - jah,

Glo - ry, glo - ry hal - le - lu - jah, His soul is march - ing on.

He captured Harper's Ferry with his nineteen men so true,
He frightened old Virginia 'til she trembled through and through,
They hanged him for a traitor, themselves the traitor's crew.
His soul goes marching on!
(*Chorus*)*

The stars above in heaven are a-lookin' kindly down,
On the grave of old John Brown.
(*Chorus*)

He's gone to be a soldier in the army of the Lord,
His soul goes marching on!
(*Chorus*)

THE BATTLE HYMN OF THE REPUBLIC
Julia Ward Howe   William Steffe

Mine eyes have seen the glory of the coming of the Lord,
He is trampling out the vintage where the grapes of wrath are stored;
He hath loosed the fateful lightning of His terrible swift sword,
His truth is marching on.

Glory, glory Hallelujah (*repeat three times*)
His truth is marching on!

I have seen Him in the watch fires of a hundred circling camps,
They have builded Him an altar in the evening dews and damps;
I can read His righteous sentence by the dim and flaring lamps,
His day is marching on.

(*Chorus*)

He has sounded forth the trumpet that shall never call retreat,
He is sifting out the hearts of men before His judgment seat;

*It should be noted that the melody of the chorus is identical in all but word rhythms with
the melody of the verse.

Oh, be swift my soul to answer Him, be jubilant my feet,
Our God is marching on!

(*Chorus*)

In the beauty of the lilies Christ was born across the sea,
With a glory in his bosom that transfigures you and me;
As he died to make men holy, let us die to make men free,
While God is marching on!

(*Chorus*)

The North

The song that served the Union forces best as a spirited and unifying win-the-war song was "The Battle Cry of Freedom." Just as the song "Dixie" served as an unofficial national anthem for the Confederacy, "The Battle Cry of Freedom" was the true catalyst in rallying people together for the cause of freedom. Musically, the song has martial rhythms and a spirited melody that stir people into action; verbally, the well-conceived lyrics detail the cause of freedom. The words and music were written by George Frederick Root, one of the more successful professional song writers of the time. Among his other "hits" were such tear-jerkers as "Just Before the Battle, Mother" and "Tramp, Tramp, Tramp." Root ran a profitable music publishing house in Chicago, Illinois. In his later years he surmounted his commercial status in music by earning a doctorate in Music from the University of Chicago.

THE BATTLE CRY OF FREEDOM

George Root   George Root

Oh we'll ral-ly 'round the flag boys we'll ral-ly 'round the flag,
Shout-ing the bat-tle cry of free-dom, We will ral-ly from the hill-side, We'll
gath-er from the plain, Shout-ing the bat-tle cry of free-dom.

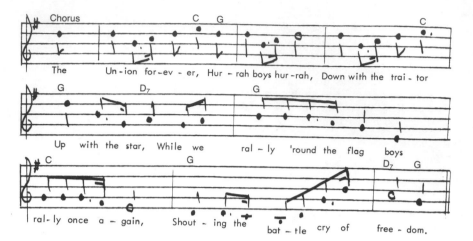

We are springing to the call of our
    brothers gone before,
Shouting the battle cry of freedom;
And we'll fill the vacant rank with a
    million freemen more,
Shouting the battle cry of freedom.
(*Chorus*)

We will welcome to our numbers the
    loyal, true and brave,
Shouting the battle cry of freedom;

And altogether they may be poor not a
    man shall be a slave,
Shouting the battle cry of freedom.
(*Chorus*)

So we're springing to the call from the
    East and from the West,
Shouting the battle cry of freedom;
And we'll hurl the Rebel crew from the
    land we love the best,
Shouting the battle cry of freedom.
(*Chorus*)

"Tramp, Tramp, Tramp" or "The Prisoner's Hope" is another of George F. Root's war songs. It is an example of the melodramatic songs that were so popular during this period. Many people, including soldiers, took comfort while singing songs such as this. It was considered quite proper for singers and listeners alike to cry their eyes out during their performance. Some other melodramatic songs of the period were "Vacant Chair," "Just Before the Battle, Mother," "Tenting Tonight," and "Weeping Sad and Lonely."

TRAMP, TRAMP, TRAMP

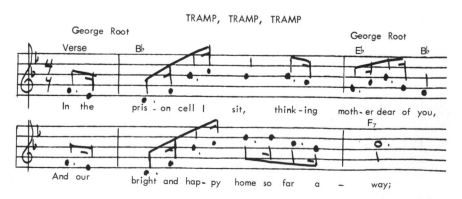

And the tears they fill my eyes, spite of all that I can do,

Tho' I try to cheer my com-rades and be gay.

Chorus

Tramp, tramp tramp the boys are march - ing

Cheer up com-rades they will come........

And be - neath the star-ry flag, We shall breathe the air a - gain,

Of the free- land in our own be - lov - ed home.

In the battle front we stood,
When their fiercest charge they made,
And they swept us off a hundred mcn
   or more;
But before we reached their lines,
They were beaten back dismayed,
And we heard the cry of vict'ry o'er and
   o'er.
(*Chorus*)

So within the prison cell,
We are waiting for the day,
That shall come to open wide the iron
   door;
And the hollow eye grows bright,
And the poor heart almost gay,
As we think of seeing home and friends
   once more.
(*Chorus*)

Large numbers of Irish immigrants rushed to become volunteers in the Union army. They were generally not emotionally involved with the slavery issue; rather, they were intent upon the preservation of the laws and freedoms of their newly adopted land which held out a better life for them. The lyrics of "Flag of the Free" aptly describe their perspective on the situation; the melody is taken from one of their best-loved tunes, "Eibhleen a Ruin," which translated, means "Treasure of My Heart." "Flag of the Free" effectively persuaded many Irish immigrants to join the struggle on behalf of the Union.

FLAG OF THE FREE

Old Irish Song

Could we de - sert you now, Flag of the Free,

When we a sol - emn vow, Flag of the Free,

You from all harm to save, Made when we crossed the wave,

And you a wel - come gave, Flag of the Free.

Are we now cowards grown,	Could we desert you now,
Flag of the Free?	Flag of the Free?
Would we you now disown,	And to black traitors bow,
Flag of the Free?	Flag of the Free?
You to whose folds we've fled,	Never! through good and ill,
You in whose cause we've bled,	Ireland her blood will spill,
Bearing you at our head,	Bearing you onward still,
Flag of the Free?	Flag of the Free.

At first glance, the song "In the Days of '76" would appear to be a Revolutionary War song; it belongs, however, to the Civil War period. Each side of the conflict had its own song designed expressly for the purpose of recruiting volunteers into the ranks. This song calls attention to those noble Yankee volunteers who fought the great battles for freedom during the Revolution. It capitalizes on these deeds and suggests that this trend should continue in an effort to preserve the freedoms for which they fought. The fourth verse strikes out at the Rebel forces who were successfully encroaching on northern soil at the time.

The days of sev-en-ty six my boys, We ev-er must re-vere,
Our fath-ers took their musk-ets then, to fight for free-dom dear;
Up-on the plains of Lex-ing-ton, they made the foe look queer,
Oh 'tis great de-light to march and fight as a Yan-kee Vol-un-teer,

Through snow and ice at Trenton, boys,
They crossed the Delaware;
Led on by immortal Washington
No danger did they fear;
They gave the foe a drubbing, boys,
Then back to town did steer,
(*Chorus*)

At Saratoga next, my boys,
Burgoyne they beat severe;
And at the seige of Yorktown,
They gained their cause so dear;
Cornwallis there gave up his sword,
Whilst freedom's sons did cheer,
(*Chorus*)

And should a foeman e'er again,
Upon our coast appear;
There's hearts around me brave and
true,
Who'd quickly volunteer;
To drive invaders from the soil,
Columbia's sons hold dear,
(*Chorus*)

O, they'd each delight to march and
fight,
Like Yankee volunteers.
Ready . . . Aim . . . Fire!

"When Johnny Comes Marching Home" is a typical war song in which members of the troops phantasize about the war's end and returning home. It has been credited to Patrick Gilmore, an Irish immigrant, writing under the name of Louis Lambert, who, like John Philip Sousa, was the leader of a military band. The song has all the characteristics of an Irish jig. Many have tried unsuccessfully to trace it to an old Irish song on which it may have been based. A set of Rebel lyrics has been added to the song here that illustrate the practice in which one side takes the other side's favorite songs and then write their own lyrics for them.

139

WHEN JOHNNY COMES MARCHING HOME

Louis Lambert

The old church bell will peal with joy,
  hurrah, hurrah,
To welcome home our darling boy,
  hurrah, hurrah;
The village lads and lassies say,
With roses they will strew the way,
(*Chorus*)

Get ready for the Jubilee, hurrah,
  hurrah,
We'll give the hero three times three,
  hurrah, hurrah;

The laurel wreath is ready now,
To place upon his loyal brow,
(*Chorus*)

Let love and friendship on that day,
  hurrah, hurrah,
Their choicest treasures then display,
  hurrah, hurrah;
And let each one perform some part,
To fill with joy the warrior's heart,
(*Chorus*)

REBEL PARODY

In 1800 and '61, Ski-ball says I (*repeat twice*)
In 1800 and '61,
We licked the Yankees at Bull Run
Chorus:
And we'll all drink stone blind
Johnny fill up the bowl.

In 1800 and '62, Ski-ball says I (*repeat twice*)
In 1800 and '62
The rebels put the Yankees through,
(*Chorus*)

140

In 1800 and '65, Ski-ball says I (*repeat twice*)
In 1800 and '65
We all thanked God we were alive,
(*Chorus*)

The Union lines answered with:

In 1800 and '61, Ski-ball says I (*repeat twice*)
In 1800 and '61
The cruel rebellion had just begun
(*Chorus*)

In 1800 and '61, Ski-ball says I (*repeat twice*)
Through a mistake we lost Bull Run
And we all skedaddled for Washington
(*Chorus*)

In 1800 and '63, Ski ball says I (*repeat twice*)
In 1800 and '63
Abe Lincoln set the Negroes free,
(*Chorus*)

In 1800 and '64, Ski-ball says I (*repeat twice*)
In 1800 and '64
Abe called for a hundred thousand more
(*Chorus*)

The South

It would be an understatement to say that the south literally robbed the north of the exuberant song "Dixie." It was considered such a gem that almost immediately after the surrender of the Confederate Army, President Lincoln took steps to "restore" the song to the Union based on a legal opinion handed down from the Attorney General stating that the song was now their lawful prize.

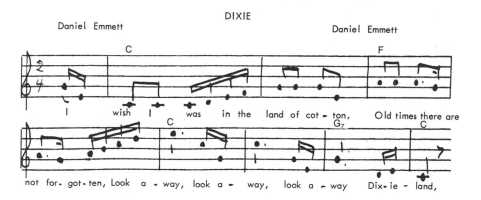

DIXIE

Daniel Emmett · · · · · · · · · · Daniel Emmett

There's buckwheat cakes and Indian batter,
Makes you fat or a little fatter;
Look away, look away, look away, Dixie land.
Then hoe it down and scratch your gravel,
To Dixie land I'm bound to travel,
Look away, look away, look away, Dixie land.
(*Chorus*)

"Bonnie Blue Flag" ranked a close second to "Dixie" as the favorite song among the people of the south. The song makes an attempt to describe and pay homage to the new flag of the Confederacy. It was written by Harry McCarthy, whose sympathies were with the south. The same Irish lilt we noticed in "When Johnny Comes Marching Home" is built into this song. McCarthy is said to have been inspired to write this after he attended a meeting in Mississippi that dealt with secession. To be sure, several parodies were written on it. Presented here are the original song by McCarthy, a

142

northern parody on the melody, and finally, a southern parody, "The Home-spun Dress." In this last version southern belles are making an appeal to their female friends to boycott northern fashions and to be proud to wear their own homespun creations. The music comes from an old Irish air.

BONNIE BLUE FLAG

As long as the Union was faithful to her trust,
Like friends and brethren, kind were we, and just;
But now, when northern treachery attempts our rights to mar,
We hoist on high the Bonnie Blue Flag that bears a single star.
(*Chorus*)

First gallant South Carolina nobly made the stand,
Then came Alabama and took her by the hand;
Next, quickly Mississippi, Georgia, and Florida,
All raised on high the Bonnie Blue Flag that bears a single star.
(*Chorus*)

Ye men of valor gather round the
banner of the right,
Texas and fair Louisiana join us in the
fight;

Davis, our loved President, and
Stephens statesmen are,
Now rally round the Bonnie Blue Flag
that bears a single star.
(*Chorus*)

NORTHERN BONNIE BLUE FLAG

We're fighting for our Union,
We're fighting for our trust,
We're fighting for that happy land,
Where sleeps our fathers' dust.
It cannot be dissevered,
Though it cost us bloody wars,
We never can give up the land,
Where floats the Stripes and Stars.

Chorus:
Hurrah, hurrah, for equal rights, hurrah;
Hurrah for the good old flag,
That bears the Stars and Stripes.

We do not want your cotton,
We care not for your slaves,
But rather than divide this land,
We'll fill your southern graves;
With Lincoln for our chieftain,
We'll bear our country's scars,
We'll rally round the brave old flag,
That bears the Stars and Stripes.
(*Chorus*)

THE HOMESPUN DRESS

O yes, I am a southern girl,
And glory in the name,
I boast of it with greater pride,
Than glittering wealth and fame;
I envy not the northern girl
Her robes of beauty rare,
Though diamonds deck her snowy neck,
And pearls bestud her hair.

Chorus:
Hurrah, hurrah, for the sunny south, I say,
Three cheers for the homespun dress,
The southern ladies wear!

Now northern goods are out of date,
And since old Abe's blockade,
We southern girls can be content,
With goods that southrons made;
We send our sweethearts to the war,
But girls, never you mind,

Your soldier love will not forget,
The girl he left behind.
(*Chorus*)

The southern land's a glorious land,
And has a glorious cause,
Three cheers, three cheers for southern rights,
And for the southern boys;
We scorn to wear a bit of silk,
A bit of northern lace,
But make our homespun dresses up,
And wear them with a grace.
(*Chorus*)

And now, young man, a word for you,
If you would win the fair,
Go to the field where honor calls,
And win your lady there;
Remember that our bravest smiles,
Are for the true and brave,
And that our tears are all for those,
Who till a soldier's grave.
(*Chorus*)

As would be expected, the southern forces had their own song for recruiting volunteers to their ranks. "Southern Volunteers" uses a slightly different tact and must have been extremely effective. It was intended to be sung by girls who would use their own persuasive tactics to enlist young men to volunteer. As a reward, each volunteer was granted the opportunity to walk with a fair and pretty maid (as the chorus section implies).

SOUTHERN VOLUNTEERS

I would not marry a lawyer, who's
   pleading at the bar,
I'd rather marry a soldier boy who
   wears a southern star,
O Soldier boy, etc.
(*Chorus*)

I would not marry a doctor who tries to
   heal the sick,
I'd rather marry a soldier boy who
   marches double quick,
O Soldier boy, etc.
(*Chorus*)

I would not be a lady that southrons
   call a belle,
I'd rather be a soldier boy and hear the
   Yankees yell;
O Soldier boy, etc.
(*Chorus*)

I would not be a nursemaid and hear
   the children squall,
I'd rather be a soldier boy and face a
   cannon ball;
O Soldier boy, etc.
(*Chorus*)

I would not be a farmer who's toiling
   in the sun,
I'd rather be a soldier boy and see the
   Yankees run;
O Soldier boy, etc.
(*Chorus*)

I would not be a miller who grinds the
   people's grain,
I'd rather be a soldier boy who walks
   through wind and rain;
O Soldier boy, etc.
(*Chorus*)

"Goober Peas" is one of the few happy, satiric songs to emerge from the war. It was sung by the southern troops as they sat around at leisure or as they marched en route to the next battle. Today, goober peas are called peanuts, a

146

native product of the south. In the song, the rebel soldiers poke fun at themselves as they munch on goober peas and momentarily forget about the hardships of war. This song is often found in grade-school songbooks because children find the tune—and especially the lyrics—so enjoyable.

GOOBER PEAS

attributed to Armand C. Blackmar

When a horseman passes the soldiers have a rule,
To cry out at their loudest, "Mister, here's your mule."
But another pleasure enchantinger than these,
Is wearing out your grinders eating goober peas.
(*Chorus*)

Just before the battle the gen'ral hears a row,
He says, "The Yanks are coming, hear their rifles now."
He turns around in wonder, what do you think he sees?
A band of Georgia soldiers eating goober peas.
(*Chorus*)

Now my song has lasted almost long enough,
The subject's interesting but rhymes are mighty rough;

I wish this war was over when free from rags and fleas,
We'd kiss our wives and sweethearts and gobble goober peas.
(*Chorus*)

In direct contrast to "Goober Peas" is one of the most bitter protest songs ever created. "I'm Just a Rebel Soldier" dramatically illustrates the hatred felt by many southerners as a consequence of the events of the war. The widespread, wholesale destruction of crops and property perpetrated by Sherman's march to the sea in itself would inspire a hatred of immense proportions. The song is based on the tune "Joe Bowers." However, the version presented here has an entirely different tune that is more suited to the lyric. (It is interesting to note that the word given in the music for proper stylistic interpretation of the song is *savagely*!)

I'M JUST A REBEL SOLDIER

ANONYMOUS

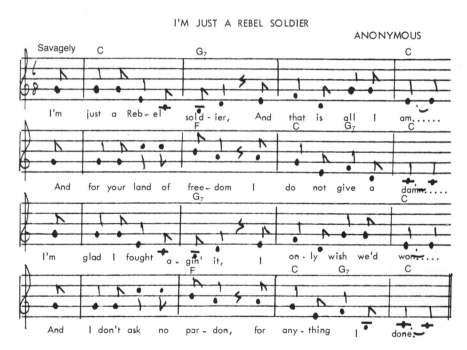

I hate your spangled banner,
Your grand republic too,
I hate your Freedman's bureau,
In uniforms of blue;
I hate your Constitution,
Your eagle and its squall,
And a lying, thievin' Yankee,
I hate's the worst of all.

My name will make no matter,
To you I will not tell,
You look to me like Yankees,
And you all can go to hell;
I'm glad I fought agin' it
I only wish we'd won,
And I don't ask no pardon,
For anythin' I done.

Three hundred thousand Yankees,
Lie moundering in the dust,
We got three hundred thousand,
Before they conquered us;
They hate the southern fevers,
And southern steel and shot,
And I wish it was three million,
Instead of what we got.

I hate the Yankee Nation,
And everything they do,
I hate the Declaration
Of Independence too;
I hate the glorious Union,
'Tis drippin' with our blood,
I hate the striped banner,
I fit' it all I could.

I followed ole Marse Robert,
For four years near about,
Got wounded in three places,
And starved at P'int Lookout;
I keetched the rumatism,
A-campin' in the snow,
But I killed a bunch of Yankees,
I'd like to kill some mo'.

I can't take up my musket,
And fight 'em now no mo',
But I ain't a-gonna love 'em,
Now that is sartin' sure;
And I don't want no pardon,
For what I was and am,
I won't be reconstructed,
And I don't give a damn.

"The Southern Girl's Reply" protests gently, yet vividly demonstrates the hurt that people can experience as a result of a war between fellow countrymen. Set to the tune of "Bonnie Blue Flag" (this is our fourth version), it sensitively summarizes the feelings of a southern girl who has suffered through the ravages of the war. Perhaps more important, it points up her difficulties in trying to forget the events of the past and considering marriage to a man who, by association, may have been a party to the killing of those whom she loved. Although the past is prologue and to forgive is divine, this young lady cannot look ahead to a life with a Yankee because the hurt she feels is so deep and penetrating. It is a lovely lyric and a fitting one with which to end this chapter on America's most shameful war.

THE SOUTHERN GIRL'S REPLY*

I cannot listen to your words,
The land's too far and wide,
Go seek some happy northern girl,
To be your loving bride;
My brothers they were soldiers,
The youngest of the three,
Was slain while fighting by the side
Of General Fitzhugh Lee.

Chorus:
Hurrah, hurrah,
For the sunny south, I say,
Three cheers for the southern girl,
And the boy that wore the gray.

*Lyrics taken from John Anthony Scott, *The Ballad of America: The History of the United States in Song and Story*. 2nd edition. Carbondale: Southern Illinois University Press, 1983. Used by permission.

My lover was a soldier too,
He fought at God's command,
A sabre pierced his gallant heart,
You might have been the man;
He reeled and fell but was not dead,
A horseman spurred his steed,
And trampled on his dying brain,
You might have done the deed.
(*Chorus*)

They left his body on the field,
Who the fight this day had won,
A horseman spurred him with his heel,
You might have been the one.
I hold no hatred in my heart,
Nor cold and righteous pride,
For many a gallant soldier fell,
Upon the other side.
(*Chorus*)

But still I cannot take the hand,
That smote my country sore,
Or love the foe that trampled down,
The colors that she wore;
Between my heart and yours there runs,
A deep and crimson tide,
My lover's and my brothers' blood
Forbids me be your bride.
(*Chorus*)

Countless volumes have been written that cover many aspects of the Civil War. It was one of the bloodiest conflicts on record with more hand-to-hand fighting than any other war. It was also a war in which huge sums of money were expended for armaments, to be sure, but also for such peripheral items as impressive uniforms and music for the troops. Because of the highly personal and deeply passionate issues underlying the dispute, strong feelings of hatred often found their expression in songs. No wonder, then, that so many songs were created during this period. The songs of the Civil War are steeped in history, yet they are good songs that can be sung anew—only this time with a more positive interpretation.

10

Songs of the American Cowboy

The end of the Civil War left the south with the ugly scars of battle and a partially impoverished society. Everywhere one turned there was evidence of death and destruction. Families that had at one time lived in luxury were now faced with the stark reality of a war that had broken up their family circle, left their properties burned or ravaged, and divested them of their slaves and servants. The younger adults, who had many more years of productive life before them, decided to follow the lure of the virgin west and seek new beginnings rather than remain on the old homesteads and work the rest of their lives to restore the grandeur that had at one time been theirs. As they ventured west they came upon the Great Plains—endless acres of flat land covered abundantly with short grass. The land was not ideal for farming, but this did not bother them because they were not anxious to become farmers or even homesteaders. Instead, they heeded the call of the borderlands of Texas where rumor had it that during the war longhorned cattle had multiplied by the millions and were there for the taking.

Before the Civil War, cattle had been slaughtered essentially for their hides. The meat from the animal was considered palatable, although not a tempting delicacy. During the war, however, with the increased demands for food, beef was found to be both inexpensive and substantial. As a result, beef became one of the mainstays of the American diet. The prospect of rounding up herds of longhorns, driving them to the grasslands for fattening, and finally, bringing them to market seemed a promising new venture. And so these young men, perhaps better described as boys, elected to work with the cattle, thus ringing up the curtain on one of the great sagas of the west with the American cowboy as its central hero.

The cowboys traveled to the borderlands of south Texas where the

151

climate was deathly hot and the thickets in which the longhorns lay in hiding were almost razorlike. Armed with ropes and a branding iron, the novice cowboy came claiming longhorns by the hundreds of thousands. In addition to the huge herds of cattle, they also found horses and ponies running wild. The horse was the ideal animal for the cattle business. To begin with, they too were available in abundance and, with a bit of work and patience, they could be tamed and trained to serve their captors. The huge expanse of land required in raising cattle necessitated a means of transportation suitable to the prairies. The horse was the perfect animal to meet this need; more important, the horse was perfect for maneuvering cattle into various positions, versatile for moving among the cattle as the need arose, and ideal as a place from which effective surveillance could be maintained over the herd. The horse became the cowboy's dearest friend and companion and was forever at his side.

Mention should be made of the buffalo, which was the first important animal of the Great Plains. The mass slaughter of the buffalo perpetrated by fur traders, bounty hunters, and desperate, starving Indians had taken its toll. The buffalo, as was soon discovered by the early cowboy, was all but extinct. Subsequently, they were placed on the endangered species list and have since been slow to multiply in their domestic settings.

The new breed of aspiring cowboys actually learned their stock in trade from the Mexican *rancheros* who had spent many years in the art of raising cattle prior to the arrival of the Americans. From the Mexicans the American cowboy learned how to handle horses in ranching situations. A special type of saddle needed for the long hours of riding and standing guard had been developed by the Mexicans. Even the kind of work clothes suited for the particular type of labor was patterned after that of the Mexicans. The horsemanship required in working the cattle was quickly mastered and advanced by the new cowboys as they perfected their skills. From the Mexicans they also learned how to live on the prairies for long stretches at a time, how to care for and fatten up cattle, and how to maneuver them skillfully from place to place. Suffice it to say that the young aspiring American cowboy fully capitalized on the art of ranching as developed by the Mexicans.

In a relatively short period of twenty years (from 1870 to 1890), ranches appeared in large numbers throughout the Great Plains states of Texas, Montana, Colorado, New Mexico, Wyoming, and the Dakotas. The migration to the west was somewhat comparable to the gold rush days with the chance once again of becoming an instant millionaire. The eastern states were becoming heavily populated once more now that the Civil War was over and the trend was toward industrialism. Immigrants were flocking to American shores by the thousands and food, especially meat, was in great demand. The prospect of ranching appeared both tempting and exciting to the adventurous soul.

As the westward push began, the critical need for railroads to expand services escalated. Thousands of Irish, Italian, and Polish immigrants, as well as the newly emancipated blacks, laid thousands of miles of track in an attempt to enable the iron horse to service the bountiful west. One of the gravest problems that faced the ranchers was getting their stock to market. They were influential, to a limited extent, in convincing the railroad barons to extend their railheads farther west and closer to the ranches with mutual benefits as incentive. The barons pushed their railheads to such places as Abiline, Newton, Ogalalla, and through the efforts of Colonel Dodge, to that much romanticized place, Dodge City. From these railheads cattle were transported to Chicago for slaughtering, and finally, shipped to the ready markets in the larger cities in the east.

The great cattle boom almost came to an abrupt halt as farmers and homesteaders bought up properties on the Plains and began to fence in their lands, thereby preventing drovers from having free access to their long-traveled grazing lands and trails. Ranching, of course, continued far beyond 1890 as a profitable and active business, but not with the zest and flair of the 1870s and 1880s.

The authentic cowboy of the period bore only the slightest resemblance to the cowboy as romanticized by Hollywood. He was essentially a hard-working laborer. The cowboy worked around the clock, seven days a week, months at a time, completely isolated from the mainstream of normal living conditions. He also labored under the most trying and hazardous of conditions. His life was continually in jeopardy as he strove to protect himself and his livestock from the throngs of outlaws who would stop at nothing short of murder to secure an easy fortune. Even renegade Indians were constantly at his heels, seeking revenge for their displacement, as well as for their next meal. Living and working conditions in the open spaces exposed him to extremes in weather over which there was little or no protection. He endured the hot, burning sun, snow and cold, tornadoes, rain, and dust storms.

For practical and personal reasons, most of the cowboys remained bachelors. They often dreamed about the "normal" life and pledged that after the next drive they would leave their cowboy life, find a pretty gal, and start a ranch. They held the "normal" life in high esteem, perhaps as much as a prisoner in a jail cell, swearing that the next drive would be their last. As honorable as their intentions were, something always seemed to go awry. At the end of the drive, they would take their back pay and literally blow it all on a "great big jag!" This was understandable, because after having spent many months apart from civilization much like a hermit, he tended to go all out to celebrate his homecoming. The big problem with this was that since he was now broke again, he had no other alternative but to sign on again for another hitch! For many a cowboy this cycle continued on and on until he finally resigned himself to the fact that he was doomed to be a cowboy for the rest of his days.

The majority of early cowboys were hardened veterans from the recent war. During the conflict they had learned how to live in the out-of-doors; they had also learned how to handle firearms and to be constantly on the alert for surprise attacks. These two vitally important experiences made him fully qualified to handle the dangerous and rough life he had to lead as a cowboy. People were quick to identify a cowboy as contrasted with other townspeople because of the long rifle he either had in hand or at easy access in his saddle slot. He had been trained to be a good shot and had plenty of opportunities on the open range to maintain and perfect his marksmanship skills. The long rifle was ideal for shooting long-distance targets; however, he also needed another kind of firearm for more immediate protection from outlaws and Indians and for such functional reasons as killing snakes, animals, and so on. Cowboys became all the easier to single out from the crowd because they carried revolvers as well on one or both of their hips. The revolver that most cowboys preferred was the repeating Colt six-shooter.

The cowboy was quite adept with his pistols because of the many opportunities he had of using them while out on the open range. Unfortunately, the easy access to firepower and the personal successes some of the more "trigger-happy" cowboys were able to realize from their skirmishes led some to abuse their firearms and revel in their self-appointed powers. It must be stated, however, that both the rifle and the revolver were considered necessary tools of the cowboy's profession; he lived in constant danger from bad men, renegade Indians, reptiles, and wild animals and it was important for him to have ready access to firearms principally for reasons of personal safety.

The slow-moving, unwieldy longhorns had to be driven many hundreds of miles along open territory in order to get them to market. Cowboys were constantly searching for the shortest and most feasible route, one on which they would be able to find an adequate supply of grass and water for their stock in order that they might retain and perhaps even gain weight, and thereby bring top prices at the railhead. He also had to find a trail where he would not come under attack from renegade Indians and outlaws. Unfortunately, the first drives followed the shortest distance from south Texas to St. Louis via the Ozark Mountains. This proved to be disastrous to the longhorns as well as to the cowboys. After much trail blazing, a route was found that was ideal in terms of safety and an adequate supply of grass and water. They called this route The Old Chisholm Trail. It ran from northern Texas all the way to Montana and the Dakotas. Often, cattle were driven north of the railheads where they were allowed to feast on a more nutritious grass in order to fatten them up and also to sweeten their meat. These particular cattle would bring in a better price because of their choice meats. The distance for the drives was always shortened as the railroads moved in closer to the trails.

Cattle drives were back-breaking hard work. Fording rivers, recovering the cattle after a stampede caused by a sudden electrical storm or other unanticipated shock, fighting intruders, and riding through dust storms that would literally fill up your lungs and kill you, presented more than the usual bundle of occupational hazards. Cowboys who were able to survive repeated drives could be compared to combat-hardened soldiers. Those cowboys who participated in the long drives were singled out from all the others and called "drovers." They were a reckless lot.

On a comparative basis, the cowboy's music is considered the most elementary of all American folk music. Like all folk, he brought with him the musical heritage of his youth and from his place of origin. Nonetheless, the cowboy soon learned that his whole rhythm of life was so completely different from anything even remotely related to anything he had experienced that he actually had to begin from scratch in building his song repertoire. The elementary quality and musical naïveté is noticeably evident in his original music. Melodically, the music is based almost entirely on the basic tones of the major scale, with only an occasional song based on the minor scale. The melodic ideas and rhythms are very simplistic, repetitive, and limited in scope. It must be stated, however, that he did introduce an original pattern into his songs, that of the gently loping figure. Harmonically, the music is generally based on the three primary chords common to basic hymns. Beyond this, more elaborate harmonizations are often the product of a modern arranger at work with a simple but potentially promising tune.

This statement of the elementary quality of cowboy music is not made to degrade the music nor to foster a negative attitude toward its merit, but rather, it is made to point up the fact that the cowboy actually had to begin from the beginning to build up a song repertoire that would genuinely represent himself. His long periods of isolation from the mainstream of life gave him the freedom of opportunity and the frame of reference within which he could create without the influence of outside factors. In the end, there emerged an elementary, yet highly original and representative kind of music.

Having spoken of the cowboy's original musical contributions, let us now mention that small quantity of music which he, like all other folk before him, adapted for use in his everyday living. The cowboy was enamored of ballads and found storytelling songs to be interesting to sing and listen to but, more important, ideal for relating the trials and tribulations connected with his way of life. At night, while he sat around the campfire or in the bunkhouse, storytelling songs would give him great personal satisfaction in return for his efforts. Some of these ballads were about people who lived in real communities and interacted socially in a manner that he admired but that he himself could not enjoy at the present time. He also found the setting of a ballad to be ideal for transmitting to the world (and temporarily, to himself) something about the rigors of the cowboy's life that needed a therapeutic outlet. In the ballad form he was able to tell about cowboys who led dangerous lives fighting off Indians, outlaws, wild animals, and dust storms; he could talk about big drives and the danger from stampedes; he could even talk about that great range in the sky, which was his way of describing heaven. The cowboy took some of the well-known ballads and added his own lyrics to them; he also contributed some originals of lasting value.

The cowboy, like the sailor and lumberjack, was a lusty singer. He worked in open spaces and interacted primarily within a male society, so he had an atmosphere in which he could sing unabashedly. The cowboy took his song repertoire and his mode of singing with him on those rare occasions when he joined the community society. As a result, members of the community were always intrigued with his unique style of singing and his songs in particular. In essence, he provided a concert for the townspeople.

Like both the sailor and lumberjack, the cowboy had songs for work and songs for leisure time. His work songs were often called "saddle songs" because this was precisely where he spent most of his work time and the place from which he sang. The leisure songs were usually sung around the campfire, in the bunkhouse, or on a visit to town. These songs, however, were considered very intimate and personal and were not often shared with outsiders. The songs are more autobiographical in nature and represent some of their better contributions.

Again, like the sailor and lumberjack, the cowboy had to use portable instruments. He could bring along a limited amount of gear and if he wished to perform on a musical instrument, he had to tote that item on his own back. Perhaps this is why the guitar became the cowboy's main musical instrument. He could carry it on his back because of the shoulder strap that was attached to the instrument. He had only to swing the instrument to the front of his body as he sat in his saddle in order to accompany himself as he sang. Like his pistol, the guitar was easily accessible when the urge to use it presented itself. The cowboy did not use the guitar for picking out melodies; rather, his style of guitar playing was confined to the playing of chordal–rhythmic accompaniment.

The cowboy was also attracted to the jew's harp, which could be easily carried in a shirt pocket and never thought of as an extra burden. It is said that just about every cowboy carried one of these around and strummed away on it whether he had any musical talent or not. They were attracted to this instrument not only because it was tiny and easy to play but also because the amount of sound it produced was perfect for the quiet music that they were often asked to make. With a little bit of doing, the gadget could be made to produce something resembling a melodic line accompanied by a rhythmic buzz.

The one rhythmic figure that immediately identifies a cowboy song is that which musically describes the gentle loping movement of the horse. Those work songs that were sung as the cowboy lazily loped along must have given birth to this rhythmic figure. One can add this loping figure to just about any tune from folk to symphonic themes and "create" a cowboy song, as in the following example:

ALMA MATER

The cowboy had his own unique set of commands or "jargon" that he used in his "conversations" with the cattle. These nonsense syllables found their way into his work songs and sometimes even into his ballads. They were used because they were a part of the cowboy's professional vocabulary and, as in other types of folk music, they were included to take up space while the singers were thinking up new or additional lyrics. Nonsense syllables such as ki-yi-yip-py, ti-yi-yo, and so forth, along with the loping rhythm, unmistakably help identify the cowboy song.

A considerable amount of the cowboy's work time was spent on guard duty watching the cattle. These songs are necessarily quiet ones, songs that were sung during the lonely, wee hours of the night. They were perfect for keeping the cowboy awake as he sat in his saddle; they were equally enjoyed by the cattle and helped settle them down for the evening. It is said that oftentimes cattle would actually follow and be close to a singing cowboy.

The cowboy's leisure songs were full of boasting and bragging about his way of life. Usually these songs told of a courageous cowboy with whom they could identify. The lyrics to these songs were real folk tales at best, containing only a smattering of actual fact. They adequately served to help the cowboy enjoy some momentary comfort and at the same time tell listeners something about his way of life.

Before discussing a few of the cowboy's representative songs, it would be well to mention two of the other instruments associated with them. The accordion and fiddle were not portable instruments, so they had to be carried on the chuck wagon. They were far more sophisticated than the guitar or jew's harp, and required a higher level of playing ability. Because of the added musical potential that these instruments could contribute to the song fest, they were included in the tons of equipment and provisions that the wagons carried on the prairies and trails.

Work Songs

Without question, "The Old Chisholm Trail" was the number one song of the cowboy. Several tunes exist with the same basic title and essentially the same lyrics; some are better than others. It is said that dozens of verses were created for this song every day of a drive. The dozens of verses that have been handed down are generally boastful and bragging, humorous, fallacious, nonsensical, even crazy; they are products of instant creativity and represent the cowboy at his level best. There is no thread of continuity in them nor any sense of story; they are simply a potpourri of personal contributions given on-the-spot. The song was perfect for taking up time as the cattle were moved at a slow, lazy pace and the men continued working at a monotonous job. The song has a definite "cowboy" flavor to it.

THE OLD CHISHOLM TRAIL

Cowboy Song

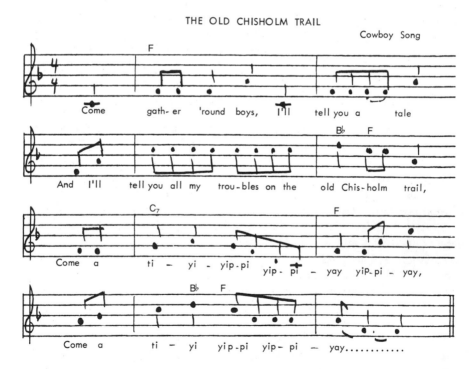

I started up the trail on October twenty-third,
Started up the trail with the Two-U head.
(*Chorus*)

On a ten-dollar horse and a forty-dollar saddle,
Started up the trail just to punch Texas cattle.
(*Chorus*)

I jumped in the saddle and grabbed a-
hold the horn,
I'm the best blame cowboy that ever
was born.
(*Chorus*)

It's cloudy in the West and it looks like
rain,
And my darn'd old slicker's in the
wagon again.
(*Chorus*)

Oh, it began to storm and the rain
begin to fall,
And we thought, by grab, we'se a-goin'
to lose 'em all.
(*Chorus*)

We hit Caldwell, we hit her on the fly,
And we bedded down the cattle on the
hill close by.
(*Chorus*)

I woke up one morning on the Old
Chisholm Trail,
Rope in my hand and a cow by the tail.
(*Chorus*)

Stray in the herd and the boss said to
kill it,
So I shot him in the rump with the
handle of a skillet.
(*Chorus*)

My hoss throwed me off at the creek
'cross the level,

A-kicking up his heels and a-runnin'
like the devil.
(*Chorus*)

Last time I saw him he was goin' 'cross
the level,
Still a-kickin' up his heels and a-goin'
like the devil.
(*Chorus*)

I popped my foot in the stirrup and
gave a little yell,
The tail cattle broke and the leaders
went to hell.
(*Chorus*)

I don't give a damn if they never do
stop,
I'll ride as long as an eight-day clock.
(*Chorus*)

We rounded them up and put 'em on
the cars,
And that was the last of the old Two
Bars.
(*Chorus*)

Goin' to the boss to git all my money,
Goin' back south to see my little honey.
(*Chorus*)

With my hand on the horn and my seat
in the sky,
I'll be punchin' Texas cattle 'til the day
I die.
(*Chorus*)

Mention has been made of the respect that the cowboy had for his companion and work partner, the horse. "Paint" was a symbolic name that the cowboy had for a horse and such songs as "Goodbye, Old Paint" or "I Ride an Old Paint" are typical "horse" songs. Obviously, the cowboy would substitute the name of his own horse for Old Paint. It is interesting to note that beyond the stereotype loping rhythm, the slow, three-quarter-time waltz rhythm was equally appropriate for use while working the horse at a walking pace.

I RIDE AN OLD PAINT

Cowboy Song

I'm goin' to Mon – tan' for to do the hool- i – an;

They feed in the cou - lees, they wa - ter in the draw,

Their tails are all mat - ted, their backs are all raw.

Ride a - round lit - tle dog - ies, ride a - round them slow,

for the fi - ery and snuf - fy are a rar - in' to go.

I've worked in the army, and worked
   on the farm,
All I've got to show is just this muscle
   in my arm;
Blisters on my seat, callous on my
   hands,
And I'm off to Montan' for to throw the
   hoolihan.
(*Chorus*)

Old Bill Jones had a daughter and a
   son,
One went to college and the other
   went wrong;

His wife, she died in a poolroom fight,
But still he keeps singin' from mornin'
   'til night.
(*Chorus*)

Now when I die, don't bury me at all,
Just saddle my pony, lead him out of
   the stall;
Tie my bones in the saddle, turn our
   faces to the west,
And we'll ride the prairie that we love
   the best.
(*Chorus*)

    Reference was also made to the cowboy's "conversations" with his herd. The following song, "Whoopie Ti Yi Yo," illustrates this habit. Dogies were young orphaned cattle whose father had run off with another cow and whose mother was either lost or dead. The dogies had no family with which to identify and consequently lagged behind the rest of the herd to become the concern of the cowboys located on the tail end of the drive. In some respects the cowboy empathized with the poor mavericks and took special pains to care for these hapless wanderers. The song contains some of the nonsense syllables that were a part of the cowboy's functional vocabulary. It has a verse and chorus structure that is adaptable to solo and group exchanges.

WHOOPIE TI YI YO

Cowboy Song

It's early in the spring time we round up them dogies,
Mark 'um and brand 'um and bob off their tails;
Drive up the horses, load up the chuck wagon,
And throw them little dogies out on the trail.
(*Chorus*)

Now some boys, they goes up the trail for pleasure,
But that's where they get it most awfully wrong;
For you ain't got no idea of the trouble they give us,
As we go drivin' them dogies along.
(*Chorus*)

It's you'll be beef for Uncle Sam's Injuns,
It's beef, heap beef I hear them cry;

Git along, git along, git along you little dogies,
You're gwin-a be beef steers bye and bye.
(*Chorus*)

Your mother was raised way down in Texas,
Where the jimson weed and sand-burrs grow;
Now we'll fill you up on prickly pear 'n cholla,
'Til you're ready for the trail to Idaho.
(*Chorus*)

When night comes on and we hold them on the bed ground,
Those little dogies that roll on so slow;
Roll up the herd and cut out the strays,
And roll the little dogies that never rolled before.
(*Chorus*)

"Doney Gal" is not as well known as it should be, although it is unquestionably one of the most exquisite songs contributed by the American cowboy. This is one of the quieter songs, best suited for night herding or a quiet campfire setting. In this song the cowboy is singing to his horse, Doney Gal, reflecting on the hardships that they have both experienced and the loyalty they have to their work. It is more effectively performed with a nonrhythmic, *ad libitum* (at liberty) treatment of the chorus and a slow but rhythmic verse.

DONEY GAL

Cowboy Song

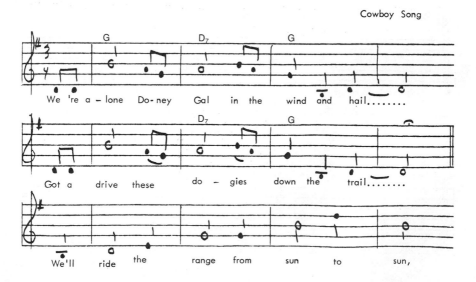

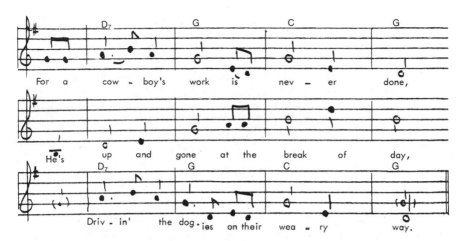

For a cow - boy's work is nev — er done,

He's up and gone at the break of day,

Driv - in' the dog-ies on their wea — ry way.

It's rain or shine, sleet or snow,
Me and my Doney Gal are on the go;
Yes, rain or shine, sleet or snow,
Me and my Doney Gal are bound to go.
(*Chorus*)

A cowboy's life is a weary thing,
For it's rope and brand and ride and
   sing;
Yes, day or night in the rain or hail,
He'll stay with his dogies out on the
   trail.
(*Chorus*)

Rain or shine, sleet or snow,
Me and my Doney Gal are on the go;

We travel down that lonesome trail,
Where a man and his horse seldom
   ever fail.
(*Chorus*)

We whoop at the sun and yell through
   the hail,
But we drive the poor dogies down the
   trail;
And we'll laugh at the storms, the sleet
   and snow,
When we reach the little town of San
   Antonio.
(*Chorus*)

"Lone Star Trail" is a song reminiscent of the "come 'ye all" songs typically associated with sailors and lumberjacks. It is a hearty, robust kind of song and should be performed at a brisk tempo. Like "The Old Chisholm Trail" it is full of boasting, bragging, and tall tales and is perfect for creating new verses and group participation on the chorus.

LONE STAR TRAIL

Cowboy Song

I start - ed on the trail on June twen - ty third,

I been punch-in' Tex-as cat-tle on the Lone Star Trail;

163

Sing- in' ki - yi yip- pi yap- pi — ye, yap - pi - ye,

Sing- in' ki - yi yip-pi yap- pi - ye....................

I'm up in the mornin' before daylight,
And before I'm a-sleepin' the moon shines bright.
(*Chorus*)

It's bacon and beans most ev'ry day,
I'd as soon be a-eatin' some prairie hay.
(*Chorus*)

My feet are in the stirrups and my rope is on the side,
Just a-show me a horse that I can't ride.
(*Chorus*)

With my knees in the saddle and my seat in the sky,
I'll be punchin' cows in the sweet by and by.
(*Chorus*)

Leisure Songs

The ballad was ideally suited for leisure singing around the campfire or bunkhouse. Some of the tunes were borrowed and adapted. A good, well-liked melody can always serve as a source of inspiration for a good lyric just waiting to be born. One of the more respected ballads is known variously as "The Cowboy's Lament," "Streets of Laredo," or "The Dying Cowboy." (Many books on folk music include a special index on first lines of songs to assist in finding a song. Titles often change, as do whole songs when handed down from one person to another.) The tune itself is a good and very ancient one, with its origin in the British isles and its hero cast as everything from a dying lover to a dying soldier. The cowboy loved his version because it beautifully described his vocation. The hero in this song is every cowboy—a hard-working, courageous man, well respected by his peers. It is amusing to glance through the different versions of the ballad just to examine the numerous anatomical sites in which the dying cowboy's bullet became lodged. This, of course, attests to the folk singer's license to present "his version" of the song along with the carefree manner in which tales such as this are changed through oral transmission.

THE DYING COWBOY

Cowboy Song

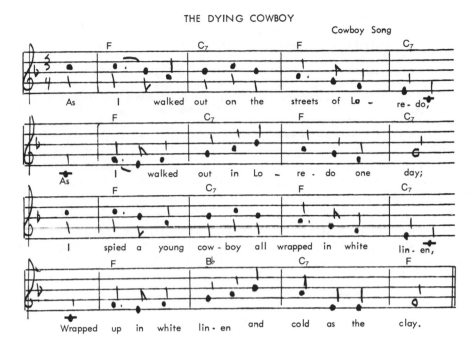

As I walked out on the streets of Lo - re - do,
As I walked out in Lo - re - do one day;
I spied a young cow - boy all wrapped in white lin - en,
Wrapped up in white lin - en and cold as the clay.

"I see by your outfit that you are a cowboy."
These words he did say as I boldly stepped by.
"Come sit down beside me and hear my sad story,
I was shot in the breast and I know I must die.

"Oh, beat the drum slowly and play the fife lowly,
Play the Dead march as you carry me along;
Take me to the green valley, there lay the sod o'er me,
For I'm a young cowboy and I know I've done wrong.

"Go gather around you a crowd of young cowboys,
And tell them the story of this, my sad fate;
Tell one and the other before they go further,
To stop their wild rovin' before 'tis too late.

"It was once in the saddle I used to go dashing,
It was once in the saddle I used to go gay;
First to the dramhouse and then to the cardhouse,
Got shot in the breast, I am dying today.

"My friends and relations, they live in the Nation,
They know not where their poor boy may have gone;
He first came to Texas and hired to a ranchman,
Oh, I'm a young cowboy and I know I've done wrong.

"Let six jolly cowboys come carry my coffin,
Let six pretty maidens come bear up my pall;
Put branches of roses all over my coffin,
Put roses to deaden the clods as they fall.

165

"Go fetch me a cup, a cup of cold
water,
To cool my parched lips," the poor
cowboy said.
Before I returned, the spirit had left
him,
And gone to his Maker. The cowboy
was dead.

So beat the drum slowly and play the
fife lowly,
Play the Dead March as you carry him
along;
Take him to Green Valley, there lay the
sod o'er him,
For he was a cowboy and knew he'd
done wrong."

The cowboy constantly pondered thoughts of dying out on the prairie. Much as the sailor who thought about dying at sea and having his body thrown into the ocean, so too the cowboy feared the idea of having his body laid to rest in the sod of the great and expansive plains. A sense of loneliness was with him most of the time and being buried out on the prairie was for him nothing but another addition to this entirely lonesome kind of existence. The song "Bury Me Not on the Lone Prairie" is said to have originally been a sailor's song. The following lyrics aptly describe the cowboy's fear and pleading:

> It matters not, so I've been told,
> Where the body lies when the heart grows cold;
> Yet grant, O grant, this wish to me,
> O bury me not on the lone prairie.

The James and Younger brothers were the most feared of desperadoes. They were feared by bankers, railroaders, and stagecoach drivers alike, yet they were truly admired and loved by their own kinfolk. The manner in which Jesse James, the leader and mastermind of the flock, met his end—by being shot in the back by one of his trusted friends—provided the perfect scenario for a folk ballad. Jesse was a cowboy, a rebel veteran, a husband, and a father; unfortunately, he lived by the gun and ultimately died by the gun. He is romanticized in "Jesse James" as America's Robin Hood. The event in the song took place around 1882.

JESSE JAMES

Cowboy Song

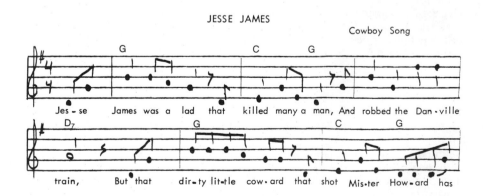

Jes-se James was a lad that killed many a man, And robbed the Dan-ville train, But that dir-ty lit-tle cow-ard that shot Mis-ter How-ard has

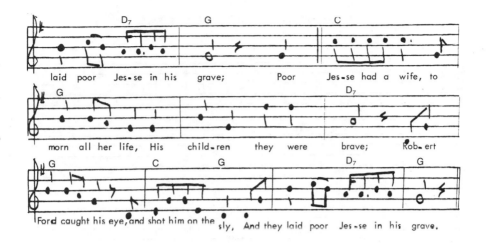

laid poor Jes-se in his grave; Poor Jes-se had a wife, to morn all her life, His child-ren they were brave; Rob-ert Ford caught his eye, and shot him on the sly, And they laid poor Jes-se in his grave.

It was his brother Frank stuck up the
   Pittsfield Bank,
And carried the money from the town;
It was in this very place that they had a
   little race,
For they shot Captain Sheets to the
   Ground.
(*Chorus*)

They went to the crossing not very far
   from there,
And there they did the same.
With the agent on his knees, he
   delivered up the keys,
To the outlaws, Frank and James.
(*Chorus*)

It was on a Wednesday night, the moon
   was shining bright,
They stopped the Glendale train;
He robbed from the rich and he gave
   to the poor,
He'd a heart and a hand and a brain.
(*Chorus*)

It was on a Saturday night when Jesse
   was at home,
Talking with his family brave;
Robert Ford's pistol ball brought him
   tumbling from the wall,
And they laid poor Jesse in his grave.
(*Chorus*)

It was Robert Ford, that dirty little
   coward,
I wonder how he does feel;
For he ate of Jesse's bread, and he slept
   in Jesse's bed;
And he laid poor Jesse in his grave.
(*Chorus*)

This song was made by Billy Gashade,
As soon as the news did arrive;
He said there was no man with the law
   in his hand,
Could take Jesse James when alive.
(*Chorus*)

Appropriately, this chapter closes with one of the more descriptive cowboy ballads. As one listens to this ballad, one empathizes with its hero, a model cowboy with a fine home background and the best of intentions to serve his tenure as a cowboy in an honorable and dedicated way. As expected, fate cuts short his dreams.

WHEN THE WORK'S ALL DONE THIS FALL

Cowboy Song

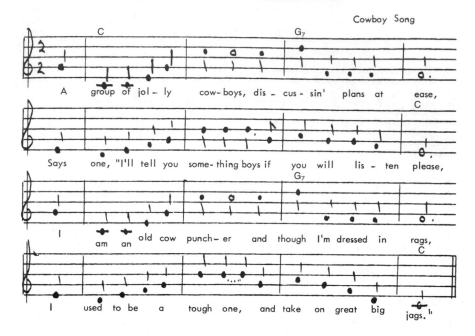

A group of jol – ly cow-boys, dis – cus – sin' plans at ease,

Says one, "I'll tell you some- thing boys if you will lis – ten please,

I am an old cow punch- er and though I'm dressed in rags,

I used to be a tough one, and take on great big jags."

But I've got a home, boys, a good one
    you all know,
Although I have not seen it since long,
    long ago;
But I'm going back to Dixie once more
    to see them all,
I'm going to see my mother when the
    work's all done this fall.

After the round-up's over, and after the
    shipping's done,
I'm going right straight home, boys,
    'ere all my money's gone;
I've changed my ways, boys, no more
    will I fall,
And I'm going home to mother when
    the work's all done this fall.

When I left home, boys, my mother for
    me cried,
She begged me not to go, boys, for me
    she would have died;
Mother's heart is breaking, breaking for
    me that's all,
So I'm going to see my mother when
    the work's all done this fall.

That very night this cowboy went out to
    stand his guard,
The weather it was stormy and raining
    very hard;
The cattle they got frightened and
    rushed in wild stampede,
The cowboy tried to head them while
    riding at top speed.

While riding in the darkness, so loudly
    he did shout,
Trying his best to head them and turn
    the herd about;
His saddle horse did stumble, and upon
    him did fall,
And he'll not see his mother when the
    work's all done this fall.

His body was so mangled the boys all
    thought him dead,
They picked him up so gently and laid
    him on his bed;
He opened wide his blue eyes and
    looking all around,
He motioned to his comrades to sit
    near him on the ground.

"Boys, send my mother my wages, the wages I have earned,
For I am afraid, boys, my last steer I have turned;
I'm going to a new range, I hear my Master's call,
And I'll not see my mother when the work's all done this fall.

"Joe, you take my saddle. Bill, you take my bed,
Peter, you take my pistol, after I am dead;

Think of me kindly, as you gaze upon them all,
And give my love to mother when the work's all done this fall.

Poor Charles was buried at sunrise, no tombstone at his head,
Nothing but a little board, and this is what it said,
"Charlie died at daybreak, he died from a fall,
And he'll not see his mother when the work's all done this fall."

The two decades between 1870 and 1890 marked the heyday of the American cowboy. His reign came to a sudden end with the coming of the Industrial Revolution and the delivery of railroad service right into the heartland of the cattle industry. The living experiences of the cowboy have been preserved in song and story and, more recently, in films. Stories of their exploits as currently portrayed not only appeal to Americans but also to people the world over. Italians, Japanese, and Russians, to mention a few, relish cowboy stories. The impact of the cowboy was strongly felt and their stories are well worth repeating. The folk music of the cowboy was simplistic, yet dramatically original and exciting. The small handful of cowboys who reigned supreme during the latter part of the nineteenth century contributed a great deal to the folk literature and music of America.

11

Songs of the
American Railroader

Throughout the nineteenth century, railroads and railroading made a profound impact on this nation and its people. The first railroads in the United States were built and operated by the Baltimore and Ohio Company in 1828. They were originally drawn by horse, providing a novelty ride for passengers as well as an economical means for transporting heavy cargo. Passenger cars were open and had canvas tops for protection from the elements. Passengers preferred the openness to afford themselves the pleasure of a full view of the area through which they were passing as well as an opportunity, in turn, to be viewed by the public. Passenger cars were found mostly in the cities and considered to be more a popular fad than a practical means of transportation. Boxed cars carrying payloads of goods to transport, however, were found to be useful, and indeed, profitable.*

In a short span of twenty years, the railroad industry expanded to the point where there were around 9,000 miles of track (mostly along the eastern seaboard) available for railroading. In the years leading up to the Civil War, railroad track miles had increased threefold. The war years gave added impetus to the practical feasibility of railroads after demonstrating their capacity for moving troops, equipment, and goods in large numbers and in record time. After the war, railroads began to spread across the continent at a phenomenal rate as labor became plentiful for laying track and building rail cars and as the demand for access to railroads exceeded all expectations. Railroads soon stretched from shore to shore, across plains and over towering

---

*The steam engine supplanted the horse-drawn trains and, as a consequence, the first steam-drawn "monsters" were referred to as "iron horses."

mountains, creating a fabulous fabric woven from thousands of threads of track.

One can easily understand the impact this new mode of transportation had within and between urban areas; people and goods could be both quickly and conveniently exchanged. The greatest impact, however, was made in the rural areas where people had traveled long distances and in large blocks of time to reach their new homesteads. Now, suddenly, they realized that with the coming of the railroads the continent had become smaller. People and goods, which had heretofore seemed to be millions of miles away from rural folks, could now be reached within a matter of a few short days. People's imaginations gushed with exotic thoughts as they witnessed the new "iron monster" dramatically altering their way of life. The steam-driven railroad was considered to be as advanced a piece of technology then as the probes that are being catapulted into outer space are to us today. Suffice it to say that the railroads drastically changed the whole pattern of living for the American public, providing this vast continent with a monumental maze of tracks that could join people and things together in an incredibly short span of time.

Additionally, the railroads provided job opportunities for hundreds of thousands of immigrants who were clamoring at America's shores. Much of the unskilled labor required to lay tracks and build engines and cars was supplied at the outset by Irish immigrants. They were soon joined by Italians, Poles, and American blacks. These people worked long and hard for meager wages; however, they were happy to have the opportunity to work and earn money in order to survive and possibly even build a little nest egg with which to better establish themselves in their new land. Semi-skilled labor was also in demand for laborers such an engineers, porters, maintenance men, baggage movers, and so on, who could operate the railroads. As with the shipping industry, railroading became a highly profitable business and many a railroad magnate surfaced to become an instant millionaire.

The railroad became such a source of excitement that a phenomenal collection of songs emerged that were contributed by every segment of the society that came in contact with it. As a result, we have the songs of the observers or onlookers, those people who looked anxiously at the passing or even the stopping of trains as they came along each day, week, or month. To them it meant that Chicago, New York, and Philadelphia were suddenly at their doorsteps. Trains brought them closer to their loved ones, relatives, and friends. Moreover, closer communication was realized through letters and packages mailed only a few short days before their arrival. Railroads made them feel closer to everything, not only because people and goods came to them but because they, in turn, could reverse the flow as easily. It is a well-documented fact that the early observers used to drop whatever they were doing to watch the trains go by. They even knew which trains were early and late, who the engineers operating the trains were, and even the particular numbers of the engines pulling the cars. It was a great day when the trains came to town or even just whistled as they passed by.

Dozens of songs were added to the song bag that were created by people who built the railroads. Some of the songs were rather American in sound; others showed definite nationalistic origins (Irish, Italian, and so forth). The early builders were fresh "off the boat" and had hardly been assimilated into the American culture. They either adapted their favorite Old World songs to their new work or created new songs based on the musical materials of their places of origin. Some of the songs came from workers who spent their time blasting and busting rocks so that mountains could be cut down to allow for a grade of incline compatible with the horsepower capabilities of the steam engine or to provide crushed rock for use in building railbeds. There were also songs contributed by those workers who laid out the tracks. Wooden ties had to be placed equidistantly along the rockbeds by workers operating as teams, who took rails off the small cars and placed them across the ties. Young boys called "shakers" (the reason being obvious) had to hold the spikes in place while steel-driving men pounded in the spikes in order to secure the rails to the ties. Songs emerged quite naturally out of the enthusiasm and inspiration experienced by the several types of laborers as they went about their work.

Like the sailor and the cowboy, the railroad worker soon learned that a song could help him pass the time away quickly and pleasantly and even make his work less fatiguing. Through their songs they told about the rigors of their work, their relationships with their fellow workers, the peculiarities connected with their occupations, and even the dangers connected with railroad building. Some of their songs are structured to accompany the rhythm of their tasks, such as busting rocks or driving spikes, both of which involved the swinging of heavy hammers.

Two unique and significant sounds connected with railroading are the rhythmic clicking of the tracks that comes as wheels run across the breaks in the rails (much like the dividers on concrete superhighways as the car tires cut across them) and the sound of the steam whistle operated by the engineer. The steady click of the tracks established a rhythmic beat that has since become the basis for a great deal of American music. This rhythmic pulse not only appears in railroad music but it is also the basic foundation of jazz.

The railroad whistle is like no other whistle in existence; its sound is best described as lonesome and haunting. Many people actually were known to tell the time of day just by listening to the sounds of the train whistles as they sped by. For some, the whistle meant joy; for others, it spelled bad news. The low-down blues that are deeply inculcated in American music are said to have been attributed to the sounds of the early train whistles as they blew away while crossing the wide open spaces. Music is said to be sound painting; therefore, it is no wonder these two unique sounds were artistically blended together in railroading music.

Several of the railroading songs were contributed by the passengers as they sat aboard the train thinking about their destinations, observing the countryside, and listening to the clicking sounds and the sounds of the whistle. As they thought, observed, and listened their creative juices began to flow and songs began to pour forth.

There were some riders who were not a part of the paid ridership. These were the so-called "bums" or hobos who rode the blinds, hung precariously onto the rods below the cars, or hid just about anyplace where the railroad security guards, whom they called "bulls," could not find them. Many of these fellows were driven to hopping trains because of lack of work, sheer poverty, or simply from the desire to start anew in some other locale. Unfortunately, many of them became addicted to their wanderlust existence and chose to live as "bums," panhandling and living in "jungles" along the tracks, completely degenerated in personal appearance, morals, and self-esteem. What was even worse, many of them were so lazy that they actively recruited curious young boys into joining their exclusive society by luring them with tales of fantastic rewards. They, too, used the medium of song to help share their unusual way of life.

The fourth and final group of railroaders whose music has been preserved and enjoyed is that of the semi-skilled workers—the engineers, conductors, porters, baggage men, and so forth. Their songs are ideally cast in ballad form to describe great events and particular hero workers. Some are true stories and others are highly fictionalized. At any rate, they gave insight into their special vocations and served to provide themselves with heroes and events with which they could identify. Hard work, and especially, dedication were hallmarks of operating a railway that sought always to be on time and always to have fulfilled a prescribed mission. Their songs are some of the finest from the collection of American railroading music.

One of the best-known songs to come from railroading and one that is highly descriptive of the onlooker's response to the emergence of the railroad is "She'll Be Coming 'Round the Mountain." The song is considered to be an adaptation of a spiritual; this may account for its singability and longevity down to our day. The song speaks of the excitement that people experienced because the railroad was able to bring loved ones closer together. The six white horses may refer to the horsepower of the steam engine. The other verses talk about the celebration to take place as a result of her "coming 'round the mountain."

SHE'LL BE COMING 'ROUND THE MOUNTAIN

Traditional Song

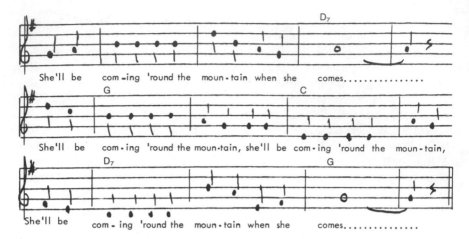

She'll be driving six white horses when she comes, etc.
Oh, we'll all go out to meet her when she comes, etc.
Oh, we'll kill the old red rooster when she comes, etc.
And we'll all have chicken 'n dumplings when she comes, etc.
Oh, she'll have to sleep with gramma when she comes, etc.

People involved in particular vocations have always had their own individual sets of fans and railroading was no exception. "A Railroader for Me" is typical of this type of song, so frequently found in folk literature, that speaks of persons associated with a number of vocations yet singles out a particular worker as being the ideal one to fall in love with and (presumably) marry.

A RAILROADER FOR ME

Traditional

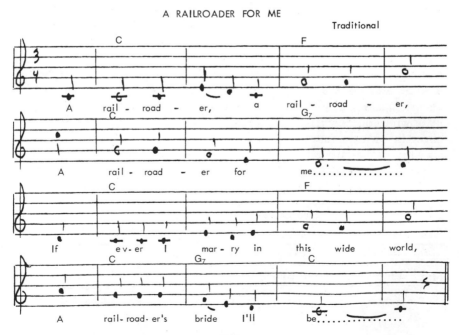

174

Now I would not marry a blacksmith,
He's always in the black;
I'd rather marry an engineer,
That throws the throttle back.

I would not marry a farmer,
He's always in the dirt;
I'd rather marry an engineer,
That wears the striped shirt.

People deeply engrossed in religion found the train to be a symbolic image that they could use to effectively illustrate a moral message about the accessibility of heaven and the means of getting there. This was especially effective with black congregations. Several fine spirituals use the train symbolically by referring to its ability to transport people as a congregation and lead them into the Promised Land. The spiritual "This Train" gives warning to all kinds of sinners—gamblers, hypocrites, liars, and street walkers. If they should continue in their sinful ways, there would be no room for them on that special train bound for glory! One should take note of the rhythm of the tracks that underlies this and the following song. It is conceivable that the songs may have been inspired as one was riding on a train, thinking religious thoughts. An effective introduction to these songs would be to establish a train-like rhythm and to continue it throughout the songs.

THIS TRAIN

Spiritual

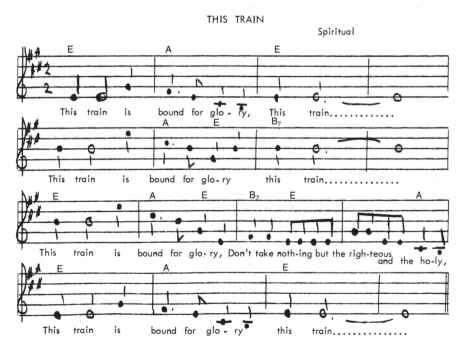

This train don't carry no gamblers, This train.
This train don't carry no gamblers, This train.

This train don't carry no gamblers,
No hypocrites, no midnight gamblers,
This train don't carry no gamblers, This train.

This train is built for speed now, This train.
This train is built for speed now, This train.
This train is built for speed now,
Fastest train you ever did see,
This train is built for speed now, This train.

This train don't carry no liars, This train.
This train don't carry no liars, This train.
No hypocrites and no high flyers,
This train don't carry no liars, This train.

This train don't pay no 'tention, This train.
This train don't pay no 'tention, This train.
This train don't pay no 'tention,
No Jim Crow and no discrimination,
This train don't pay no 'tention, This train.

This train don't carry no rustlers, This train.
This train don't carry no rustlers, This train.
This train don't carry no rustlers,
Sidestreet walkers, two bit gamblers,
This train don't carry no rustlers, This train.

"Get On Board" is another of these spirituals in which the train is used symbolically to get a religious message across to the congregation. Again, in this song the train is, in essence, a gospel train with its ultimate destination being the Promised Land!

GET ON BOARD

Spiritual

The passenger car is empty,
The doors are open wide;
There's room for ev'rybody,
So please just step inside.

The little black train's a long train,
A fast train, you will find;
The red caboose is coming,
It's tagging on behind.

I hear the train a-coming, a-coming
  round the curve,
She loosened all her steam and brakes,
She's straining every nerve.

The fare is cheap and all can go,
The rich and poor are there;
No second class aboard this train,
No difference in the fare.

Songs representative of the riders definitely contain that unflagging rhythm of the train clicking over the tracks. There are a number of songs that mention the name of the community where the passengers came aboard as well as the stops along the way and the point of destination. "Kalamazoo to Timbucto" is just such a song. One of the more interesting of these songs, which helps the rider "check" off the miles, is one that the twentieth-century balladeer Woody Guthrie helped popularize. "900 Miles" is based on a tune used many times over by folk in the southeastern section of the United States. It contains the rail rhythm along with some of the lonesome blues feelings inspired by the train whistle. This song travels at the speed of a train.

900 MILES

Traditional

Well I'm walk-ing down the track, I've got tears in my eyes... Try-'n to read a let-ter from my home.. If that train runs me right I'll be home 'fore to-mor-row night.... 'cause I'm nine hun-dred miles from my home.... And I hate to hear that lone-some whis-tle blow........

Well, I'll pawn you my watch,
And I'll pawn you my chain,
I'll pawn you my gold diamond ring,
If that train runs me right,
I'll be home 'fore tomorrow night,
'Cause I'm nine hundred miles from my home
And I hate to hear that lonesome whistle blow.

Well, this train I ride on
Is a hundred coaches long,
Hear the whistle blow a hundred miles.
If that train runs me right,
I'll be home 'fore tomorrow night,
'Cause I'm nine hundred miles from my home
And I hate to hear that lonesome whistle blow.

Engineer's Verse:

If my woman says so,
I'll railroad no more.
I'll sidetrack my train and go home.
If that wheeler runs me right,
I'll be home 'fore tomorrow night,
'Cause I'm nine hundred miles from my home
And I hate to hear that lonesome whistle blow.

As has been mentioned, the hobo was a special kind of train passenger. He was addicted with wanderlust and cared little for the respectable life or settling down. He was so lazy and carefree that wherever he went he was always out to recruit young assistants whom he called "punks" to wait on him hand and foot. These punks would have to serve their apprenticeship on their way to becoming a full-fledged bum. Through this process the bums were allowed to lead their own type of "better life" and at the same time replenish their ranks with new members. "You Wonder Why I'm a Hobo" beautifully summarizes their philosophy of life and riding the rails—a luxury, to be sure, that every man could afford. This song was sung in the hobo jungles alongside the tracks as the hobos sat around the campfire eating their "take" for the day. The song perhaps helped them to rationalize their existence and carry on for another day.

YOU WONDER WHY I'M A HOBO

Railroader Song

You won·der why I'm a ho·bo, and why I sleep in a ditch,

Well it ain't be-cause I'm la-zy, I just don't want to be rich;

Now I could eat from dish-es, It's just a mat-ter of choice,

But when I eat from an old tin can, There ain't no dish-es to wash.

Dee-dle-dy dee, dee, dee, dee, Dee-dle-dy dee dee doo.

Taken from *A Treasury of Railroad Folklore* edited by B. A. Botkin and Alvin F. Harlow. Copyright 1953 by B. A. Botkin and Alvin F. Harlow. Used by permission of Crown Publishers, Inc.

Now I could ride the pullman,
But there it is again;
The plush they put on the pullman
    seats,
It tickles my sensitive skin.
Now I could be a conductor,
And never have a wreck;
But any kind of a railroad man
To me is a pain in the neck.
(*Chorus*)

Now I could be a banker,
If ever I wanted to be;
But the very thought of an iron cage,
Is too frightening to me;

Now I could be a banker,
Without the slightest excuse,
But look at 1929
And tell me what's the use.
(*Chorus*)

Now I could be a doctor,
My duty I never would shirk;
But if I doctored a railroad bull,
He'd never go back to work;
Now you wonder why I'm a hobo,
And why I sleep in the ditch,
Well, it ain't because I'm lazy,
No, I just don't want to be rich.
(*Chorus*)

To be sure, not all trains were alike. There were the several ordinary trains; however, there were also some very special trains. People who lived in the northeastern section of the United States during the first half of the twentieth century remember such special trains as the *Empire State Express,* the *Phoebe Snow* and the *Wolverine.* These trains had very special accommodations and were especially fast. One such train from the latter half of the nineteenth century was romanticized in song, the "Wabash Cannon Ball." This song was usually sung with a trainlike rhythmic introduction garnished with train whistle sounds made with either the singing voice or a real whistle.

The lyrics of the song give the full story of railroading during the pioneer days and the music vividly portrays the rhythmic sounds uniquely connected with the media.

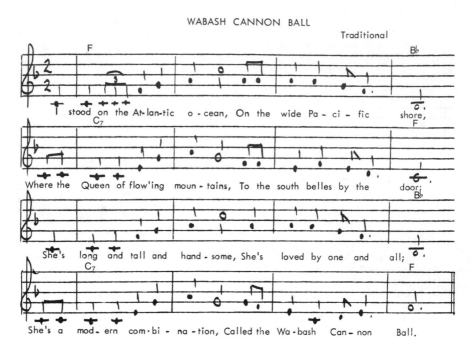

WABASH CANNON BALL

Traditional

I stood on the At-lan-tic o - cean, On the wide Pa - ci - fic shore,
Where the Queen of flow'ing moun - tains, To the south belles by the door;
She's long and tall and hand - some, She's loved by one and all;
She's a mod - ern com-bi - na -tion, Called the Wa -bash Can - non Ball.

Now listen to the jungle,
The rumble and the roar;
Riding through the woodland,
Through the hills and by the shore;
Hear the mighty rush of engine,
Hear that lonesome hobo squall,
Riding through the jungles
On the Wabash Cannon Ball.

Now the eastern states at Andes,
So the western people say,
From New York to St. Louis,
And Chicago by the way;
Through the hills of Minnesota
Where them ripling waters fall,

No chances can be taken,
On the Wabash Cannon Ball.

(*Verse 2*)

Here's to daddy Claxton
May his name forever stand,
Will he be remembered
Through parts of all our land?
When his earthly race is over,
The curtain 'round him falls,
We'll carry him on to victory,
On the Wabash Cannon Ball.

(*Verse 2*)

The songs of the builders and operators of the early railroads represent some of the finest from this segment of American society. Irish immigrants were connected in greater numbers in the laying of tracks than any other ethnic group. "Pat Works on the Railway" tells, in a humorous yet poignant way, about the Irish affiliations with this undertaking. Similarly, the song "Drill Ye Tarriers, Drill," written by an Irish railroad worker or tarrier turned vaudevillian, tells of their participation in railroad building. The songs are considered to be American folk songs, yet they are as Irish as the Irishmen who created them and sang them.

PAT WORKS ON THE RAILWAY

Traditional

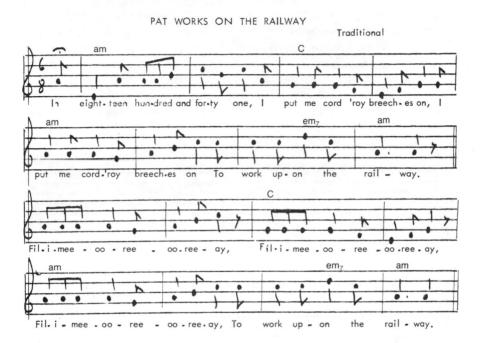

In eighteen hundred and forty-two
I left the old world for the new,
Bad cess to the luck that brought me
    through
To work upon the railway.
(*Repeat chorus after each verse*)

When we left Ireland to come here,
And spend our latter days in cheer;
Our bosses, they did drink strong beer
While Pat worked on the railway.

Our boss's name, it was Tom King,
He kept a store to rob the men;
A Yankee clerk with ink and pen,
To cheat Pat on the railway.

It's "Pat do this and Pat do that,"
Without a stocking or cravat;
And nothing but an old straw hat,
While Pat works on the railway.

One Monday morning to our surprise,
Just a half an hour before sunrise;

The dirty divil went to the skies
And Pat worked on the railway.

And when Pat lays him down to sleep,
The wirey bugs around him creep;
And divil a bit can poor Pat sleep,
While he works on the railway.

In eighteen hundred and forty-three,
'Twas then I met Miss Molly McGhee;
And an elegant wife she's been to me,
While working on the railway.

In eighteen hundred and forty-seven,
Sweet Molly McGhee went off to
    heaven;
If she left one child, she left eleven,
To work upon the railway.

In eighteen hundred and forty-eight,
I learned to take my whiskey straight;
'Tis an elegant drink and can't be bate,
For working on the railway.

Another ethnic group, the Italians, are beautifully described to us in the song "Where Do You Worka, John?" One cannot help but be amused with the Italian immigrant whose limited English vocabulary consists of the name of the company for whom he is working and another word explaining what he does at his job. The Italian language is filled with vowel sounds, and Italians, in their early attempts at mastering the English language, would add vowels to the ends of just about every English word, such as "worka" for "work," "pusha" for "push," and so on. The third verse of the song deals with the female counterpart of the Italian immigrant who works for the telephone company. It shows that Marie was no more adept at speaking English than was John, the railroad worker.

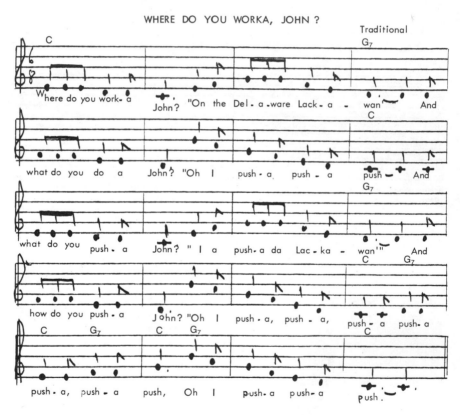

WHERE DO YOU WORKA, JOHN ?

"What-a you eat-a, John?"
"I eat-a da big salam."
"And how do you eat-a, John?"
"Oh I push-a, push, push."
"And how do you push-a, John?"
"I push-a da big salam."
"And how do you push-a, John?"
"Oh I push-a, push-a, push-a," etc.

"Where do you work-a, Marie?"
"In the telephone company."
"And what do you do-a, Marie?"
"Oh I push-a, push-a, push."
"And what do you push-a, Marie?"
"I push-a da company."
"And what do you push-a, Marie?"
"Oh I push-a, push-a, push-a," etc.

The song used to help lay countless miles of track was the ever-popular "I've Been Working on the Railroad." The origin of the song is unknown; however, it is thought to be derived from the southern spiritual "I've Been Working on the Levee," a likely coincidence. In its present form it is actually two songs in one. In some places in the United States the song goes by the

I'VE BEEN WORKING ON THE RAILROAD

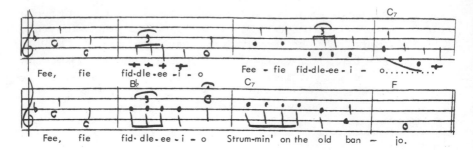

title "Dinah." Regardless of its genealogy, it remains a favorite of such group singers as campers, barber shoppers, and service club members.

John Henry was the folk hero of the steel-driving men. His dedication and phenomenal strength has been lyricized in more than half a dozen songs. Legend has it that John Henry, a black steel-driving man, could whop spikes into ties faster than any other man. People came from far and near to watch him swing his heavy hammers while his shaker boys would sing and hold spikes for him to drive. Most of the songs about John Henry tell their story in ballad form. Others are structured to be sung while driving steel. These songs not only enticed the whopper into making more rhythmically coordinated swings, but also gave him a psychological lift as he worked. As the story goes, a salesman from the industrial north came to Georgia where a new railroad track was being built to promote the double jointed steam drill, a new invention used in driving steel. The salesman boasted that his new piece of equipment could do the work of several whoppers. A contest was arranged between the steam drill and the best black whopper on the line, John Henry. The song vividly relates what happened at the competition.

JOHN HENRY

Railroaders Song

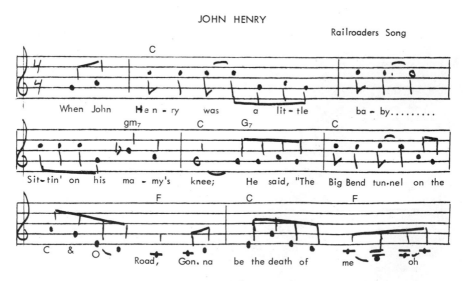

184

Lord, Lord, Lord; Gon-na be the death of me oh Lord.

When John Henry was a little baby
Sittin' on his daddy's knee;
He point his finger at a little piece of
  steel
Said, "That's gonna be the death of me,
  Lord, Lord,
Gonna be the death of me, oh Lord."

Oh, the captain says to John Henry,
"Gonna bring me a steam drill 'round.
I'm gonna take that steam drill out on
  the job
Gonna whop that steel on down, Lord,
  Lord,
Gonna whop that steel on down."

Then John Henry told his captain,
"A man ain't nothin' but a man.
And befo' I'd let that steam drill beat
  me down
I'd die with my hammer in my hand,
  Lord, Lord,
I'd die with my hammer in my hand."

Oh, John Henry started on the right
  hand,
Steam drill started on the left;
Fo' I'd let that steam drill beat me
  down,
I'd hammer myself to death, Lord, Lord,
I'd hammer myself to death."

Oh, John Henry told his shaker,
"Shaker, why don't you sing?
I'm throwin' nine pounds from my hips
  on down,
Just listen to that cold steel ring, Lord,
  Lord,
Just listen to that cold steel ring."

Oh, John Henry told his shaker,
"Shaker, why don't you pray?
'Fore if I miss this six foot steel,
Tomorrow'll be your buryin' day, Lord,
  Lord,
Tomorrow'll be your buryin' day."

Oh, the man who invented the steam
  drill
He thought that he was mighty fine.
But John Henry drove his steel fifteen
  feet
And the steam drill only went nine,
  Lord, Lord,
The steam drill only went nine.

Oh, John Henry hammered in the
  mountain
Handle of the hammer caught fire.
He drove so hard that he broke his
  heart
Then he laid down his hammer and
  died, Lord, Lord,
Laid down his hammer and died.

Oh, they took John Henry to the tunnel,
Buried him in the sand;
And ev'ry locomotive come rollin' by,
Says, "There lays a steel drivin' man,
  Lord, Lord,
There lays a steel drivin' man."

Now some say he come from England,
Some say he come from Spain;
But I say he's nothin' but a Louisiana
  man,
Leader of the steel-drivin' gang, Lord,
  Lord,
Leader of the steel-drivin' gang.

The highlights of the John Henry story are adapted to the steel-driving song that follows, "This 'Ole Hammer." The song accommodates the full swing of the hammer forcing the rhythmic spacing of whops.

THIS 'OLE HAMMER

Work Song

This ole' ham-mer........... killed John Hen-ry...........

This ole' ham-mer........... killed John Hen-ry...........

This ole' ham-mer........... killed John Hen-ry........... But it

won't kill me............... but it won't kill me...........

This ole hammer . . . shine like silver . . .
This ole hammer . . . shine like silver . . .
This ole hammer . . . shine like silver . . .
But it ring like gold . . . but it ring like gold . . .

Gonna lay my head . . . on the railroad track . . .
Gonna lay my head . . . on the railroad track . . .
Gonna lay my head . . . on the railroad track . . .
When the train come along . . .
Gonna snatch it back . . .

Engineers, like whoppers, were singled out as heroes and represented ideally in song. "Zack, the Mormon Engineer" was not the greatest hero among the engineers but he certainly was a very interesting one. Being a Mormon, and therefore a polygamist, made him the brunt of some well-intended puns. The song is a modified version of "Oh Susannah."

ZACK, THE MORMON ENGINEER

Railroad Song

Old Zack he came from U-tah way Back in sev'-ty two, A

186

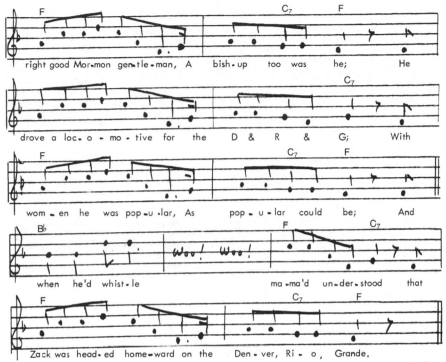

right good Mor-mon gen-tle-man, A bish-up too was he; He
drove a loc-o-mo-tive for the D & R & G; With
wom-en he was pop-u-lar, As pop-u-lar could be; And
when he'd whist-le Woo! Woo! ma-ma'd un-der-stood that
Zack was head-ed home-ward on the Den-ver, Ri-o, Grande.

Taken from *A Treasury of Railroad Folklore* edited by B. A. Botkin and Alvin F. Harlow. Copyright 1953 by B. A. Botkin and Alvin F. Harlow. Used by permission of Crown Publishers, Inc.

Old Zack, he had a wifey,
In every railroad town;
No matter where he stopped he had
A place to lay him down;
And when his train was comin'
He wanted her to know,
So as he passed each wifey town,
His whistle he would blow.
(*Chorus*)

Old Zack, he claimed to love his wifeys,
And love them all the same;
But always little Mabel was,
The one that Zack would name;
And as he would pass her,

He'd blow his whistle loud,
And when she'd throw a kiss at him,
Old Zack would look so proud.
(*Chorus*)

Now listen everybody,
Because this story's true,
Old Zack he had a wife in every town,
That he passed through;
They tried to make him transfer,
On to the old UP,
But Zack said No because his wives,
Were on the D,R&G.
(*Chorus*)

The greatest hero among engineers was Casey Jones. Casey was so dedicated to his job that he risked life and limb to ensure that the train he was driving would always be on time. Some of the fatalism brought to our attention by such early Americans as the pioneers is again in evidence as we scrutinize those lines in "Casey Jones" that relate to Casey's bereaved wife upon hearing that Casey had died in a train accident. She tells her children to go to bed and hush their crying because they would have (or, as in some versions, already had) another poppa on the Salt Lake Line. This ballad has the railroad rhythm of the clicking tracks as well as a great story of a dramatic occurrence in the early days of railroading.

CASEY JONES

Railroader Song

"Put in your water and shovel your
coal,
Your head out the window watch them
drivers roll.
I'll run her 'til she leaves the rail
'Cause I'm eight hours late with that
western mail."
He looked at his watch and his watch
was slow,
He looked at the water and the water
was low,
He turned to the fireman and then he
said,
"We're goin' to reach Frisco but we'll
all be dead."

Chorus:
Casey Jones, goin' to reach Frisco,
Casey Jones, but we'll all be dead;
Casey Jones, goin' to reach Frisco,
We're goin' to reach Frisco but we'll all
be dead.

Casey pulled up that Reno Hill,
He tooted for the crossing with an
awful shrill,
The switchman knew by the engine's
moan
That the man at the throttle was Casey
Jones.
Casey got to that certain place,
Ol' number nine stared him right in the
face,

He turned to the fireman, said, "Boy,
you better jump,
'Cause there's two locomotives and
they're bound to bump."

Chorus:
Casey Jones, two locomotives,
Casey Jones, that's bound to bump;
Casey Jones, two locomotives,
There's two locomotives that's a-bound
to bump.

Casey said just before he died,
"There's two more roads that I'd like to
ride."
The fireman said what could they be?
"The Southern Pacific and the Sante
Fe."
Mrs. Casey sat on her bed a-cryin',
Just received word that her Casey was
a-dyin',
Said, "Go to bed, children, and hush
your cryin',
'Cause you got another papa on the Salt
Lake Line."

Chorus:
Casey Jones, got another papa,
Casey Jones, on the Salt Lake Line,
Casey Jones, got another papa,
You've got another papa on the Salt
Lake Line.

The invention of the steam engine and its adaptation to the railroads made a profound impact on America and its people. Trains were the source of considerable excitement which, among others things, manifested itself in a potpourri of great folk songs handed down for our enjoyment. It is sad to say that in today's modern, impersonal society the railroad has become yet another victim of progress. Conductors as train callers no longer sing, engineers remain anonymous figures, and riders sit quietly reading their newspapers and magazines. Unfortunately, the thrill of railroading is gone, as is the source of inspiration that gave birth to so many great songs.

12

Songs of Minstrelsy
& the Gay Nineties

During the second half of the nineteenth century, the field of entertainment served as the dominant inspirational source for music, giving new shape and purpose to song materials in America. Songs created expressly for popular theatre found their way into the hearts and voices of millions of Americans and ultimately became the new folk music of the times. The gradual trend from a purely agrarian society to a more urbanized one, brought on by a concerted drive toward industrialism and big-city living, provided the perfect mold for new recreational activities to whet the appetites of the emerging middle class. City dwellers were working in factories and mills earning, for the first time, a few more dollars beyond what was absolutely essential for mere survival. They worked hard and for long hours each day; nonetheless, they found time for some leisure activities. What was more important, they felt they deserved some fun time as a reward for their efforts.

The mere gathering together of folks to sing their favorite songs was perfect for those people who lived in rural areas and served as a most satisfying recreational activity. This practice, however, did not work as well in heavily populated urban areas where tenement houses and neighborhood streets abounded. Moreover, urban folks had money in their pockets and yearned for the opportunity to be entertained rather than to find ways of entertaining themselves.

The answer to their wishes came in the form of theatre, namely, minstrelsy, variety shows, and vaudeville. In retrospect, we can safely say that collectively these types of theatre served as the forerunners to the musical comedies of the twentieth century, a unique genre of musical theatre for which Americans can be singularly proud.

During this time, songs presented in the various types of "people theatre" were patterned on the format of the emerging folk music of America. They were songs of the people, by the people, and for the people. Theatergoers heard them being sung and walked out of the theatre singing them. These songs, in turn, became the "pop" tunes of the day. Yet, unlike ordinary "pop" tunes, they were songs of genuine musical substance and, as a result, people never tired of singing and hearing them. Literally thousands of songs were cranked out by the songwriters connected with musical theatre, and the great majority of them sustained their popularity. They were performed again and again at community dances, band concerts in the park, and holiday activities; they were sung in barber shops, backyards, and just about any place where people were gathered together in social settings.

American folk music, as a result, took on a new character by finding a new wellspring for the outpouring of people music. Music of all types fully flowered during the latter half of the nineteenth century. No longer were songs inspired solely as a result of significant happenings in people's lives, such as working on a railroad, searching for gold, moving cattle, or winding the capstan. Songs began to lose their autobiographical roots and were now being produced for the people. Interestingly enough, the songs of the common people continued to flow in abundance, only now they came from known individuals who performed their materials in the American folk song mold and made them available in printed form. Their level of musical sophistication was only slightly above that which had been produced anonymously during the first century of America's existence.

On the other side of the ledger, members of the wealthy upper class were actively engaged in assuming all of the niceties identified with persons of their station in society. This included living in large, luxurious homes, wearing the latest in European fashions, and being affiliated with cultural activities that befitted their high places in society. In terms of music, this required their active support of and attendance at symphony concerts, operas, parlor performances featuring chamber groups and solo singers, as well as grand ballroom dances. As a consequence, they went along their own musical path, identifying with the music of the European master composers; meanwhile, the members of the lower and emerging middle classes sought the more unsophisticated brand of American music to bring them pleasure.

Minstrelsy

Slaveholders, members of their families, and friends were the only people who had had the opportunity to witness blacks carrying on and having fun singing and dancing on the plantations in their seemingly wild and uninhibited manner. Even the blacks' unique dialect and uncanny way of telling stories and jokes had been somewhat confined to the large plantations. With the coming of the emancipation and the black's exposure to a wider public, more and more people got the opportunity to observe and enjoy their unique manner of entertaining themselves. Despite this, only a small percentage of the American public actually had any close contact with the black man. Suffice it to say that in the middle of the nineteenth century the manner in which the American black made his fun singing, dancing, and storytelling was unique and was shared by only a small number of people.*

A number of enterprising white entertainers seized on the idea of capitalizing on the uniqueness of black humor and adapting it to musical theatre. At the outset, these entertainers worked individually and appeared on stage with their faces blackened with burnt cork. They sang songs while moving back and forth across the stage, they cracked jokes in black dialect, and they played instruments identified with blacks, such as the banjo and the bones. In short, they entertained their audiences by making them happy in a way they had never before experienced. These performers were immediate sensations and were soon joined by teams of black-faced entertainers who created shows that ultimately came to be known as "Negro extravaganzas." Thus was born minstrelsy, which dominated the American scene from the larger cities to the most remote hamlets. Some of the troupes of entertainers were top professionals who toured the country from coast to coast and even as far away as Europe. Many of them were rank amateurs, hometown folks who were "hams" at heart and who yearned for the chance to get into show biz.

Although it is true that minstrel shows can be seen as merely another example of white entertainers "robbing" American blacks and exploiting their wares, it must be stated most emphatically that minstrel shows, by themselves, were not an attempt to poke fun at blacks. Theatergoers were laughing *with* the black-faced entertainers, *not* at them. Ironically, there is evidence available today to indicate that the concept of black-faced minstrelsy actually began in the British isles, thus predating its initial appearance in America.

Among the many black-faced entertainers involved in the so-called "Ethiopian business," there were two who stood out most prominently— George Washington Dixon and Thomas Dartmouth Rice. These two gentlemen, along with their several professional peers, did much to establish the media of entertainment during what has been identified as the "pre-minstrel show period." G. W. Dixon was one of the earliest and most successful of these entertainers. He put together an act consisting of songs, dances, and repartee that was reported to have played in Albany and New York City as early as the 1820s. Two of the top songs in his repertoire were "Coal Black Rose," described as the "first burnt-cork song of comic love," and "Long Tail Blue," which musically characterized a black "dandy" elegantly attired in a blue, swallow-tailed coat strutting down the street.

---

*Their fun-loving ways are enjoyed even today in television sitcoms that feature black entertainers exclusively.

Thomas Dartmouth Rice, better known as "Daddy" or "Jim Crow" Rice, traveled more extensively with his act (even to England) and garnered for himself the title of "Father of American minstrelsy." The song that made "Daddy" Rice the sensation of his day was "Jim Crow," a catchy song with innumerable sets of stanzas based on the black dialect. The song not only made Rice a household name but also went on to become a national and international hit. "Daddy" Rice developed a style of song delivery in which he imitated the black man's shuffling manner of walking. As he sang and walked around, he even threw in a few sudden jerks and jumps at appropriate places in the song, which would evoke thunderous applause from his audiences. Dixon, Rice, and their fellow performers laid the groundwork and lined up the eager audiences for the more extravagant minstrel shows of the mid-fifties.

From these one-man acts emerged a famous four-man act known as the Virginia Minstrels, whose members were Daniel Decatur Emmett, Billy Whitlock, Frank Brower, and Dick Pelham. These four men put together a show that was reported to have had a long run of packed houses in the Bowery Amphitheatre in New York City in 1843. These four black-faced entertainers performed on such instruments as the violin, banjo, bones, and tambourine; they could sing, dance, and exchange stories to the sheer delight of their audiences. The Virginia Minstrels soon gave way to Bryant's Minstrels. This company was made up of four black-faced entertainers, an interlocutor who served as a kind of master of ceremonies and straight man, and a chorus of singers and entertainers. Dan Emmett joined Bryant's Minstrels in 1858 and achieved fame as an outstanding black-faced entertainer whose "walk-arounds" were considered to be as authentic as that of the southern blacks and whose original songs were received as immediate hits.

Dan Emmett was the creator of the song "Dixie" that we have discussed in Chapter 9. Emmett also claimed authorship for such songs as "Old Dan Tucker" and "De Boatman's Dance," which he popularized and which, as a consequence, was identified with him.

Another minstrel troupe of the period that waged a long-standing battle with Bryant's Minstrels over which of the two was organized first was the E. P. Christy Minstrels. E. P. Christy, like Dan Emmett, was an entertainer fully emersed in the performance end of the business; unlike Emmett, he was also an owner–promoter of the medium. Having organized his troupe in Buffalo, New York and having toured several parts of the country, Christy finally settled in New York City, packing houses for a period of about ten years. (The New Christy Minstrels, a group that will be discussed in Chapter 13, was patterned after the original Christy Minstrels.)

The search for new and appealing songs for the minstrel stage was an ongoing process. Because of this, Christy sought out Stephen Foster, who had written him expressing his desire to prepare song materials for his show. Foster's folklike songs were already becoming popular with the common folks. Christy, a shrewd businessman, worked out an agreement with Foster whereby Christy's name would appear on the sheet music as the composer of "Foster's" songs; Foster, in turn, would receive the sum of ten dollars in advance, for each song submitted. One of the most notable of these hoaxes was "Old Folks at Home" ("Way Down Upon the Swanee River"), which went on to become the number one song of the day and which had Christy's name on the sheet music as the composer–lyricist. Foster, a proud, deeply troubled man, was utterly frustrated at hearing his music being thoroughly enjoyed by audiences while he was deprived of the recognition due him as the music's real composer. This, as well as a number of other problems, led to excessive drinking, poverty, and an early death at the age of thirty-seven. Foster was one of the most gifted melodists of his time; he wrote songs not only for the minstrel stage but also sentimental "parlor" songs filled with lush melody and proper English lyrics. The strong influence of a black maid who practically raised him, the familiarity and fascination he shared with the work of "Daddy" Rice, the keen observations he enjoyed in watching and listening to the singing of the black man's roustabouts as they worked on the warf in Pittsburg, where he was employed as a kind of bookkeeper, all contributed to his ability to write minstrel tunes with great authority and authenticity.

Stephen Foster's songs made a tremendous impact on the progress of folk music in America. Everyone was familiar with his songs, both minstrel and nonminstrel. Because of his tremendous musical output and its quality, Foster was accorded the affectionate titles of "American Folk Composer" and "America's Minstrel," even though he had never been a performer but only a producer of songs. Foster's songs have since been rightfully restored to his credit. Pittsburg, his home town, is the depository of Foster memorabilia. A museum, located on the University of Pittsburg campus, houses his memorabilia and serves as a living tribute to his contribution to American folk music.

Another important contributor to minstrelsy was the composer–performer, James Bland. A son of a black slave, Bland served at one time as a page in the House of Representatives and was later educated in law at Howard University. He became infatuated with minstrels, and he eventually sang with groups and produced some of the finest songs for the medium, including "Carry Me Back to Old Virginia," "In the Evening by the Moonlight," "Golden Slippers," and "Hand Me Down My Walking Cane." Bland claimed to be "the best Ethiopian songwriter in the world."

Mention was made earlier of the banjo and its popularity with the blacks as well as the fascination it held for mountain folk. The instrument received unprecedented use in minstrel settings. Joel Walker Sweeney is credited with developing the five-stringed banjo, considered by some to be a marked manual and musical improvement on the earlier four-stringed gourd. A number of quasi-virtuoso banjoists developed special musical selections for the instrument that became showstoppers. It was essential for every minstrel show to have a banjoist on stage or at least in the pit band. In addition to being used in solo settings, the instrument was also used to accompany the singing and dancing that gave the show a touch of black authenticity.

The minstrel show opened with an overture, a potpourri of tunes arranged to prepare the audience for the show as well as to take up sound while the latecomers found their seats. The music came from the theater pit and consisted of anything from one or two pianos to a small or large instrumental ensemble. At the end of the overture and without pause, the curtain would open. On stage the entire troupe stood and sang a medley of songs arranged in the best tradition of great show openers of musical theater. At the end of the opening medley, the interlocutor, who stood in the middle of the front row before a chair that resembled a king's throne, would say in a loud, commanding voice, "Gentlemen, be seated!" After this, the show proceeded with a series of songs, instrumentals, jokes, and repartee, all organized in a lively, moving manner. The second part of the show was made up of a series of variety acts that culminated in a grand finale, again involving the entire cast. The entire show called for practically no set changes and, as a matter of fact, no special stage requirements. Performers on stage were seated in a semicircular, tiered arrangement in a number of rows that depended on how many people were in the group. The front-row seating arrangement was always the same, that is, the end men (the black-faced entertainers, two or four in number) sat at opposite ends with the interlocutor in the center. In between them were seated the featured soloists, the barbershop quartet, a banjoist, a dancer, and so on. In the early shows only the end men would appear black-faced; in some of the later performances, however, everybody wanted to get into the act and often the entire cast appeared in black-face.

The great majority of the music used in the early minstrel shows was taken from folk songs, those songs that could easily be adapted to the medium of show business. They were reworked to fit the idiom, given new lyrics, and altered with each personal rendition. This, as has already been stated, was part and parcel of the folk process. Because of this, these songs and those written later expressly for the minstrel theater all made a smooth transition into the field of American folk music.

The songs of minstrelsy had all the characteristic qualities of the best folk music. The melodies were short, catchy, and most of all, easily remembered. Likewise, the lyrics contained simple messages that could be easily understood. As with all folk tunes, there was considerable repetition both in the music and the lyrics. One of the most distinctive contributions of minstrel music to the mainstream was its frequent use of syncopated rhythms. Syncopation, as discussed earlier, neither originated with nor became the exclusive property of jazz or Latin-American music where it is used extensively. Such master composers as Bach, Handel, Mozart, and others, all of whom predated this era, used it in their compositions. The rhythmic pattern, however, was showcased in a more pronounced fashion in music that came from the West Indies islands and it was quickly infused into the songs that emerged from the American South. The rhythmic technique realized its full potential in jazz, whose roots were just beginning to be nurtured during the heyday of minstrelsy. Syncopation produces an upsetting of the normal sequence of rhythmic accents or pulses, causing the listener to move, walk around, dance, clap hands, or to do just about anything except sit idly by! Syncopated rhythms were ideal for the minstrel shows because excitement had to be generated and momentum sustained.

The following examples illustrate the use of syncopation. The first examples are from older traditional folk songs; these are followed by a few examples taken from some of the minstrel show literature.

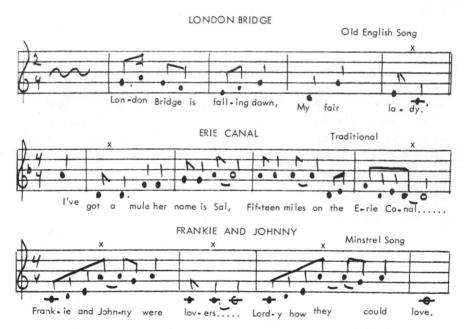

LONDON BRIDGE
Old English Song

Lon-don Bridge is fall-ing down, My fair la-dy.

ERIE CANAL
Traditional

I've got a mule her name is Sal, Fif-teen miles on the E-rie Ca-nal......

FRANKIE AND JOHNNY
Minstrel Song

Frank-ie and John-ny were lov-ers..... Lord-y how they could love.

Appropriately enough, fast-moving (up-tempo) songs were used as show openers and grand finale tunes. Also included in the show were a number of slow, romantic songs for the newly organized and highly successful barbershop quartets. These songs offered the perfect change of pace from the fast-paced tunes. However, the key ingredient implicit in all the songs of minstrelsy, be they fast-paced or slow-moving, was entertainment. Songs had to have immediate audience appeal. A good song delivered well by the entertainer(s) would guarantee a good audience response. Minstrelsy was essentially musical theatre; as such, the public continually demanded new and exciting songs as well as exceptional delivery of the standard repertoire.

One of the earliest and most widely performed of the black-faced songs was "Jim Along Josie." Interestingly, the song appears in a number of settings, but all the versions are consistently based on the pentatonic or five-tone scale.

The song has a verse/chorus structure and has found its way into present-day song collections as a play-party song of the early American pioneers. After singing the song one can easily understand how it would have been quickly snatched up by the Western travelers and used to keep their children entertained. The tune lends itself to play-party dance movements or singing games.

JIM ALONG JOSIE

Traditional

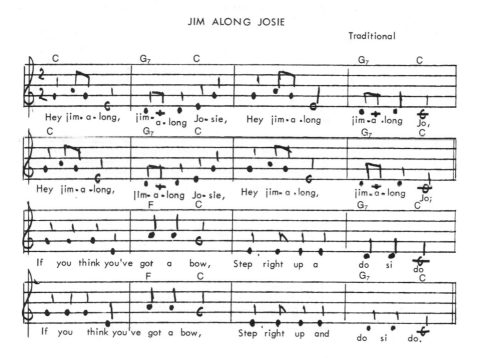

Another of the more successful minstrel songs of the early days is "Ole Zip Coon." This song has had a long and mysterious history. Some authorities point to its Irish antecedents. Both Bob Farrell and G. W. Dixon, who featured the song in their acts, laid claim to its authorship. Today, we find its more easily identifiable version under the title "Turkey in the Straw." At any rate, the song was well suited for the minstrel stage and a perfect vehicle for displaying sparkling technique on the fiddle or banjo, both of which were featured instruments.

OLE ZIP COON

Old Fiddle Song

Another early minstrel song of undetermined origin is variously known as "Luby Fan," "Bowery Gals," "Buffalo Gals," and "Charlestown Gals." (One can only speculate that minstrel troupes must have tactfully adapted the song to the town in which the show was appearing!) As with "Jim Along Josie," which also had its full flowering in minstrelsy, "Buffalo Gals" is most often classified in the nonminstrel section of folk songs, with those songs that are connected with the Erie Canal. "Buffalo Gals" has all the qualities of a good show tune; it has a verse/chorus format to which innumerable sets of lyrics could be added.

BUFFALO GALS

I asked her if she'd stop and talk,
Stop and talk, stop and talk.
Her feet took up the whole sidewalk,
And left no room for me.
(*Chorus*)

I asked her if she'd be my wife,
Be my wife, be my wife.
Then I'd be happy all my life,

If she would marry me.
(*Chorus*)

I asked her would she have some
   dance,
Have some dance, have some dance;
I thought that I might get a chance
To shake a foot with her.
(*Chorus*)

Daniel Emmett claimed authorship of "Old Dan Tucker," and he very well may have created it, words, music, or both. As with a lot of other minstrel songs, this tune went west with the settlers who braved the wilderness and the trials and tribulations of traveling over land. These songs made them feel good and remembrances of life in the more civilized east kept them amused

during leisure times. One can easily visualize Old Dan, black-faced and dressed in bizarre clothing, walking around singing and dancing to this great song.

OLD DAN TUCKER

Daniel Emmett

Old Dan Tucker was a fine old man, he
   washed his face in a frying pan,
Combed his hair with a wagon wheel
   and died with a toothache in his
   heel.
(*Chorus*)

Now Old Dan Tucker and I fell out, and
   what do you think it was all about?
He borrowed my old setting hen and
   didn't bring her back again.
(*Chorus*)

Old Dan began in early life to play the
   banjo and win a wife,
But every time a date he'd keep, he'd
   play himself right fast asleep.
(*Chorus*)

Now Old Dan Tucker he came to town
   to swing the ladies all around,
Swing them right and swing them left,
   then to the one he liked the best.
(*Chorus*)

And when Old Dan had passed away, they missed the music he used to play,

They took him on his final ride and buried his banjo by his side. (*Chorus*)

Because Stephen Foster's contributions to the medium were so many and varied, it is difficult and a bit frustrating to single out just a few representative examples of his works. All his songs have become staples in American folk music. Foster's "Camptown Races" is certainly a foot stomper. This song was written in 1850 and became the hit song of the year (and practically every year after that). Originally it went by the title "Gwine to Run All Night." Like so many of the great Foster tunes, this song was appropriated by the water route forty-niners who added new words to suit their particular needs. In their version called "Sacramento," the nonsense syllables "do-da-day" are changed to "hoo-da-day."

CAMPTOWN RACES

Stephen Foster

The long tail filly and the big black
  horse, doo-da, doo-da,
They flew the track and both cut across,
  Oh, doo-da-day.
The blind horse sticking in a big mud
  hole, etc.
Couldn't touch bottom with a ten foot
  pole, etc.
(*Chorus*)

See them fly on a ten mile heat, doo-da,
  doo-da,
Around the track and then repeat, Oh,
  doo-da-day.

I win my money on de bob-tail nag, etc.
I keep my money in an old tow bag,
  etc.
(*Chorus*)

Old muley cow came on de track, doo-
  da, doo-da,
The bob-tail threw her over his back,
  Oh, doo-da-day.
Then flew along like a railroad car, etc.
Like runnin' a race with a shootin' star,
  etc.
(*Chorus*)

Melodies constantly danced through Stephen Foster's head, and it is
said that he sometimes arose in the middle of the night to put his latest
inspiration down on paper so that he could get back to sleep. There were also
times when he would be walking along and suddenly scramble to find a piece
of paper on which to draw a musical staff so that he could scribble out his
latest creation in musical notation. Foster was unusual in that he wrote both
the words and the music. His songs were conceived by sheer inspiration.
"Ring, Ring, the Banjo" is included here because, even though it is another of
Foster's spirited songs, it is a good illustration of a minstrel song set in
characteristic syncopated rhythmic figures. To be sure, it may have been
inspired by Foster's fascination with the picking sounds of the banjo. Perhaps
the song was used to showcase a singer or group of singers; it also must have
been used to feature the banjoist who could display his technique and gift for
embellishing tunes with all manner of ornamentations in this song.

RING, RING, THE BANJO

Stephen Foster

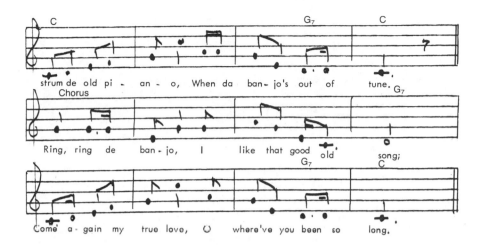

strum de old pi - an - o, When da ban-jo's out of tune.

Chorus

Ring, ring de ban - jo, I like that good old song;

Come a-gain my true love, O where've you been so long.

Oh, never count the bubbles when there's water in the spring,
There's no one who has trouble when he has dis song to sing;
The beauties of creation will never lose their charm,
While I roam de old plantation with my true love on my arm.
(*Chorus*)

My love, I'll have to leave you while the river's runnin' high,
But I will not deceive you, so don't you wipe your eye;
I'm goin' to make some money but I'll come another day,
I'll come again, my honey, if I have to work my way.
(*Chorus*)

It would be short-sighted to omit an example of one of Foster's beautiful, slower-moving minstrel melodies. Aside from his nonminstrel parlor songs, most of which were slow-moving and exquisitely lyrical, "Old Black Joe" is undoubtedly one of the most expressive songs from the minstrel show series.

OLD BLACK JOE

Stephen Foster

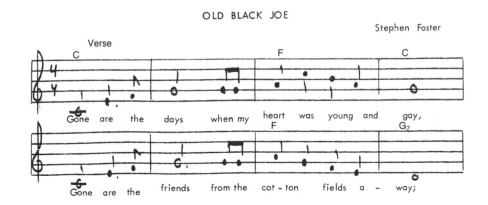

Gone are the days when my heart was young and gay,

Gone are the friends from the cot - ton fields a - way;

203

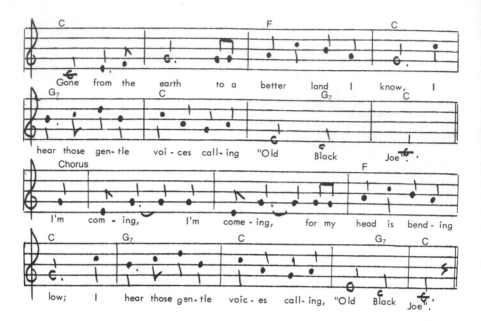

Why do I weep when my heart should feel no pain?
Why do I sigh that my friends come not again?
Grieving for forms now departed long ago,
I hear those gentle voices calling "Old Black Joe."
(*Chorus*)

James A. Bland, a black songwriter who specialized in minstrel tunes, contributed a number of outstanding songs, some peppy, others slow and lyrical, to the repertoire. "Golden Slippers," based on the verse/chorus structure, has some interesting lyrics in the black dialect as well as a highly singable melody. In recent years this song has been used as a standard square dance tune. The song has all the qualities of a good show tune and includes a number of the syncopated rhythms that were so much a part of the music of this genre.

GOLDEN SLIPPERS

James A. Bland

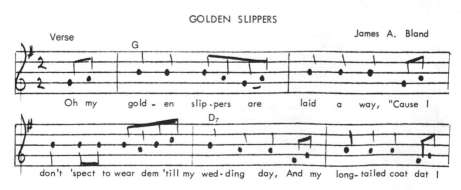

loved so well, I will wear up in de char-iot in de morn;

Chorus

Oh, those gold-en slip-pers, Oh those gold-en slip-pers,

gold-en slip-pers I'm gon-na wear, Be — cause they look so neat;

Oh those gold-en slip-pers, Oh those gold-en slip-pers,

gold-en slip-pers I'm gon-na wear, To walk da gold en streets.

There's the long white robe dat I
  bought last June,
Dat I must go and change 'cause it fits
  too soon;
And de old grey hoss dat I always drive,
I will hitch up to de chariot in de
  morn.
(*Chorus*)

And my banjo still is hanging on de
  wall,
For it hasn't had a tune-up since way
  last fall;
But de folks all say we'll hab a fine old
  time,
When we ride up in de chariot in de
  morn.
(*Chorus*)

So it's goodby, children, I will have to
  go,
Where de rain can't fall and de wind
  won't blow;
And your ulster coats you never there
  will need,
When you ride up in de chariot in de
  morn.
(*Chorus*)

Now your golden slippers must be
  shiny clean,
And your gloves de very whitest dat
  were ever seen;
And be sure you're ready when it's time
  to go,
When we ride up in de chariot in de
  morn.
(*Chorus*)

Perhaps the most soul-searching melody by James Bland was the lovely song, "Carry Me Back to Old Virginny." Bland achieved great success as an entertainer and songwriter during the heyday of minstrelsy. His international reputation took him to England where he became popular and prosperous.

205

After an absence of nineteen years he returned to the United States to find that he had become an unknown and forgotten man. He died in 1911, a completely impoverished and dejected man. In 1940 Virginia declared this song as its official state song. Unfortunately, as has happened with so many creative artists throughout history, Bland did not live to see this honor bestowed upon him.

CARRY ME BACK TO OLD VIRGINNY

James A. Bland

Carry me back to old Virginny,
There let me live 'til I wither and decay;
Long by the old dismal swamp have I wandered,

There's where this old darkey's life will pass away.
Massa and Missis have gone on before me,
Soon we will meet on that bright and happy shore;
There we'll be happy and free from all sorrow,
There's where we'll meet and we'll never part no more.

The Gay Nineties

The full impact of the Industrial Revolution in America was experienced in the 1880s. Prior to the mid-nineteenth century, it was the agricultural, mining, and construction industries that expanded at a rapid rate and spread the population westward. Manufacturing accounted for less than one-fifth of American productivity. Shortly after the mid-century, however, manufacturing accounted for approximately one-third of America's production. Goods began to be produced by power-driven machinery and were assembled in factories. Initially, the center of industrial activity was concentrated in the southern New England states. Within a few short years, however, it spread rapidly all along the eastern half of the nation. The railroad, the steamship, the telegraph, and a host of other inventions helped reduce the cost of communication and transportation so that for the first time American goods became competitive with British goods. More and more job opportunities became available, the population increased by leaps and bounds, people swarmed to the cities, and standards of living were on the upgrade. In sum, America was beginning to "bloom"; things were beginning to move quickly in every phase of life. Industrialization demanded a more routinized, disciplined way of living. Money was more plentiful and people were having to adjust to an entirely new way of living in an industrialized society.

The traditional structure of family life was experiencing sudden changes. For one thing, both men and women were now becoming breadwinners and the traditional roles played by young women as housewives, homemakers, and mothers changed to that of secretaries, retailers, and factory workers. Young women were earning their own money and were beginning to achieve personal independence. Societal habits, values, and class mobility changed drastically. Marriages, which had traditionally been arranged between consenting families, were no longer the prevailing custom. Women dressed in much more attractive and enticing fashion and men followed suit in an attempt to attract the prettiest of them. Needless to say, this "liberal" manner of courting was considered shocking by members of the older generation.

The 1890s was a lighthearted and sentimental decade, and for this reason it has been referred to as the Gay Nineties. It was a time of overeating, overdrinking, and conspicuous self-indulgence. Pleasure was king and glamor the focus of attention. In a nutshell, the 1890s was considered by many to be a very naughty period in American life. The lyrics of the tune "Bridget Maguire" illustrate the effect of the times on a poor father of a once respectable and honorable family. He pours out his heart in a song that tells how his daughter Bridget's behavior has changed now that she has gone to work and become independent.

BRIDGET MAGUIRE

My daughter's as fine a young girl as you'll meet,
In your travels day in and day out;
But she's getting high-toned and she's putting on airs,
Since she has been working about.
When she comes home at night from her office,
She walks in with a swag like a fighter;
And she says to her ma, "Look at elegant me!"
Since my daughter plays on the typewriter.

Chorus:
She cries in her sleep, "Your letter's to hand,"
She calls her old father "esquire";
And the neighbors they shout when my daughter turns out,
"There goes Bridget Typewriter Maguire."

She says she's a regular daisy,
Uses slang 'til my poor heart is sore;
She now warbles snatches from operas,
Where she used to sing "Peggy O'Moore."
Now the red on her nails looks ignited,
She's bleached her hair 'til it is lighter,
Now perhaps I should always be mad at the man,
That taught her to play the typewriter.

Sociologists and musicologists consider the 1890s to have been a very exciting time in American history. People enjoyed having a good time and sought every available opportunity to indulge in social activities. They met in local parks and dance halls; they went to the theaters; every day they seemed to find new places to sing, dance, and have fun. Men and women enjoyed dressing up. Women held the rounded, hourglass figure in high esteem and they achieved it by wearing boned corsets and other fancy devices. They wore magnificent dresses, gored shirts with fancy blouses, stunning shoes, dazzling jewelry, gigantic hats, makeup, and nail polish! Men, on the other hand, took to wearing heavily starched collars, fancy shirts, colorful vests, spats over their shoes, straw hats (in season, otherwise they wore caps), and moustaches of individual creation and endless variety. Young men took pleasure in being referred to as "gay" blades. (Today, such a label might well elicit a punch in the nose.) The older generation accused the younger of "going to pot." (The word *pot,* as well as the word *gay,* has obviously acquired other connotations today.)

In addition to the minstrel shows as "the" popular social attraction, the

Variety Show came on the scene around the 1870s, which gave way to the Vaudeville Show of the 1890s. Theater owners went all out to attract a female audience in addition to the usual male clientele. Tony Pastor, considered the "Father of Vaudeville," advertised his theatre by stating that the jokes were clean and the girls covered up. Vaudeville shows were simple to organize. They accommodated individual or group singers accompanied by a single piano or small orchestra, stand-up comedians doing slapstick routines, jugglers, magicians, escape artists, dog acts, and so on. These acts were simply staged and programmed, which lent variety to the show.

There is an axiom in music that says when times are good, music thrives; when times are bad, music becomes suddenly very quiet. Times were exceptionally good during the 1890s, so music was created on demand and in great abundance. Everyone (literally) was singing and dancing and music was the prime ingredient used to satisfy their fondest yearnings.

One of the most distinctive types of music to emerge during this era was barbershop singing. It is speculated that the practice originated in England where barbershops actually were known to be centers of musical activity. Today, our barbershops provide waiting customers with magazines to read and soft background music to listen to as they pass the time waiting for their turn. In those days, however, barbers provided their waiting customers with musical instruments to play and encouraged them to sing as well. Barbershop singing took on some rather sophisticated airs as two or more gentlemen would attempt to create some standard (or even some elaborate) harmony in support of a well-known, favorite melody. This was done entirely by ear through the trial-and-error approach; thus, a considerable number of hours was spent searching out agreeable and pleasing harmonies.

Harmony received unprecedented attention during the 1890s. As a matter of fact, anyone who was relegated to singing the melody considered himself to be a second-rate singer. To be able to sing harmony was the "in-thing." Barbershop singing was exported to America and spread far beyond the confines of the barbershop itself, all the way to college campuses, dance halls, fraternal clubs, and anywhere else that people gathered together to work out harmonized arrangements to good tunes.

Barbershop singing was done in "close" harmony because men's voices encompass only a small range of sounds. The music was written for four voice classifications—first tenor, second tenor, baritone, and bass. The melody was ordinarily sung by the second tenor (a singer with a high voice who cannot reach the highest tenor tones and who has a darker quality in sound). The first tenor would sing a harmony part just above the melody. The baritone, in turn, would sing a harmony part just below the melody. The bass was often the featured singer and would perform the lowest and most fundamental tones, adding fancy embellishments as well. Duets, trios, quartets, quintets, sextets, and full male choruses performed this music and "arrangements" on certain songs eventually became standardized. After considerable experimentation, the barbershop quartet emerged as the ideal combination. The four singers could work out their specials to include elaborate harmonizations, the creation of beautiful blending, and the devising of some eye-appealing theatrical movements. Ultimately, all-female (the Sweet Adelines, for example) and mixed male–female groups were formed. The Society for the Preservation and Encouragement of Barber Shop Quartet Singing in America (SPEBSQSA), founded in 1938, is actively involved today in the organization across the nation of hundreds of male and female groups of outstanding musical quality.

The Irish tenor was one of the main ingredients in the popular success of the barbershop quartet. This singer could employ his falsetto (false) voice in a manner that made it impossible to detect the difference between his mature, manly voice (changed voice) and his false (boy soprano) voice. Not only did this provide a more extensive range of vocal sounds to enrich and expand the limited range of sounds available to male singers, but the quality of the Irish tenor voice was one of consummate beauty. It is no wonder that barbershop quartets stole the hearts of the American public in the 1890s and that they still continue to amaze listeners even to our day. In addition to their amazing singing, members of barbershop quartets are true "hams" as performers. Traditionally, these singers are decked out in straw hats, striped shirts, white flannel pants, spats, and white shoes; they may even have a mug of beer in hand. Then, they offer a routine of hand, leg, and body movements that is sure to leave their audiences pleasantly entertained.

In the 1890s bicycle riding served a practical purpose, that is, it was an important and inexpensive mode of travel. However, it held a social value as well, because now boys and girls could go biking together out of sight of their parents. The old model with a large front wheel and a small one in the rear gave way to a bicycle that had wheels of the same size and air-filled tires. There was also a model manufactured for women that allowed them to pedal in long, full dresses without danger of injury and, most especially, while still looking "ladylike." The model that evoked the most excitement was the tandem bicycle, which had two seats, one behind the other. This novelty could accommodate two boys, two girls, or especially, one boy and one girl. Bicycling, then, progressed from being a practical means of transportation to being one of the social delights of the era.

Music has always been known to reflect social aspects of the period and, as such, a number of bicycle songs were produced and popularly enjoyed during this time. The first of these was a song introduced by Tony Pastor that became an immediate hit. Its lilting, waltzlike rhythm touched the heartstrings of both the American youth and their elders. They danced, sang, and harmonized the tune as they pedaled their bikes. "A Bicycle Built for Two," sometimes known as "Daisy Bell," is representative of the happy songs of this period in American history. Its popularity has continued both here in America, and indeed, around the world for the past one hundred years.

A BICYCLE BUILT FOR TWO

Harry Dacre

Romantic songs were produced in great abundance during this time that ran the gamut of boy–girl associations. People enjoyed singing them and could somehow identify with the verbal and musical messages they contained. A popular tune of the day was "The Man on the Flying Trapeze." It is the sad tale of a young lover whose sweetheart was purloined (stolen) by a traveling circus trapeze artist.

THE MAN ON THE FLYING TRAPEZE

Traditional

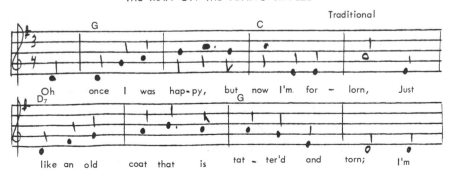

left in this wide world to fret and to morn, be -
tray'd by a maid in her teens.......... The
girl that I loved she was hand - some to see; I
tried all I knew her to please............... But
I could not please her one quar - ter as well, As the
man on the fly - ing tra - peze.......... Oh, He
flies thru' the air, with the great - est of ease, That
dar - ing young man on the fly - ing tra - peze; His
move - ments are grace - ful all girls he does please, And my
love he has pur - loined a - way.................

Another representative song of the 1890s, also in the popular waltz-time rhythm of the period, is "The Sidewalks of New York," or as it was sometimes identified, "East Side, West Side." This song is English in origin; it was written by Charles B. Lawlor, a vaudevillian, and James W. Blake, a hat salesman. It was published in 1894 and first sung by Lottie Gilson in a London theatre. Because the song was about America, it was quickly claimed by Americans as their own.

THE SIDEWALKS OF NEW YORK

Charles Lawlos
James W. Blake

Down in front of Ca - sey's,.........
Old brown wood - en stoop...............
On a sum - mer's eve - ning............ We
formed a mer - ry group...................
Boys and girls to - geth - er...............
We would sing and waltz............. While
To - ny played the or - gan on the
side - walks of New York...............

Things have changed since those times, Some are up in "G",
Others, they are wanderers, but they all feel just like me;
They'd part with all they've got, could they once more walk
With their best girl and have a twirl on the sidewalks of New York.
(*Chorus*)

During the 1890s Americans were showered with all kinds of new inventions that drastically changed their way of life. The incandescent bulb, the telegraph, the steam engine, the typewriter, and the telephone all had a tremendous impact on people's lives. Like the bicycle, the telephone served a functional purpose; however, it soon became a medium for the conduct of romantic relationships as well. The song "Hello, My Baby" portrays the burning love that one young man is experiencing and the way in which he is going about getting his answer.

HELLO, MY BABY

Joseph E. Howard & Ida Emerson

Hel-lo my ba-by, hel-lo my hon-ey, hel-lo my rag-time gal..... Send me a kiss by wire, Ba-by my heart's on fire; If you re-fuse me, hon-ey you'll lose me, then you'll be left a — lone, oh ba-by tel-e-phone and tell me I'se your own...........

One of the most serious of the songs of the Gay Nineties and perhaps the simplest and most expressive of all American songs is the inimitable "Tell Me Why." This song easily lends itself to harmonization and is therefore a favorite at community sings and campouts.

TELL ME WHY

Traditional

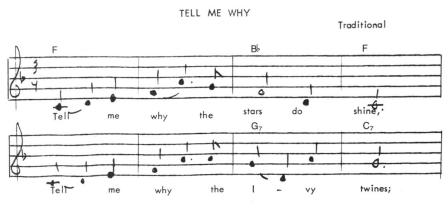

Tell me why the stars do shine; Tell me why the i — vy twines;

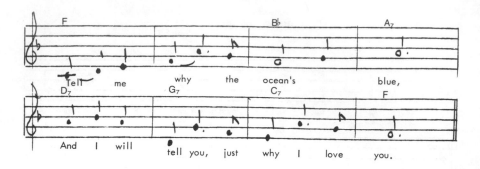

Because God made the stars to shine,
Because God made the ivy twine,
Because God made the ocean blue,
That is the reason why I love you.

The list of songs from this grand decade in American history is seemingly endless. Some of the more popular tunes are: "Ta Ra Ra Boom Te Aye," "My Sweetheart's the Man in the Moon," "The Bowery," "After the Ball," "The Band Played On," "A Hot Time in the Old Town Tonight," "Sweet Rosie O'Grady," "When you Were Sixteen," "Frankie and Johnny," "My Wild Irish Rose," "While Strolling Through the Park One Day," "In the Good Old Summertime," "You Tell Me Your Dreams," "Up in a Balloon," and "Sweetheart of Sigma Chi."

It should be stressed that American folk music during the nineteenth century made a transition from a more personal (individual or group), anonymous, rural, and highly simplistic type of music to one where songs were produced for the people, printed, had known authors or composers, were slightly more sophisticated in development, and were more urbanized. There was wider socialization among people, new modes of living, and more demand for recreational activities and a variety of popular musical theatres. What was important was that Americans were continuing to sing and sing as they never had before, in more places and with greater participation. This trend reached its apex with the ushering in of the twentieth century. With it came a sudden change from singing to dancing as the fashionable social activity. Chapter 13 addresses this turn about.

13

Folk Song Survival and Revival

With the beginning of the twentieth century Americans embarked on a high-speed chase that predictably led them to sudden disaster. The crash came in 1929 that brought the American economic bonanza to an abrupt halt and ushered in its subsequent depression. The factors that were the main ingredients in the brewing cauldron of disaster were many and varied. The American Industrial Revolution had given rise to the creation of a technological revolution that in turn gave birth to such significant inventions as the gasoline- and electrical-powered motors. These inventions were ingeniously adapted to power automobiles, airplanes, ships, and trains, thereby making communication between people and places incredibly fast. The whole pace of living was accelerated because these modern monsters were able to move objects and people faster than anything man had ever previously known or experienced. Additionally, these motors were wisely used in factories and industry to power new machines devised to make the manufacture of goods and gadgets a precise and seemingly effortless process.

As if the invention of the new motors in and of itself was not phenomenal enough, the cost of operating them was of comparatively little consequence. For one thing, Americans had discovered literally thousands of bottomless reservoirs of "black gold" that could be refined into a number of highly useful petroleum products. Gasoline to power motors became abundant, relatively inexpensive, and therefore, in great demand. Likewise, the thousands of natural rivers and waterways across the country became prime targets for civil engineers who began damming them up with incredible-looking structures to help provide the water power necessary to produce electricity, again at an unbelievably low dollar cost. Cheap energy then became the catalyst to industrial success. America was definitely on the move and cheap and abundant power was the underlying key to the movement.

An additional factor that played a significant role in the economic thrust of the twentieth century was the mass migration of immigrants to our shores. America had been the haven of refuge for thousands of immigrants during the eighteenth and nineteenth centuries. Many of these people were primarily seeking religious and personal freedom. The new breed of immigrants of the twentieth century were coming primarily to better their standards of living. The rapid pace at which immigrants were flocking to America was beyond comprehension. In the short span of twenty years a total of over fifteen million people had immigrated to the American mainland. Mostly, they came from eastern and southern Europe. They were Italians, Poles, Czechs, Hungarians, Greeks, Rumanians, Frenchmen, Germans, Russians, Ukranians, and especially, Jews. As a matter of fact, approximately ten percent of the European immigrants were of Jewish extraction, people who had been treated repressively and who therefore sought religious and personal freedom along with a chance for survival. Orientals, too, arrived in large numbers. They were transported to our shores both legally and illegally. So, too, Canadians and Mexicans invaded from the north and south, respectively. America had opened its hands and hearts, inviting the world's "tired and poor." The response was overwhelming as these oppressed people sought the better life.

This huge pool of immigrants provided our eager industries with another ingredient needed to achieve quick success, and that was, cheap labor. Immigrants crowded into endless rows of tenement houses in the dirtiest and dingiest sections of the cities; they worked six full days a week, ten to twelve hours a day, in crowded, airless, and comfortless factories, for peasant wages. These factories came to be known as *sweatshops*. The "sweater" was a foreman whose job it was to dole out the work, determine the wages, and deliver his profits to the industrial barons who, without the burden of personal and corporate income taxes, could store away their fortunes or scurrilously invest them in the stock market. Most of the immigrants were ignorant, or rather, uneducated. Their pressing need was for a job that would provide them with the basic necessities of life—food and shelter. They were perfect targets for exploitation. Thus, along with cheap power, an abundant source of cheap labor made the industrial dream a reality.

The eastern seaboard no longer remained the sole center of industrial activity. As the central and western sections of the nation became more heavily populated, there began to appear a sudden growth of cities and other urban settlements in these parts of the country as well. Thus, the trend from a primarily rural to a primarily urban nation was swiftly taking place during the first two decades of the twentieth century. There were some other factors that played an important role in determining the sociological and economic changes that would have an impact on the way of folk songs in America. However, the two we have mentioned here—cheap power and cheap labor— were perhaps the most important in altering the course of American life of this period.

The first half of the twentieth century could aptly be described as a "folk song void." All the ingredients necessary for the creation, dissemination, and popularization of folk music had suddenly disappeared. Group traditionalism was temporarily shelved and attention was given instead to progress, modernization, and social mobility. Society suddenly became interested in seizing every available opportunity to better itself; thus, the rich became richer, the enterprising aspired to become middle class, and the poor became less poor. Pride in one's place in life (as, for instance, a railroader, cowboy, miner, or lumberjack) gave way to a primary interest in bettering one's position for the ultimate goal of accumulating wealth. Success was the key word and the main preoccupation was on seeking out all available opportunities and capitalizing on them.

Workers in rural America interacted in a slow-moving, quiet environment, so a song could occupy their time and enrich their spirits. On the other hand, workers in an industrial society interacted in a fast-moving, noisy environment. They were more intent on completing tasks on a piece-work basis, so they had no time to waste in singing. Thus, Americans suddenly just stopped singing. Folk music was supplanted by jazz, the new American craze. America was on the move and jazz more appropriately identified with this new trend. Jazz was essentially an instrumental expression, so as a result, it inspired dancing and singing became a mere by-product. Dancing replaced singing as the primary focus of social interaction. Collectively, Americans gave birth to the great Jazz Age where both men and women gathered together in saloons and nightclubs to drink and dance to jazz or to attend the newest form of musical theater, the Broadway musical, where jazz greatly influenced the music that was heard.

Some members of the musical intelligentsia of the day claimed that jazz was essentially folk music. According to them, Americans were still involved in producing, disseminating, and enjoying folk music, only in this instance it was instrumental folk music rather than vocal folk music. It is true that both forms are essentially "people" music; however, the similarity stops there. There are many characteristics of folk music and jazz that are similar and could lead to the (superficial) conclusion that they are identical. What separates the two, however, is the purpose and intent of their expressions. Folk music is involved in the communication of a tale, story, or significant thought in which the performer uses words and music combined to get his message across. On the other hand, jazz is involved in the use of a musical theme or tune and the development of a series of variations, spontaneous or intentional, to communicate an essentially musical message.

People of different ethnic origins continued in their "old world" ways as they clustered together in their separate areas in the cities' ghettos. Their main concern was survival, but they took whatever pleasure they could in singing and dancing to their "old world" music, while at the same time they slowly absorbed the music of their newly adopted country. In summary,

Americans turned their attention to the new craze for jazz, which was more compatible with the social mores of the period. Singing did not come to an abrupt halt, although it was not as popular with the people as it had been in the immediate past.

Fortunately, there was a small group of dedicated and determined folk singers and folklorists who, despite the trend of the times, held tenaciously to their love and respect for American folk music. They worked to unearth, collect, preserve, protect, and perform our national musical treasures. For the most part, they worked quietly and received little, if any, national attention; but they derived personal satisfaction from their involvement with American folk music, whether it was vocationally or, more often, avocationally. Their outstanding work has since received the highest praise. Without their efforts, much of what we have today that represents our national treasury of folk songs may very well have been lost because the transmission of folklore depends to a great degree on an unbroken chain of generations for their safekeeping.

It is difficult to know where to begin to give credit for this heroic effort, who to include and who to exclude. Fortunately, there are a number of persons about whom there is general agreement regarding their place in this great society of friends.

A charter member of the older generation who was a pioneer in the collection and preservation of American folk songs was John A. Lomax. Lomax grew up along the Chisholm Trail and, as a small boy, he was intrigued with the singing of the cowboys. With the help of a fellowship at Harvard University, he initiated the first bona fide survey of American folk music, which concentrated on the music of the cowboy and blacks living in the west and southwest areas of the country. With the publication of his book, *Cowboy Songs,* he aroused interest in research into the musical heritage of America. In the 1930s, with the use of the phonograph and the generosity of the Carnegie and Rockefeller Foundations, Lomax and his son Alan ventured out into America in search of folk music to record, document, and codify. These recordings became the basis of a more extended collection that now comprises the Archives of American Folk Song, located in the Library of Congress in Washington, D.C.

The contributions of Carl Sandburg, eminent Lincoln scholar, must be acknowledged. Sandburg's *American Songbag* contains a representative selection of tunes with interesting anecdotal information. Sandburg availed himself of every opportunity to talk about the rich depository of folk music that abounded in America, waiting to be discovered. He would take out his guitar at the slightest provocation and share his favorite songs accompanied with some supporting chatter. Sandburg's prominence as scholar–teacher did much to give folk music some degree of credibility.

The English folklorist, Cecil J. Sharp, rightfully deserves membership in this most illustrious group. Although he was a British subject that came to

America to search for the "lost" folk music of his country, Sharp shared his findings with the American public and helped awaken them to the wealth and variety of American folk music that was ripe for discovery. His book, *English Folk Songs from the Southern Appalachians,* is a definitive work and held in high esteem by our scholar–folklorists.

Charles Seeger was deeply involved in the early attempts at unearthing and preserving our folk heritage. As a trained musicologist, he gave his scholarly attention not so much to the Bachs and Beethovens of classical music but rather to American music per se. Seeger was an inspiration to his several disciples and he took a more scholarly approach in his folklore involvements. He was witness to a number of movements connected with the drive to collect, codify, and have songs published. Interestingly, he witnessed both the sterile times in American folk song production and the grand, glorious times.

Finally, among the older generation, John Jacob Niles holds an esteemed place. Niles, a trained singer with a high tenor voice of chilling quality, has been labeled "the dean of American balladeers." A native Kentuckian, Niles scoured the Southern Mountains to coax songs out of the hill folk; he wrote them down in musical notation and popularized them in performance. He was content to remain in the region of his birth and ventured away from it only when he was on tour. A few of the well-known songs associated with Niles are "Black Is the Color of My True Love's Hair" and "I Wonder as I Wander." Niles should be given credit not only for his work in collecting American folk music and reviving its popularity, but also as one of the first to gain success as a singer of American folk songs.

The second generation of staunch friends of American folk music had a great deal more in common amongst themselves than did the first generation—that is, they were all balladeers. The younger group were primarily itinerant singers who roamed the countryside sharing their favorite songs and, in turn, picking up any new ones that seemed of exceptional quality. These people worked tangentially with members of the older group, profiting from their advice, counsel, friendship, and especially, from the bag of songs that they had already compiled. Perhaps their most important contribution was the example they set concerning what a good American balladeer or folk singer should be. It was their model that the younger singers of the second half of the century emulated. To say that they were extremely influential would be an understatement. Again, it is difficult to know where to begin and who to include or exclude. Certainly, the select few we shall mention here have made an indelible mark on folk music in America.

The legendary Leadbelly (born Huddie Leadbetter) vividly characterizes the American stereotype of the solitary collector and presenter of folk songs in the 1930s and 1940s. However, there was one notable exception—his violent nature was in direct contrast to the peaceful, compassionate folk singer of the ensuing years. Leadbetter's life was made of the stuff that produces a best-selling book or movie. Leadbelly was a living embodiment of the old adage about "wine, women, and song." In and out of prison, with a girlfriend in every town, desperately poor at times, then a winner at others, Leadbelly would sing for anyone who would listen. His listeners ranged from audiences of one to several hundred. (He actually sang his way out of two prison terms!)

Large in physical stature, his voice was deep, powerful, and highly resonant. He once heard someone playing a twelve-string guitar (each of the strings doubled) at a circus and decided that was what he needed to match his big voice. Leadbelly claimed to be the king of the twelve-string guitar players of the world. He worked with John and Alan Lomax in the 1930s, traveling, collecting, performing, and recording folk songs, especially in the prisons of the land. He soon gave this up to live the rest of his life doing what he loved best—wandering, womanizing, and singing.

Leadbelly carried in excess of one thousand songs in his head and he could sing for hours without ever repeating himself. The song by which he was first widely known was "Goodnight, Irene." It is a beautiful tune and contains that magic which makes a folk song's popularity last forever.

GOODNIGHT, IRENE

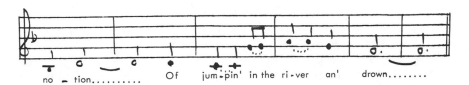

no - tion......... Of jum-pin' in the ri-ver an' drown.......

I asked your mother for you,
She told me you were too young;
I wish to the Lawd I'd never seen your
    face,
I'm sorry you ever was born.
(*Chorus*)

Last Saturday night I got married,
Me an' my wife settled down;
Now me an' my wife have parted,
Gonna take me a stroll uptown.
(*Chorus*)

Stop ramblin' an' quit your gamblin',
Quit stayin' out late at night;
Go home with your wife an' your
    family,
Sit down by the fireside bright.
(*Chorus*)

I love Irene, God knows I do,
Love her 'til the sea runs dry;
And if Irene turns her back on me,
I'm gonna take morphine and die.
(*Chorus*)

Burl Ives was born into a singing family of English–Irish extraction. He left college in 1929 to begin his life as a "wayfaring stranger," a label that he was destined to retain throughout his professional career. Ives leaned toward the country-type folk literature in his early years and later developed a much broader repertoire that even included English ballads. He exemplified the ideal model of the relaxed storyteller, a style widely emulated by the upcoming generation of American folk singers. His wanderings eventually took him to the coffee houses of New York City where he began his dual career as folk singer and actor.

Ives was content to work as a loner in the field of folk music. He completely detached himself from the "people movements" in which several of his professional folknik peers became involved. Whatever his reasons may have been for this, Ives did leave an indelible mark on the manner in which a musical tale should be communicated and exerted a lasting influence on his many disciples. Ives concentrated on selecting the best folk songs for his style and then presented them in the most effective and authentic manner possible.

Pete Seeger also shares an enviable reputation as folk singer and role model. Basically a common, humble man with simple, basic human values, Seeger has enjoyed a long and successful career as collector, performer, and creator of folk songs. His most notable contribution, however, was stimulating people into participating in various kinds of folk activity. As such, he has played a dominant role in the folk revival movement of the 1960s and in getting concerts and gatherings organized in which people and music could be joined together in joy and personal satisfaction. In this capacity, Seeger interacted with everyone who was involved in the folk survival and revival movements. He assisted John and Alan Lomax with their research projects on

American folk music; he sang with the Almanac Singers and with the trend-setting Weavers; he worked passionately and sincerely with the forces for peace and human rights; and finally, he achieved great success as a balladeer and songwriter. Suffice it to say that Seeger's contributions to American folk music have been multifaceted and deeply profound. His songs will be discussed in Chapter 14.

Woody Guthrie's contributions were incalculable. Not content with the task of collecting songs and performing them, Woody made his greatest mark as spokesman for the various peoples with whom he interacted. In this role he became an innovator within the broad spectrum of folk music. He wrote songs that helped convey to the general public that which these people were keeping in their hearts or conveying awkwardly in speech and actions. Woody could communicate a message in a song so profoundly and yet so simply. Thus, he became a most effective spokesman for his people. It is in this facet of his career that Woody made his greatest impact on America's aspiring folk singers. One of his most promising admirers, Bob Dylan, later went on to win all the "Oscars" as spokesman of the people. He learned his craft well from his great teacher.

Woody Guthrie's songs range from the simplistic, those patterned on the early, rural-type of American folk songs, to the most profound, those filled with poetry of deep meaning and music of high sophistication. "This Land Is Your Land" is sung and revered by every American. Most assuredly, it will always enjoy a place in the American Heritage songbooks. The song describes America in simple terms, yet with a majesty to equal that in "America the Beautiful."

THIS LAND IS YOUR LAND

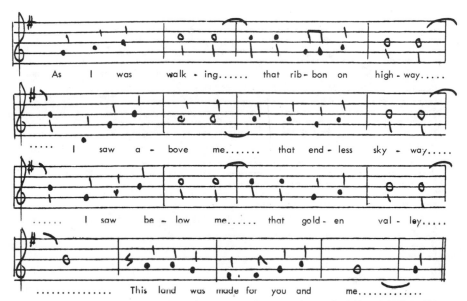

As I was walk-ing...... that rib-bon on high-way.....

..... I saw a - bove me....... that end-less sky - way.....

...... I saw be - low me...... that gold - en val - ley.....

.... This land was made for you and me.............

Words and music by Woody Guthrie. TRO—© Copyright 1956, 1958 and 1970 Ludlow Music, Inc., New York, N.Y. Used by permission.

I've roamed and rambled
And I followed my footsteps,
To the sparkling sands of
Her diamond deserts;
And all around me
A voice was sounding
This land was made for you and me.
(*Chorus*)

When the sun comes shining,
And I was strolling,
And the wheatfields waving,
And the dust clouds rolling,
And the fog was lifting,
A voice was chanting,
This land was made for you and me.
(*Chorus*)

Likewise, "So Long, It's Been Good to Know Yuh" holds a permanent place in the song repository of America. After "Auld Lang Syne," it ranks as the most popular parting song of this century. The song is so singable and easy to remember that it is no wonder it has been a favorite with the general public.

SO LONG, IT'S BEEN GOOD TO KNOW YUH

C   G₇

I've sung this song but I'll sing it a - gain, Of the

C   G₇   C

place where I lived on the wild, wind - y plains; In the month called

225

April, the coun·ty called Gray
Here's what all of the
peo - ple there say;(sing-ing) So....... Long, it's been good to
know yuh, So........ Long it's been good to know yuh,
So........ Long it's been good to know yuh, This dust-y old
dust is a get - tin' my home, And I've got to be
drift - in' a - long........

Words and Music by Woody Guthrie. TRO © Copyright 1940 (renewed 1968), 1950 (renewed 1978) and 1951 (renewed 1979). Folkways Music Publishers, Inc., New York, N.Y. Used by permission.

A dust storm hit and it hit like a
    thunder,
It dusted us over and covered us under;
It blocked out the traffic and blocked
    out the sun,
And straight for home all the people
    did run.
(*Chorus*)

We talked on the end of the world, and
    then,
We'd sing a song, and then sing it
    again;
We'd sit for an hour and not say a
    word,

And then these words would be heard.
(*Chorus*)

The sweethearts sat in the dark and
    they sparked,
They hugged and kissed in that dusty
    old dark;
They sighed and cried, hugged and
    kissed,
Instead of marriage they talked like this,
    honey.
(*Chorus*)

Now, the telephone rang and it jumped
    off the wall,

226

That was the preacher a-makin' his call;
He said, "Kind friend, this may be the end,
You've got your last chance of salvation of sin."
(*Chorus*)

The churches was jammed and the churches was packed,

And that dusty old storm blowed so black;
The preacher could not read a word of his text,
And he folded his specs and he took up collection, said,
(*Chorus*)

"Pretty Boy Floyd" is Woody's masterpiece. It is beautifully constructed, both in words and music. It tells of a modern-day Robin Hood who is in a constant race with the law. He restores to the poor those things that they have been deprived of due to their unfortunate positions in life. The lyrics "Some will rob you with a six-gun, And some with a fountain pen," aptly described the situation that existed among the poor and destitute in the Oklahoma dustbowl during the 1930s.

PRETTY BOY FLOYD

PRETTY BOY FLOYD by Woody Guthrie. © Copyright 1961, 1962 by FALL RIVER MUSIC INC. All rights reserved. Used by permission.

It was in the town of Shawnee,
It was Saturday afternoon;
His wife beside him in the wagon,
As into town they rode.

There a deputy sheriff approached him,
In a manner rather rude,

Using vulgar words of language,
And his wife she overheard.

Pretty Boy grabbed a log chain,
And the deputy grabbed a gun;
And in the fight that followed,
He laid that deputy down.

He took to the trees and timbers,
And he lived a life of shame;
Every crime in Oklahoma,
Was added to his name.

Yes, he took to the trees and timbers,
On that Canadian River's shore;
And Pretty Boy found a welcome,
At many a farmer's door.

There's many a starvin' farmer
The same old story told;
How this outlaw paid their mortgage
And saved their little home.

Others tell you 'bout a stranger
That come to beg a meal;
And underneath his napkin,
Left a thousand dollar bill.

It was in Oklahoma City,
It was on Christmas day;
There came a whole carload of
   groceries
With a letter that did say,

"You say that I'm an outlaw,
You say that I'm a thief;
Here's a Christmas dinner
For the families on relief."

Now through this world I ramble,
I see lots of funny men;
Some will rob you with a six-gun,
And some with a fountain pen.

But as through this life you travel,
As through this life you roam;
You won't never see an outlaw,
Drive a family from their home.

The last and the youngest of the influential folk singers is a woman, one of the first of her sex to enter the scene and to earn a place among the giants of the art. Because of her efforts and her dedication, Joan Baez has earned the title "high priestess of American folk music." Be this as it may, her most impressive quality is her consummate musicianship. Joan Baez has a truly distinctive voice, with a fast vibrato and a throaty tone that combine with incredible fluidity to produce a pleasing sound that is both hauntingly beautiful and entirely unmatched. Her artistic singing and guitar playing are testimonials to her superior sensitivity to music.

Joan Baez's first encounter with music came at the beginning of the rock and roll era, when she was twelve years of age. Visiting a coffee house at the age of seventeen with her dad, Dr. Albert Baez, she became enamored with folk music and launched a career that has rarely veered from the straight and narrow path. She first appeared in a larger than intimate setting at the Newport Folk Festival in 1959. The invitation came from Bob Gibson, and her name didn't even appear on the printed program. One year later, at the same festival, it was Joan Baez whom everyone was raving about.

Joan Baez has focused her musical attention on both the old and the new songs which she finds to be vehicles of musical and verbal worth, songs she prefers to share with her listeners in an intimate setting rather than in a concert hall. In recent years, she has refused many offers to appear on television, in films, even in nightclubs; she prefers, rather, to work in intimate settings. She produces one recording per year and tours only two months during the year. Joan Baez will always hold a lasting place in the annals of American folk history. Her contributions are well chronicled in recordings and written testimonials; her influence has touched the lives of all contemporary folk singers, both male and female.

Thus, the first half of the twentieth century may be described as a period of folk survival during which Americans immersed themselves in their fast-moving sociological milieu with the prime focus of attention on the accumulation of wealth. In the sphere of music, dancing and jazz music held sway. Only a handful of dedicated folk artists carried on the courageous fight to collect, preserve, and transmit our vast heritage of American folk music.

Revival

Around the middle of the twentieth century, with the economic boom that followed the aftermath of World War II, a dramatic sociological phenomenon began to sweep the nation. A number of significant factors underlaid the movement that helped trigger the change. Youth, especially a frightened and disenchanted youth, have always been at the heart of a concerted demand for societal change. American youth, in great abundance, was to be found in the very eye of the hurricane. Despite the fact that World War II had been fought on foreign soil, the population figures in the United States revealed that the total casualties from the conflict amounted to over one million with nearly 300,000 of those deaths incurred in battle. This figure was offset by a population explosion composed of "war babies" who, when considered against the whole, constituted roughly one-third of the total population of the country. This bulging segment of the populace, narrow in age range, had all kinds of implications, politically as well as economically and socially. It was a group to be acknowledged and carefully monitored. Astonishingly enough, the mean age of living Americans in 1950 plummeted to an incredible all-time low of 30.2 years of age.*

During the mid-fifties, these "war babies" were entering their teen years. They began to look at their future with jaundiced eyes. For one thing, they witnessed the events revolving around the civil rights of minority groups within our borders. These events were legally resolved in the hallmark decision of the Supreme Court of May 17, 1954 that declared segregation unconstitutional. It seemed unconscionable that a nation that had just recently fought in a war to preserve the democratic principle of human rights could, at the very same time, deny some of its own people that precious privilege of freedom. Needless to say, this seeming conflict of values was difficult to comprehend, especially by youth who were living in a "land of plenty" where day-to-day survival was not a factor. These youths, therefore, were able to turn their attention to ideological and human interest issues.

Closely connected with the human rights issue were the McCarthy trials in which people were being persecuted for any word or action that could in any way be construed as "un-American." The Bill of Rights had long guaran-

---

*With the post-war economic boom the birth rate continued to rise; the mean age was 29.5 years in 1960 and 28.0 years in 1970.

teed all Americans the freedom to speak and write without reprisal. Suppression of one's right to express an opinion was contrary to the spirit and letter of the Constitution, yet the trials continued unabated in which leading Americans—such as Pete Seeger from the folk community—were subjected to strong-arm tactics under the guise of Congressional investigation. These goings-on were difficult for our young Americans to understand.

American youth also began to question the particular goals to which Americans were now addressing themselves, that is, the accumulation of material goods and money. They also witnessed the dishonest means through which large corporations and individual businessmen pursued their goals. Ruthless and dishonest business practices were routinely dismissed by their "perpetrators" as the way of the American jungle. American youth looked hesitantly at this way of life and pondered the thought of having to become a part of this commercial morass. Again, the majority of American youth had everything they needed and most of what they wanted; money was not a real problem, so they could afford to concern themselves with moral values.

These youths were conceived during World War II, grew up with the Korean conflict, the Cold War with Communism, and the constant threat of nuclear destruction. It was more than they could tolerate. Almost at once, these "war babies" turned their backs on the "great society" that their forefathers had created and chose instead a simple, uncomplicated life reminiscent of early, rural America. They elected to identify with such cherished human values as honesty, brotherhood, love, and peace.

Their rejection of the American dream took on many forms. With regard to music, theirs was a highly positive movement that heralded a return to group traditionalism. Renewed attention was given to the songs of early Americans, songs sung by whole groups of people in a simple, nonprofessional, strictly casual manner. It was an attempt on the part of youthful Americans and of later Americans in general to rediscover themselves through the singing of songs created at a time when America was composed of genuine, simple-hearted people. Folk music is inextricably bonded to the history and sociology of the people, that is, to their deepest feelings. It was no wonder that youth turned to the folk songs of their forefathers in order to assist them in rediscovering themselves and charting a new course for the future. They searched for their roots in a place and at a time when Americans were a great people engaged in building a new nation for free and morally honest individuals.

The folk revival that came about as a result of their actions was more than a musical phenomenon; it was a musical renaissance! Ironic as it may seem, Americans as a people suddenly began doing what a few devoted folk artists had been doing throughout the first half of the century—bringing back the songs of America's glorious past. At first, the movement confined itself to the singing of selected songs from the past, songs that exemplified America in its finest hours, especially songs that emphasized freedom in its broadest and most idealistic framework. These songs were performed in traditional and casual settings, but with a new purpose—that of voicing a gentle protest on life in America as it was being lived. At the same time they were suggesting a return to the "good life" as a goal for the future. This countercultural movement began to produce new songs that would pointedly express people's innermost feelings on the present state of things and their desires for the future. The process involved in the production of the new songs was no different than that which people had always employed to express their personal feelings—with one notable exception. This time the creators became well-known individuals and their utterances appeared in a single, original version.

College campuses became the main centers of folk activity. Students could be found carrying their guitars, gathering together in informal groups, singing and playing their favorite songs. When they tired of playing their guitars, they passed the instruments on to the persons next to them who, surprisingly, could manage to play with equal, if not surpassing, skill. Parents of students flippantly referred to their offspring as "my son (daughter) the folk singer." The "hootenanny" soon became the "in-thing." Campus "hoots" showcased group traditionalism in its purest form. People gathered together to listen to and participate in the singing of a wide variety of both familiar and new folk songs. The hootenanny was to folk music what the jam session was to jazz, that is, a gathering of the faithful where a nucleus of musicians were on hand to perform. The invitation was always open for anyone to "sit in." Hootenannies provided an excellent outlet for personal emotions as well as an opportunity for whole groups of people to engage in some fun.

Besides "hoots," folk songs were also performed by aspiring musicians in coffee houses, which were fast appearing in several cities across the nation. Additionally, folk festivals were being organized that ranged from intimate to those that would attract thousands of eager enthusiasts. Folk groups could also be heard on (the recently invented) television. Americans could also listen to folk music at their leisure through recordings that were now being made, as well as on long-playing, nonbreakable discs or tapes. Suffice it to say that the folk song revival produced a ready market for the commercially enterprising as well as for the sincere lovers of the art. It would be safe to say that the song repertoire of the 1950s and 1960s was restrictive enough to be labeled "generation music." The American youth movement had fairly well determined, through their participation and dollars, which songs would be rediscovered and even provided the basis of inspiration for the creation of songs that would speak for their generation.

Before proceeding to a discussion of particular individuals and groups, it might be well to point up a number of new, representative songs that emerged during this period in America's musical history. These songs come under the umbrella of "generation songs"; however, they are rather special and could better be identified as "message songs." The quality of the poetry found in their lyrics is on a considerably higher level than that which appeared in earlier folk materials. The words are far more profound, carry a deeper meaning, and cannot be interpreted superficially. In early American folk music, the words were simple and easy to understand; in the new songs the words had a deeper significance.

"If I Had a Hammer" was written in the late 1950s by Pete Seeger (music) and Lee Hayes (words), both of whom were members of the folk group, the Weavers. The lyrics cannot be taken on face value, for to do so would be to completely miss the song's message. In this song the hammer is used symbolically as an instrument to try to signal people all over this land of the dangers that are befalling them. At the same time the hammer is used to help mold people back into loving their brothers and their sisters. The fourth and final verse spells out what each individual is capable of doing given the proper symbolic tools. The song has all the usual qualities of a great folk song, but it also carries a provocative message that is delivered in much the same way as a church sermon, only in song.

IF I HAD A HAMMER

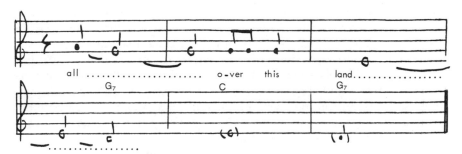

all .... o-ver this land...............

G₇   C   G₇

Words and Music by Lee Hays and Pete Seeger. TRO © Copyright 1958 and 1962. Ludlow Music, Inc., New York, N.Y. Used by permission.

If I had a bell,
I'd a-ring it in the morning;
I'd a-ring it in the evening,
All over this land.
I'd a-ring out danger,
I'd a-ring out warning,
I'd a-ring out love between
My brothers and my sisters
All over this land.

If I had a song,
I'd a-sing it in the morning;
I'd a-sing it in the evening,
All over this land.
I'd a-sing out danger,

I'd a-sing out warning,
I'd a-sing out love between
My brothers and my sisters
All over this land.

Well, I got a hammer,
And I've got a bell,
And I've got a song,
All over this land.
It's the hammer of justice,
It's the bell of freedom,
It's the song about love between
My brothers and my sisters
All over this land.

Bob Dylan's first major contribution to the world of American folk music, and especially to the troubled youth of the fifties, was the trend-setting song, "Blowin' in the Wind." The song had a singable melody that was easy to remember. More than that, however, it had the kind of lyrics that were unmatched in folk music in terms of sheer poetic beauty and depth of content. Dylan's song raised the pertinent questions of the day and asked them with artistic flair. The answers to these questions, he told his friends, were "blowin' in the wind." The song became the unofficial "alma mater" of the youthful protesters who demanded immediate solutions to such problems as world injustice, hunger, nuclear war, environmental pollution, and so on. The song was so good that it went beyond its initial purpose for presentation and became a song for old and young alike, regardless of their personal beliefs and involvements.

Even though youthful protesters fought diligently yet peacefully to achieve their objectives, many found the obstacles before them to be insurmountable and as taking too long to effect. As a recourse, they sought some kind of temporary escapism. Alcohol was available, but it was considered to be the tranquilizer of the older generation from whom many had alienated themselves. "Their world" would become completely detached from the source of their problems. Foolishly, they chose drugs that ranged from marijuana on up to such hallucinogenic and mind-boggling drugs as LSD. Several songs cut on the folk song mold were created that dealt with this type of adventurism in a kind of cleverly disguised language. The general public sang these songs purely on the level of their musical appeal, never purposefully delving into their underlying messages. They were certainly understood and enjoyed by the members of the drug culture.

"Mr. Tambourine Man," also by Bob Dylan, has all of the earmarks of a simple, enjoyable contemporary folk song. Adults and young children alike sang this song with complete abandon and never questioned its lyrics. On the surface, the message of the song was innocent enough. The song described a Tambourine Man, a presumably poor, physically handicapped person looking for coins to be deposited in his tambourine in exchange for a song. The general public never read into the story that the Tambourine Man was really a drug pusher and that the product to be exchanged was on the surface "a song," but in reality, some kind of drug. Obviously, within the commercial world the latter interpretation of the lyrics was strongly denied.

By the sixties, folk music had become big business and highly commercialized. A tremendous market was in operation for sheet music, instruments, public appearances, and recordings. Many of the producers and consumers of the new revival were more than traditionalists, they were purists. These people continued to fight the good fight for integrity and authenticity as the commercialists waved millions of dollars before their eyes to bend just a little and give the larger audiences more of what they wanted. The "folkniks," as they were called, courageously stuck to their guns, preferring to sing in intimate settings and to perform their songs with orthodox authenticity.

There was also a growing number of "new wing" folk artists who wanted to move with the times and make their presentations relevant. They took liberties with traditional songs, embraced with open arms the new literature of the day, and protested both gently and pointedly in addition to performing before huge audiences. The cold war was fought between the two factions for fully two decades, with each group claiming victory and going on its separate way.

The Weavers were trendsetters. Originally composed of Pete Seeger, Ronnie Gilbert, Lee Hayes, and Fred Hellerman, Seeger left the group in 1958 to seek his own career and was replaced by Erik Darling. The Weavers represented the perfect blending of four outstanding musicians who adhered to one philosophy, blended beautiful music, and created some very satisfying arrangements on each of their well-chosen songs. Struggling at first in a sea where American folk music was still an unknown entity, they finally made their mark at a Christmas Eve concert in Carnegie Hall in 1955. Their singing and playing was bright, cheerful, and very entertaining. They were the first group to expose the general public to the joy of folk songs, singing such tunes as Leadbelly's "Good Night, Irene," the traditional "On Top of Old Smoky," and their big hit, "Kisses Sweeter Than Wine."

The Weavers were soon followed by a host of singing balladeers, all differing in size of membership, gender, instrumentation, and so forth, but all presenting their wares with the same kind of cheerful abandon as did the Weavers. The Kingston Trio (Nick Reynolds, Bob Shane, and David Guard) presented themselves as three clean-cut Americans with no special axe to grind. They were just interested in sharing their songs and informal fun with whomever would come to listen. They topped the charts with their rendition of an old traditional Southern mountain song, "Tom Dooley." The Kingston Trio was the sensational box office attraction of the time.

TOM DOOLEY

Traditional

Hang your head Tom Doo - ley, Hang your head and cry.......
Killed poor Lau -ra Fost - er you know you're bound to die.

Words and music collected, adapted, and arranged by Frank Warner, John A. Lomax, and Alan Lomax. TRO © Copyright 1947 (renewed 1975) and 1958. Ludlow Music, Inc., New York, N.Y. Used by permission.

You took her on the hillside,
As God Almighty knows;
You took her on the hillside
And there you hid her clothes.

You took her on the roadside
Where you begged to be excused;
You took her on the roadside,
Where there you hid her shoes.

Take down my old violin,
And play it all you please,
At this time tomorrow,
It'll be no use to me.

I dug a grave four feet long,
I dug it three feet deep;
And throwed the cold clay o'er her
And tramped it with my feet.

This world and one more then,
Where do you reckon I'd be;
If it hadn't been for Grayson,
I'd-a been in Tennessee.

This old time tomorrow,
Reckon where I'll be;
In some lonesome valley,
A-hangin' on a tree.

The Mitchell Trio was another early group that attained considerable success. The trio was formed at Gonzaga University in Spokane, Washington in 1958 and went through several changes in group members. The particular combination that achieved the greatest popularity was Joe Frazier, Mike Kobluk, and John Denver (who went on in the seventies to become a top solo performer and song writer). The group never had any intentions of becoming famous as folk artists or even as singers of topical-protest songs; they merely wanted to sing songs of their choosing and to sing them with complete freedom. Some of the topical targets addressed in their songs caused a great deal of controversy, yet they stuck to their guns. Their repertoire included traditional songs from the world's library of folk music.

Such solo folk singers as Pete Seeger, Joan Baez, Theodore Bikel, Bob Gibson, Jean Richie, Josh White, and many others enjoyed playing dates in coffee houses, college campuses, and on television and recordings. They all flourished and were successful. One rather unique group was formed that gave the public a choral sound as compared to an individual or the one-on-a-part sound of smaller vocal combinations. This group was the New Christy Minstrels, which took its name from the Christy Minstrels of the Stephen Foster days of minstrelsy. The group was composed of nine (sometimes more) members. They were well-disciplined musically and presented a clean, bouncy, cheerful act. They sang, played a variety of instruments, and moved around as they performed. Their music had integrity, but it was also entertaining. Usually, the group was made up of seven men and two or more women; the personnel roster changed frequently, and they set an example for choral-styled folk performance that was imitated by several aspiring folknik groups. One of their most popular renditions was "The Big Rock Candy Mountain." This song properly belongs in the chapter on railroad songs, but it was purposely withheld to be identified with the New Christy Minstrels who gave it recognition through their splendid singing. It is a song said to have been created by the railroad "bums" to entice young "punks" into joining them in their itinerant, carefree life. As you examine the lyrics, try to wonder why it would be impossible for a lonesome young person to pass up the "promised land" as described in this song.

BIG ROCK CANDY MOUNTAIN

Traditional

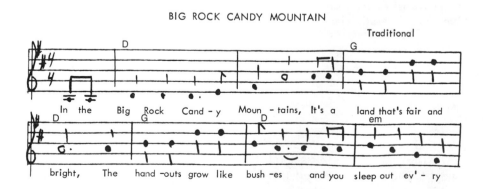

In the Big Rock Cand - y Moun - tains, It's a land that's fair and bright, The hand -outs grow like bush -es and you sleep out ev' - ry

night; The box cars all are emp- ty and the sun - shines ev' - ry day, I'm bound to go where there ain't no snow, where the sleet don't fall and the wind don't blow, In the Big Rock Cand - y Moun - tain,.......... Oh the buz -zin' of the bees in the cig - a - rette trees, The so - da wa - ter foun - tain; Where the lem-on - ade spring and the blue -bird sings, In the Big Rock Cand - y Moun - tain.

In the Big Rock Candy Mountains you never change your socks,
Little streams of alky-hol comes trickling down the rocks,
Oh, the shacks all have to tip their hats and the railroad bulls are blind,
There's a lake of stew and ginger ale, too,
And you can paddle all around it in a big canoe,
In the Big Rock Candy Mountain.

In the Big Rock Candy Mountains the cops have wooden legs,
The bull dogs all have rubber teeth and the hens lay soft-boiled eggs.
The box cars all are empty and the sun shines every day.

I'm bound to go where there ain't no snow
Where the sleet don't fall and the wind don't blow,
In the Big Rock Candy Mountain.

In the Big Rock Candy Mountains the jails are made of tin,
You can slip right out again as soon as they put you in;
There ain't no short-handled shovels, no axes, saws, nor picks.
I'm bound to stay where you sleep all day,
Where they hung the jerk that invented work,
In the Big Rock Candy Mountain.

Peter, Paul, and Mary (known as P P M in the trade) was a group that had as its members Peter Yarrow, Paul Stookey, and Mary Travers. Each of these singers had a voice worthy of solo performance. Their great vocal blending and their constant attention to musical perfection made them a group to be envied. Their guitar playing (Peter and Paul) was expert, as attested to by the infinite variety of tasteful accompaniments that they skillfully devised to support each of their songs. Their rendition of "Puff the Magic Dragon" is considered a classic.

The 1950s and 1960s represented a period of great excitement and ferment for American folk music. Many of the folk artists followed the straight and narrow path and gave the listening public the best of the old songs and a smattering of the new in an honest and authentic mode of delivery. At the same time there were a number of others who subscribed to the new wing of folk singers. They felt strongly that a folk singer or folk group should be the spokesmen of their own time and as such should have the choice of veering to the right or left of dead center. Still others fell prey to the golden opportunity for glory and dollars, and as such, quickly commercialized their art to meet the whims of the buying public. It would be safe to say that American folk music enjoyed two full decades of prime attention from the listening public, especially that large segment of the public made up of those once-youthful "kids" known as the "war babies."

In scrutinizing the movement of style in the history of art, and especially music, it is difficult to pinpoint with any degree of accuracy where one style ends and another begins. New movements take time to germinate and even when an innovative kind of music makes it appearance while another is still in vogue, it is difficult to predict if that new voice will survive the rigid tests of people preference. This is relevant to the materials found in Chapter 14, which deals with a new type of folk music known as urban folk music. At the opening of this chapter we said that folk music produced during the twentieth century reflected a more urban orientation as compared to the music produced during the eighteenth and nineteenth centuries, which could properly be characterized as rural in nature. The first fifty years of the twentieth century served as the incubation period for that mature expression known as urban folk music, which made its full-blown appearance in the late 1960s. Tangentially connected with urban folk music is folk rock, which resulted from the marriage of these two styles of "people" music.

14
Urban Folk Songs

The folk revival of the 1950s and 1960s provided fertile soil for the nurturing of a new species of musical expression called urban folk music. The revival not only helped Americans rediscover their musical heritage but, more important, the joy of singing. Once again, folk music and singing had come to the forefront, even in an affluent society, as the popular vehicle for describing the American way of life and as an important social activity. No generation, however, can be completely contented with merely unearthing and reliving events of the past. Being people of the present, and especially living in tumultuous times, they did what their forefathers had done for generations, that is, they shared their legacy of life through artistic expressions. Contemporary folk artists responded in the truest of broadside traditions, only in a more modern fashion. Americans of the late 1960s and the 1970s, after having had the folk process taken off the shelves, took up their task and began speaking for their time and place in American history through folk music.

What features of contemporary American life would they deem significant, inspirational, influential, and worthy of transmission? To be sure, Americans were living in a highly advanced and technological form of civilization. How could folk music, with its simplicity, naïveté, and provincialism, reflect a society that had become complex, highly educated, and constantly "on-the-go"? The challenge was definitely there; nonetheless, it must be remembered that folk artists had also become better educated verbally and musically, were more worldly-minded and more perceptibly aware of life. Let us examine for a moment a few of the more significant happenings of this era that folk artists had to take into account as chroniclers of their times.

To begin with, television was having a marked effect on the lifestyles of the American society. To be socially acceptable and just to make life more

239

bearable, everyone had to have a TV set in their homes. Millions of TV sets were sold in a matter of a few short years as evidenced by the thousands of ugly-looking antennas that projected from the rooftops of every home in the communities. People became the recipients of a communication media that provided them with news as it was actually happening and with an impact that no newspaper or movie could ever hope to project. For example, the ravages of war, which had previously been transmitted via editorial comment and black-and-white photographs, hours after their occurrence, were now being televised on location and being transmitted in "living" color! Each viewer, sitting in the comfort of his living room, felt that he was actually on the battlefield participating in a real war. He was privy to the sight of real blood being shed, limbs being blown off, and young soldiers and civilians dying. This kind of unprecedented realism was at the very heart of a movement that incited millions of Americans into active protest of the inhumanities of war and the futility of its ability to resolve man's indifferences.

On the brighter side, television served as the great entertainment medium of the day. Music of every possible genre could be seen and heard at almost any hour of the day. Aside from recordings and concert hall performances, television was the ideal medium for the presentation and mass reception of musical materials. Folk singers, who insisted on performing in intimate settings, could still have this intimate atmosphere through televised presentation, and yet share it with millions of "hidden" people. Moreover, each performance could be preserved on videotape for replaying at the flip of a finger. Television impacted the communication media; tangentially, it impacted folk music in every conceivable way from creator–performer to consumer–fan.

Of greater sociological and technological importance, this was also the age of the computer, a gadget that could retain millions of items of information that could be retrieved or used to solve problems with split-second timing. The very same operations would take the efforts of hundreds of the best minds and several hours of concentrated work to effect the same results. Computers became the key element in the successful probes into space which ultimately led to man's exploration of the moon, the placement of space weather stations that beamed pictures to earth on weather patterns, and the transmission satellites that helped relay signals making it possible for an event to be taking place on one side of the earth while being viewed on the opposite side at the very same moment. This was only the beginning. Who could predict, with any degree of certainty, the full impact that the computer would have on life, even in the foreseeable future. These were only two of a number of inventions that altered the quality of life in America.

There were also a series of happenings that had a significant effect on the people: the Vietnam war; rising crime rates; increased violence both in real life and in movies, books, and TV; staggering inflation; surge in the cost of energy; the breakdown of the family as the strong social unit; the feminist movement; high unemployment among youth and minority groups; the use and abuse of drugs; pornography; and so on. The speed and enormity of change was more than most people wanted or could cope with. This caught the attention of the younger generation looking at their future lives in America; it also caught the attention of Bob Dylan, a highly perceptive folk poet, who addressed the situation in his song, "Times They Are A-Changin'." Dylan, however, was not altogether happy with just noting these changes; he went on in the song to editorialize on them. In addition to spelling out a number of sociological facts, Dylan struck out at the mothers and fathers, telling them to stop criticizing what they could not understand about the new movement to counteract these ongoing trends, and further, that their sons and daughters were beyond their command! His final warning to parents was to get out of the new road if they could not lend a hand " 'cause the times they are a-changin'." It would be safe to say that these were times not only of inventiveness and staggering sociological change, they were also times of frank and unabashed criticism. Topical songs dominated the scene and words often took precedence over the musical materials involved.

Creative-perceptive Americans who wished to use the folk song to chronicle their times and feelings found the traditional mold for folk song communication to be impractical. Their world, according to them, was a troubled one; it was also a technologically sophisticated one. As a result, a new type of folk song had to be devised to better reflect the era about which they would speak. Lyrics for their songs would be more sophisticated, a deeper, higher quality of poetry which would be appreciated and better understood by a more educated populace. Parenthetically, the musical materials contained in the songs would be more complex in nature and more demanding in performance. People's tastes and understandings of music had become more elevated. Folk artists, at the time, were dealing with some weighty world issues. Preparing and performing music for an audience composed of better educated and more highly sensitive persons was indeed a challenge. The answer came in the form of music of high quality both in terms of musical materials and poetic content. The label, urban folk music, was selected to pinpoint its genealogy and to help differentiate its sophisticated content from the more traditional, simplistic folk music of the past.

On the surface, the decision to move into the direction of an urban-type folk seemed not only plausible but quite logical. To implement this within an expressive and artful framework, however, was indeed another thing. For example, how could anyone expressively and artfully deal with such current items as environmental pollution, genetic mutation, H-bombs, atomic fallout, Kent State, Watergate, Wounded Knee, computerized conformity, and so on? No matter how talented the lyricist or how gifted the musician, these words just do not have a place in an expressive art form.

Wisely, the word masters came to rely on metaphor, a literary technique in which a term or phrase is applied to something to which it is not literally applicable, yet which suggests a strong resemblance. For example, one well-known metaphor is "A Mighty Fortress is our God." To be sure, God is not a fortress; however, his strength and power is likened to a grand fortress as protector of his people.

The use of the metaphor by folk artists is beautifully illustrated in Pete Seeger's incomparable song, "Where Have All the Flowers Gone?" This song was written at the height of the protest movement against the Vietnam War. The song does not deal with flowers per se; rather, it deals basically with the young men going into uniform and off to war. The analogy of the flower as a symbol of youthful beauty picked prematurely is an ingenious one. Like the song "Blowin' in the Wind," as in so many other songs of this period, pertinent questions are raised as a way of getting people to think about life as it was unfolding before their very eyes. The use of the word "flowers," with its attendant symbol of living beauty, allows for a more expressive musical line to support it. The end result is a song that gets its message across and at the same time is a thing of beauty.

WHERE HAVE ALL THE FLOWERS GONE ?

WHERE HAVE ALL THE FLOWERS GONE? by Pete Seeger. © Copyright 1961, 1962 by FALL RIVER MUSIC INC. All rights reserved. Used by permission.

Where have all the young men gone?
Long time passing,
Where have all the young men gone?
Long time ago;
Where have all the young men gone?
They're all in uniform.
Oh, when will they ever learn?
Oh, when will they ever learn?

Where have all the soldiers gone?
Long time passing,
Where have all the soldiers gone?
Long time ago;
Where have all the soldiers gone?
They've gone to graveyards, ev'ry one,

Oh, when will they ever learn?
Oh, when will they ever learn?

Where have all the graveyards gone?
Long time passing,
Where have all the graveyards gone?
Long time ago;
Where have all the graveyards gone?
They're covered with flowers, ev'ry one.
Oh, when will they ever learn?
Oh, when will they ever learn?

(Repeat verse one)

At the same time that urban folk music was struggling for identity, a new teen-age craze came to the forefront called Rock and Roll. The music was nurtured on rhythm and blues, had a hard, driving beat with lyrics aimed directly at the huge teen population who had money in their pockets and a zest for good times. The "folkniks" held tenaciously to their new-found art, allowing for the two streams of music to flow their own individual ways. People selected whatever brand of music was to their liking. All went well until one of the greatest and most respected of the contemporary, traditional folk singers, Bob Dylan, went "electric" at the 1965 Newport Jazz and Folk Festival. The fans who came to the festival were die-hard folkniks. They were shocked and flabbergasted to see their hero, the main attraction of the program, walk onstage with a wire connected to his guitar and supported by a rock group! Only acoustic guitars were considered "proper" for folk performance. Dylan was booed right off the stage!

In retrospect, this occurrence could be seen as the birth of a hybrid form of music known as folk-rock music. Dylan, as a consequence of his transgressions, was forced into seclusion while the expression took shape and musical form. Within a few short months the hybrid form began reappearing in the song presentations of a large number of respected folk traditionalists. Simon and Garfunkel, two soft-spoken singers whose music was reminiscent of the ancient troubadors, came forth with a hit recording of their "Sounds of Silence," which at first presentation was a moderate flop; however, with an overdubbed, modified rock beat added to their soundtrack it surged into a smash. The Byrds, one of the newer and highly successful folk groups that followed in the footsteps of the Weavers, Kingston Trio, and others, came out with their outstanding version of Dylan's "Mr. Tambourine Man" in folk-rock style, thus helping to establish the expression. Folk-rock actually was aimed at and found to have immediate appeal with the disenchanted youth, the drug-heavy rock culture, and those who cared to protest strongly and through music. It served the needs of certain members of the American society who found the marriage of the two expressions perfect for use in getting their messages across to the general public. Folk-rock, as a definitive form of folk expression, was short-lived, yet it served as an influential base from which a number of tangential expressions emerged.

With the advent of urban folk music, American folk expression actually switched gears. A number of changes were infused that set it apart as a musical expression. The following list presents some generalizations to support this statement about the transition from traditional (or rural) folk to urban folk.

1. From songs descriptive of groups of people speaking (singing) for themselves *to* that of an individual(s) speaking (singing) for the group.
2. From songs whose creator(s) is unknown and perhaps the product of several people contributing something to the "final" version *to* songs whose creator(s)/composer(s) is a known individual.
3. From songs that display the elements of simplicity and naïveté both in words and music *to* songs that are highly sophisticated in both verbal and musical content.
4. From songs that do not require a great deal of musical ability in creation and performance *to* songs that demand considerable musical ability to create and perform effectively.
5. From songs that were initially shared by small numbers of people *to* songs that are performed for the masses via recordings, radio, television, and public performances.
6. From songs that were handed down essentially via oral transmission or through broadsides *to* songs that are available in huge quantities in the form of sheet music publications or recordings.
7. From songs that were constantly being changed as singer personalized it and passed it on to another *to* songs that become fixed entities in the sense that they are published with interpretive changes held to a bare minimum.
8. From songs descriptive of people addressing interactions among human beings on a small scale *to* topics of major sociological, political, and moral implications.
9. From songs whose subjects pertain to a small geographic area and a small number of people *to* songs that reach beyond national boundaries and are universal in scope.

Writers of urban folk songs assumed the status of "composer" as contrasted to "creator," making the study of urban folk songs best approached through a scrutiny of the works of a "composer" rather than with a representative group of Americans (that is, songs of the American cowboy vs. the songs of Bob Dylan). Successful writers of urban folk songs received considerable notoriety and were accorded praise commensurate with their creative abilities. In the following pages, we will discuss a select group of representative urban folk artists who achieved fame and helped establish the new expression.

Bob Dylan (born Robert Zimmerman) served his apprenticeship under the tutelage of Woody Guthrie, mirroring his every image as wandering minstrel with a country folk style. Not content with imitating Guthrie for the rest of his professional life, Dylan switched for a short time to rock and roll. He did not find this musical form personally satisfying, so he returned to folk and soon found a place for himself using the music as a vehicle for acting as "spokesman" of the people or as "critic in residence." Dylan secured an honored place for himself as this spokesman with his song "Blowin' in the Wind." The song captured the attention of the leading folk groups, many of whom immediately recorded it, and within a few short weeks the song became the "alma mater" for the socially conscious college and youth groups.

Joan Baez was among the established folk artists who saw in Dylan a talent bordering on genius. Dylan, through his subsequent song offerings, soon found favor with the masses as a songwriter and especially with the "folkers" as a singer well within the purist, traditional mold.

In his early years, Dylan considered himself to be more a poet than a songwriter. He would write a lyric and then search for a tune, either borrowed or of his own creation, to effectively support it. Later, as he matured into a superstar, his music unquestionably equalled the quality of his lyrics. During his professional career Dylan went full circle from country-folker Dylan to protest-Dylan to folk-rock-Dylan and again to country-folker-Dylan and protest-Dylan. A songwriter–performer, Dylan gave the world over one hundred songs, most of which will long be remembered.*

Although she was already sporting a full head of gray hair by the time she became a leading writer–singer, Malvina Reynolds was definitely among the greats of her time. She went the full academic route and held a doctorate degree. Unable to find a teaching position, she jobbed around as a newspaper reporter. Reynolds was a compassionate person who was highly sensitive to the direction in which her world was moving. She soon found it necessary to exchange her typewriter for a guitar. The result was a number of social commentaries with more wisdom and bite than any well-delivered lecture or film could ever have hoped to impart. Her song "Little Boxes" is a gem. In it she describes the social system in contemporary America. Reynolds accomplished as much in this brief but profound song as the study of the same subject materials in a college course in introductory sociology.

LITTLE BOXES

---

*Regrettably, permission to reprint Dylan's songs cannot be obtained.

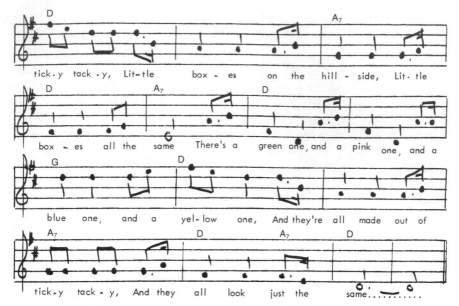

tick-y tack-y, Lit-tle box - es on the hill - side, Lit-tle
box - es all the same There's a green one, and a pink one, and a
blue one, and a yel-low one, And they're all made out of
tick-y tack-y, And they all look just the same..........

And the people in the houses,
All went to the university,
Where they all were put in boxes,
And they all came out all the same.

And there's doctors and there's lawyers,
And bus'ness executives,
And they're all made out of ticky tacky,
And they all look just the same.

And they all play on the golf course,
And drink their martinis dry.

And they all have pretty children,
And the children go to school.

And the children go to summer camp,
And then to the university,
Where they are put in boxes,
And they come out all the same.

And the boys go into business,
And marry and raise a family,
In boxes made of ticky tacky,
And they all look just the same.

In keeping with the trend of the times, Malvina Reynolds wrote one of her finest songs, "What Have They Done to the Rain?" In it she raises questions that many of her colleagues had raised in an attempt to solicit public awareness of what was happening to them. The song is definitely a protest song; however, as Joan Baez commented in introducing the song, "It protests rather gently."

WHAT HAVE THEY DONE TO THE RAIN?

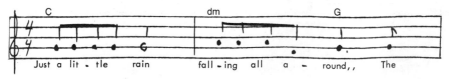

Just a lit - tle rain fall-ing all a - round,, The

grass lifts its head to the heav-en-ly sound,

Just a lit-tle rain Just a lit-tle rain

What have they done with the rain? Just a lit-tle boy

stand-ing in the rain, The gen-tle rain that falls for years; And the

grass is gone the boy dis-ap-pears the rain keeps fall-ing like

help-less tears And what have they done to the rain...........?

Reynolds' most lyrical song, and certainly one of her most expressive, is "Turn Around." The message is a wholesome one and the musical line has an eminently singable contour.

TURN AROUND

Where are you go-ing my lit-tle one, lit-tle one)

Where are you go-ing my ba-by my own; Turn a-

round   and you're two,   turn a - round   and you're four,   turn a -

round   and you're a   young girl go-ing   out   of   the   door.   Turn a -

chorus

round,   turn   a - round,   turn a - round and you're a young girl go- ing

out   of   the   door.

Where are you going my little one, little one?
Little girl with a petticoat,
Where have you gone?
Turn around and you're tiny,
Turn around and you're grown,
Turn around and you're a young wife
With babes of your own.
(*Chorus*)

Buffy Sainte-Marie holds a unique spot in American urban folk music. A strikingly attractive woman with coarse black hair and colorful clothes, she was able to win over an audience even before strumming her first chord. Sainte-Marie is of Indian descent and fully immersed in her culture, so she was able to speak convincingly of her minority people with both authority and artistry.

She was first attracted to folk music as a senior in high school. Later, she went to college, graduated with honors, and established a reputation as a folk singer and writer as well. Buffy Sainte-Marie fully capitalized on her exotic qualities by singing, with genuine human compassion, songs that ranged from the soft, quiet kind to the blistering "Cod'ine." Her contemporary comment on the merciless slaughtering of the buffalo during the early nineteenth century in order to keep the Indian in check is entitled "Now That the Buffalo's Gone." The song speaks for itself very well.

NOW THAT THE BUFFALO'S GONE

Can you re-mem-ber the times........... That you have
am
held you hand high......... And told all your friends of your
In - di - an claim.... Proud good la - dy and proud good
man? Your great, great grand-fa - ther from In - d'an blood sprang, And you
feel in your heart for these ones........... Oh it's
Now that the buf - fa - lo's gone...................

When a war between nations is lost,
The loser we know pays the cost,
But even when Germany fell to your
  hands,
Consider, dear lady, consider, dear
  man,
You left them their pride and you left
  them their land,
And what have you done to these ones?

Has a change come about, Uncle Sam,
Or are you still taking our lands?
A treaty forever George Washington
  signed,

He did, dear lady, he did, dear man,
And the treaty's being broken by Kinsua
  Dam
And what will you do for these ones?

Oh, it's all in the past, you can say,
But it's still going on here today,
The government, now, wants the
  Iroquois land,
That of the Seneca and the Cheyenne.
It's here and it's now you must help us,
  dear man,
Now that the buffalo's gone.

Buffy Sainte-Marie's song of great wisdom and strong protest is "Universal Soldier." In this song she presents a historical overview of soldiers down through the ages. The thrust of her commentary is found at the end of the song.

UNIVERSAL SOLDIER

He's five foot two and he's six feet four, He fights with mis-siles and with spears, He's all of thir-ty one and he's on-ly sev-en-teen, Been a sol-dier for a thous-and years.

He's a Catholic, a Hindu, an atheist, a Jane,
A Buddhist and a Baptist and a Jew;
And he knows he shouldn't kill and he knows he always will
Kill you for me, my friend, and me for you;

And he's fighting for Canada and he's fighting for France,
He's fighting for the U.S.A.,
And he's fighting for the Russians and he's fighting for Japan,
And he thinks he'll put an end to war this way;

And he's fighting for democracy,
He's fighting for the Reds;
He said it's for the peace of all,
He's the one who must decide who's to live and who's to die,

And he never sees the writing on the wall;

But without him how could Hitler have condemned them at Dachau,
Without him Caesar would have stood alone.
He's the one who gives his body as a weapon of the war
And without him all this killing can't go on;

He's the Universal Soldier and he really is to blame,
His orders come from far away no more,
They come from him [*slowly to the end*] and you and me, and brothers, can't you see [*increase volume and intensity*]
This is not the way we put an end to war!

Folksinger supreme, Judy Collins, contributed to the establishment of the new image for contemporary urban folk singers. Through her interpretive stylings, folk songs both traditional and contemporary approached the lofty position of the classical art songs. Each song, whether quiet and reserved or lively and boisterous, was presented with artistic polish and refinement. The selection, preparation, and final presentation of her songs reflected her meticulous attention to detail. Perfection, deep insight, and sensitivity were at the heart of each song. Trained as a pianist in the traditions of classical music, she was able to transfer her disciplined training into the musical–dramatic presentations of her songs. Collins was at her best when singing songs that dealt with hardship and pain. Through her voice and guitar, she made one feel that she had actually experienced what she was singing about. She influenced young, aspiring singers into accepting the challenge of singing the more sophisticated and demanding urban folk songs and singing them effortlessly and convincingly. Although not known as a songwriter, her renditions of both old and new songs were without equal.

Two popular songwriter–singers who belonged in a class by themselves were Phil Ochs and Tom Paxton. They represented a narrow, yet important, segment of the topical–urban folk expression of the period. Their satirical commentaries, oftentimes pointed and brusque, were just what "peacenicks" and "counterculture" folks wanted to hear. As a result, they were hailed as folk heroes. Phil Ochs was an engaging man who thrived among provocative and caring people. He was a military academy graduate, so he had a first-hand base from which to write his anti-military songs, such as "Talking Vietnam Blues" and "I Ain't Marching Anymore." His poetry was filled with sarcasm and wit; his music was always bouncy and jaunty.

Tom Paxton was more the musician and melodist of the two. As a concerned citizen, Paxton used his talents to communicate in sardonic terms and easily remembered melodies his candid opinions on the world as he saw it. His song, "What Did You Learn in School Today?" amply illustrates his talents as well as the unique contribution he and Ochs made to the field of folk music.

WHAT DID YOU LEARN IN SCHOOL TODAY ?

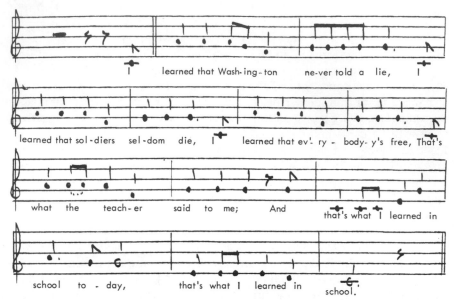

learned that Wash-ing-ton ne-ver told a lie, I learned that sol-diers sel-dom die, I learned that ev'-ry - body-y's free, That's what the teach-er said to me; And that's what I learned in school to - day, that's what I learned in school.

(*Second chorus*)

I learned that policemen are my friends,
I learned that justice never ends,
I learned that murderers die for the crimes
Even if we make a mistake sometimes;
That's what I learned today,
That's what I learned in school.
(*Chorus*)

I learned our government must be strong,

It's always right and never wrong,
Our leaders are the finest men,
And we elect them again and again;
That's what I learned in school today,
That's what I learned in school.
(*Chorus*)

I learned that war is not so bad,
I learned about the great ones we have had.
We fought in Germany and in France,
And some day I might get my chance;
That's what I learned in school today,
That's what I learned in school.

Finally, mention must be made of an urban folk duo who were true superstars—Paul Simon and Art Garfunkel. These two young men developed a musical sound that was the ultimate in sheer beauty; moreover, their songs were comparable in finesse and refinement to the art songs of Schubert and Brahms. They were able to keep large audiences musically spellbound. As singers, they certainly were worthy of the acclaim they received; and as songwriters, they were of the highest caliber. They communicated their messages in artful poetry that was filled with word pictures and compelling conversations, all carefully honed. One of their finest successes was their interpretation of the ancient English air, "Scarborough Fair." With some lovely alterations and a finely designed harmonic line in support of the melody, they took a long-neglected tune and turned it into a "classic beauty and a joy forever." Many believe their finest contribution to the literature of urban folk music to be "Bridge Over Troubled Water." The song deals with a provocative subject, yet it is handled with sensitivity, refinement, and affirmation. This is a difficult song to perform, and their recording features Art Garfunkel at his lyric-singing best.

BRIDGE OVER TROUBLED WATER

When you're trou-bled wa-ter

I will lay me down...............

Sail on·

sil-ver girl, sail on by............

your time · has come to shine........ All your

dreams are on their way..... See how they

shine........... Oh .... If you need a friend

I'm sail-ing right be-hind........... Like a

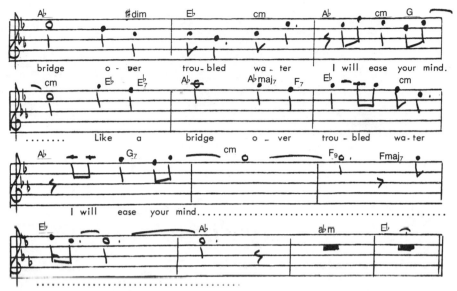

A host of outstanding urban folk singer–writers whose styles cut across all kinds of lines are busy carrying on the great tradition while at the same time searching for new paths for the future. Such performers as Carole King, Seals and Crofts, John Denver, Carly Simon, James Taylor, and Kris Kristofferson are only a few of the many folk singers who are writing and presenting materials of real worth today. Comparatively speaking, urban folk music is still in its infancy stages and time alone will reveal the direction it will take as well as the depth of its utterances.

The sea of American folk songs is bottomless and of indescribable variety. Through these songs our people have shared their innermost feelings and experiences. Down through history we have always had people who were deeply aware of their place in life and who had the irresistible yearning to put into song what they thought had to be communicated. By examining, performing, and listening to their songs we can enjoy the exquisite privilege of momentarily sharing with them an intimate vignette from their lives. Folk music will continue to pour forth from the American people. It is an integral part of human nature, and as such, becomes a part of our heritage and legacy.

Index